Sacred and Secular Agency in Early Modern France

Sacred and Secular Agency in Early Modern France

Fragments of Religion

Edited by
Sanja Perovic

continuum

Continuum International Publishing Group

The Tower Building	80 Maiden Lane
11 York Road	Suite 704
London SE1 7NX	NY 10038 New York

www.continuumbooks.com

British Library Cataloguing-in-Publication Data
A catalogue record for this book is available from the British Library.

ISBN: HB: 978-1-4411-8529-7

Library of Congress Cataloging-in-Publication Data
Sacred and secular agency in early modern France: fragments of religion/edited by Sanja Perovic.
  p. cm.
Includes bibliographical references (p.) and index.
1. Secularism – France. 2. France – Religion. 3. France – Church history – 18th century. 4. Civilization, Modern. I. Perovic, Sanja.

BL2747.8.S235 2011
211′.60944 – dc23

2011021834

Typeset by Newgen Imaging Systems Pvt Ltd, Chennai, India
Printed and bound in Great Britain

Contents

Contents

Notes on Contributors

Craig Carson is Assistant Professor of English at Adelphi University and a former Harper-Schmidt Fellow and Collegiate Assistant Professor at the University of Chicago. His current book project, *Eighteenth-Century Society of the Spectacle: Ethics and the Marketplace*, examines eighteenth-century British literature, political economy, and commodity culture.

Charly Coleman is Assistant Professor in the Department of History and the Interdisciplinary Project in the Humanities at Washington University in St. Louis. His work has appeared in *The Journal of Modern History* and *Modern Intellectual History*. He is currently completing a book on theological, philosophical, and political polemics surrounding the concept of selfhood in eighteenth-century France.

Denis Crouzet is Professor of History at the Université de Paris IV-Sorbonne and Director of the Centre Roland Mousnier as well as the Institut de recherches sur les civilisations de l'Occident Moderne. He has published numerous articles and 12 books on early modern France, including *Les Guerriers de Dieu. La violence au temps des troubles de religion (v. 1525–v. 1610)* (Champ Vallon, 1990); *La nuit de la Saint-Barthélemy. Un rêve perdu de la Renaissance* (Fayard, 1994); *La Genèse de la Réforme française 1520–1562* (SEDES, 1996); *Le haut cœur de Catherine de Médicis. Une raison politique aux temps de la Saint-Barthélemy* (Albin Michel, 2005); *Dieu en ses royaumes: Une histoire des guerres de religion* (Champ Vallon, 2008); and *Nostradamus* (Payot, 2011).

Stephanie Frank is completing a PhD in the Divinity School of the University of Chicago. She works on the intellectual–historical valence of secularization. Her current project pertains to disciplinarity and the social sciences in twentieth-century France.

Sophie Fuggle is Lecturer in Cultural Studies at Goldsmiths, University of London. Her research interests are focused on the relationship between continental philosophy and theology.

Francesco Manzini is a Junior Research Fellow in French at Oriel College, Oxford. He is the author of *Stendhal's Parallel Lives* (Peter Lang, 2004), as well as of various articles on Joseph de Maistre, Stendhal, Balzac, Borel, and Barbey d'Aurevilly. His second monograph, *The Fevered Novel from Balzac to Bernanos* (IGRS), is currently in press.

Ellen McClure is Associate Professor of French and Francophone Studies at the University of Illinois, Chicago. She is the author of *Sunspots and the Sun King: Sovereignty and Mediation in Seventeenth-Century France* (University of Illinois Press, 2006), as well as various articles on authors such as Corneille, Racine, Molière, and Mme de LaFayette.

Sanja Perovic is Lecturer of French at King's College London. She is the author of *The Calendar in Revolutionary France: Perceptions of Time in Literature, Culture, Politics* (forthcoming from Cambridge University Press), as well as articles on French theatre, revolutionary culture, encyclopedias, and other aspects of the French Enlightenment.

Erik Thomson teaches history at the University of Manitoba. His work has appeared in many journals, including *French History*, the *Scandinavian Journal of History*, and the *Journal of the History of Ideas*.

Dale Van Kley is Professor of History at Ohio State University. He is the author of numerous articles and several books on French Catholicism, including *The Jansenists and the Expulsion of the Jesuits from France* (Yale, 1975); *The Damiens Affair and the Unraveling of the* Ancien Régime (Princeton, 1984); *The Religious Origins of the French Revolution* (Yale, 1996); and *The French Idea of Freedom* (Stanford, 1994). His more recent "comparative" work on European Catholicism has appeared in several articles and the edited book *Religion and Politics in Enlightenment Europe* (Notre Dame, 2001). His latest publication is the co-edited book (with Thomas E. Kaiser) *From Deficit to Deluge: The Origins of the French Revolution* (Stanford University Press, 2011).

Introduction

Sanja Perovic

Secularization is arguably the last master narrative that remains an article of faith in Western society. It is so fundamental to the notion of modernity that the opposition between "religious" and "modern" has assumed the status of a self-evident truth. Recently, however, there has been a growing realization that religion may indeed be more resilient and compatible with "modern" forms of social life than was previously assumed. A number of recent books have begun to reconsider the secularization thesis and its related metanarratives.[1] What these works share is a concern with how the narrative of secularization undergirds a whole series of cultural and political categories premised on the notion of a political and historical distinction between an archaic, religious past and a "modern," secular present. This development is particularly striking in France and French studies, where *laïcité* has long held the status of official doctrine. Scholars on both sides of the Atlantic – including Marcel Gauchet, Denis Crouzet, and Dale Van Kley – have written studies signaling what Thomas Kselman and others have called a "religious turn" in French historiography.[2]

If distinctions between secular and sacred are far less stark than is commonly assumed, then how did these two categories interact? Did religion slowly wither away, or is it possible to identify theological dynamics that remained at work even after the supposed conclusion of secularization? This book seeks to answer these questions by exploring the persistence of religious categories in the cultural landscape of early modern France. France was the birthplace of Europe's first secular state and the center of two movements considered indispensible to secularization – the Enlightenment and the Revolution of 1789. In contradistinction to the political evolution of Britain and America, in which religion was never explicitly opposed to a secular political order, the absolutist French state originated in part as a way to end the Wars of Religion and was eventually succeeded by the establishment of the French Republic. This raises the question both of what became of the religious antecedents that had previously informed politics and culture, and whether they continued to inform modern political institutions and ideals. The study of France is thus vital for understanding not just the role played by religion in forging a resolutely self-proclaimed secular state, but also the way in which this oppositional structure of religion versus modernity might be deployed in other parts of the world that are often imagined to be in thrall to theology and therefore "in need of democracy."

This book takes as its starting point the observation that many studies aiming to reconsider secularization are still predicated on a notion of an epochal "divide" between a modern age and a religious past. Even Hans Blumenberg's *Legitimacy of the Modern Age* (1966), which contributed so much to emphasizing the differences between a narrative/descriptive and conceptual understanding of secularization, nonetheless takes as its starting point an epochal distinction.[3] The legitimacy of the modern age, Blumenberg claims, lies in its successful distinction from a religious past even if, at times, this difference is still residually informed by the vocabulary and questions arising from this past.[4] This issue of legitimacy is a crucial point for, as Kathleen Davis has recently argued, secularization functions essentially as a "periodizing operation," which reproduces the very break between premodern and modern, religious and secular, static and historical that it seeks to investigate and explain.[5] This book aims to address this "periodizing operation" through a series of essays, each of which examines the role of religion in shaping categories most often associated with modernity – the state and society, capitalism and individualism, and even the category of secularization itself. What the essays as a whole show is that secularization was not a process with a clear beginning or end, but rather that strong cultural currents associated with religion, such as the millenarian dynamics of the Wars of Religion, persisted even in such self-consciously secular moments as the dechristianization campaign during the French Revolution. From this perspective, it becomes apparent that the death of religion, pronounced many times and in many contexts, has yet to come to pass.

This volume's contribution to this reassessment of secularization is four-fold. First, it offers an interdisciplinary perspective drawing on insights from history, religion, literature, and philosophy. This emphasis on the interpretative human sciences constitutes a departure from the traditional ways of evaluating secularization, which have tended to be either sociological or philosophical/theoretical in orientation.[6] Sociologists, following in the footsteps of Auguste Comte, Emile Durkheim, Max Weber, and others, have tended to focus on how religion has become displaced by a society that is increasingly differentiated into different social and political fields, each with their own universalizing claims. Philosophers, in contrast, have focused less on the thesis that religion has been replaced by modern forms of social life and more on the question of "how religion itself was made modern."[7]

An example of the latter approach is the famous debate between Karl Löwith, Carl Schmitt, and Hans Blumenberg in the mid-1960s in Germany. Löwith argued for a conceptual continuity between Christian theology and modern beliefs in progress,[8] while Schmitt claimed that there existed a "structural analogy" between theological and political concepts.[9] Against both, Blumenberg emphasized the distinctness of the modern age, which drew its legitimacy from new sources of authority, most notably a view of reason that did not seek legitimacy outside of its own immanent sphere and thus steered clear of "transcendent" sources of authority.[10] Blumenberg identifies this will to transform the world to reflect human goals as a drive toward "self-assertion."[11] All three arguments, however, concur in defining secularization as a conceptual change that also implies a historical rupture that occurred between 1500 and 1800. Around 1500, and especially in the context of theological debates about nominalism, the loss of confidence in an Aristotelian conception of a natural order became definitive (for Blumenberg and Löwith, it is the "late medieval" abdication of understanding God by reason that enables a "modern" relation to the world).[12] Around 1800, of course, represents the end of the revolutionary period when fantasies of 'self-assertion' arguably reached their peak.

However, the fact that religion has not only persisted but even strengthened in recent years has led to a shift from philosophical claims, which remain deeply embedded in a linear narrative of progress *away* from religion, toward a renewed scrutiny of the context or framework of religious belief or unbelief. This volume's second contribution is thus to reorient the focus from exclusively theoretical accounts, which all too often reproduce the metanarratives they seek to undo, toward issues of agency and practice. Charles Taylor, in *A Secular Age,* has insisted that secularization cannot simply be a story about the loss of faith, because it is also a story about how Western European modernity gained a new understanding of the self and the place of society. One important way in which faith changes in the "secular" age is that it becomes one choice among many for the potential believer. Taylor is one thinker who remains deeply wedded to the master narrative of secularization, while at the same time acknowledging the way in which this narrative tends to flatten out emergent and vibrant cultural understandings of selfhood and agency.[13] Taylor's solution, which is to emphasize a shift in the "background" or "horizon" of expectations in which these changes took shape, thus raises a third question that this volume attempts to answer: how do we track a shift in background and how do we do so in the absence of a stable definition of religion?

One way to answer this question is to correlate this issue of sacred and secular agency back to the historical context in which the concept of an "early modern period" first emerged. As the complicated terminology of this label suggests – neither premodern nor quite modern – it was in this period that the vital break between a religious past and modern present was first actively constructed. Yet, it can also be argued that one of the functions of the label "early modern" is to attenuate such a break and draw it out for analysis. If we consider that the so-called early modern period contained multiple conceptions of time and multiple ways of relating past and future, two things become immediately clear. First, agency cannot simply be a story about increasing self-assertion, because it takes the form of an ongoing negotiation between sacred and secular conceptions of identity, power, and praxis. Second, the notion of a cultural divide between a "premodern" "religious" past and a "modern" present within the European context itself presupposes a certain politicization of historical categories. This brings us to the fourth and final contribution of this volume, which is to relate the issue of periodization to the emergence of secular politics in France, thus offering a crucial historical perspective from which to assess contemporary debates about religion and politics.

The notion that these emerging concepts of human agency contain their own spiritual vision gained full force during the Enlightenment era – the key period in which the binary opposition between the religious past and the modern secular present first became firmly established. Dale Van Kley is one scholar who has tirelessly argued for a reframing of this central Enlightenment conceit. In a series of highly influential publications, Van Kley has challenged the notion of a single Enlightenment, much less a secular one, by reclaiming the central role played by religious controversy in paving the way for the eventual downfall of the French monarchy. Van Kley's chapter opens this volume with a highly personal look back at the last fifty years of scholarship on the "religious question," clarifying the numerous affinities between Enlightenment thinkers and defenders of Catholic Christianity.

As Van Kley notes, what makes France unique in Catholic Europe is the tripartite division between Jesuits, Jansenists, and the secular *philosophes* that opposed them both. Thus, for the Jesuits, following the seventeenth-century theologian Luis Molina, what mattered most was that human nature could be rehabilitated, because it had been endowed with reason. However, if the Jesuits converged with the secular ethics of the *philosophes*, they diverged from them in their attitude to authority, insisting on a dogmatic adherence to the Church and supporting a strictly hierarchical structure in the Church. For a disobedient and at times openly defiant relation to authority, we need to look instead to the anthropologically "conservative" Jansenists. Although well known for their reluctance to stress the autonomy of human will because of their belief in God's predestination of the elect, the Jansenists, Van Kley argues, nonetheless opposed a rational "obedience" to the blind obedience advocated by the Jesuits. As Van Kley has extensively documented in his several books on this subject, by challenging the "despotism" of bishops and taking a stance against the combined power of the monarchy and the Gallican Church, the Jansenists contributed to the eventual downfall of the French monarchy. Van Kley thus implicitly demonstrates that secularization theories and debates are often dependent upon a simplistic vision of the "will" that equates it with unproblematic self-assertion. Jansenism in particular was characterized by what he calls a "paradoxical convergence of a politics of the will with a denial of the freedom of the will."[14]

If Dale Van Kley has shown how the Enlightenment was far more religious than commonly assumed, Denis Crouzet has shown how France's period of religious violence was far more enlightened than commonly assumed. In a series of magisterial publications, Denis Crouzet has demonstrated how the Wars of Religion remade the religious and political orders of France before these were overturned by the Revolution. In particular, the traumatic event of the St. Bartholomew Day massacre on August 24, 1572, is revealed to be the outcome not simply of religious and political violence, as it is commonly thought, but also the failure of a government policy based on tolerance and enlightenment. As is well known, the attempted assassination of the Huguenot Admiral Gaspar de Coligny by Catholic hardliners, on August 22, 1572, prompted Charles IX to strike pre-emptively against all the Protestant lords assembled in Paris for the wedding of Henri de Navarre. Although intended to forestall further violence, this act only served to escalate it. The entire Parisian population rose up to answer this "call from God" and defend their king by massacring the thousands of Protestants who had the misfortune to find themselves within the city walls. Crouzet's detailed analysis of the traumatic event of the St. Bartholomew Day massacre situates the dream of tolerance and religious concord – so often associated with the ideals of the "secular"

Enlightenment – squarely back in the Renaissance. By demonstrating the limitations of an enlightened and pacific humanism to deal with violence, Crouzet asks us to question the limits of our own secular understanding of the authoritative structure of the state.

In his contribution to this volume, Crouzet returns to the regency period (1561–3) when Catherine de Medici first formulated the policy of religious tolerance that would mark the early years of the reign of Charles IX (1560–74). Crouzet emphasizes how Catherine de Medici constructed her self-image as a mediating figure by combining a maternal representation of self-sacrifice with a Neo-Platonic idea of enlightenment and learning: she was the one destined to expel ignorance and bring France out of the world of darkness and internecine warfare. Central to this construction was a policy of religious and political reconciliation, which opposed words and the logos of reason to violence and ignorance, in the attempt to overcome the differences between Catholic and Protestant factions.

As Ellen McClure demonstrates in her discussion of the novel *Heptaméron*, this feminine humanitarianism had much in common with Marguerite de Navarre (1492–1549), sister of François I (1515–47) and defender of the early French Reformers, who also opposed the brutal and violent honor of men to the more "prudential" humanity of women. Prudence, as we know, was a key Renaissance virtue tied to a Stoic ideal of control over the passions, and equally compatible with both secular and sacred understandings of human agency. What links Crouzet and McClure's articles is a concern with the role of arts and literature in promoting a humanitarian ideal of religious tolerance that remained theologically informed. This contrasts with conventional accounts of how the French literary and artistic canon has shaped the French national identity, which, as McClure argues, has tended to oppose religion as an ideological totality against a "secular" and precociously "modernist" understanding of authorship and agency.

Central to the self-fashioning of both these women is the Latin concept of *auctor*, the term meaning both actor and author, itself modeled on an understanding of God as embodying both these essential elements of "authority." The role of God as simultaneously actor and author of divine justice is addressed by Erik Thomson's chapter, which elaborates the role of economic thinking in Renaissance France. One of the merits of Thomson's contribution is to highlight how free trade, protectionism, and competition for scarce resources – all central elements of "modern" economic science – also featured in early modern economic theory, which was based on notions of plenitude, self-sufficiency, stability, and a providential understanding of justice. As with Crouzet and McClure, female agency plays a surprisingly central role in Thomson's account, which focuses on a little-known text by the female entrepreneur and alchemist Martine de Bertereau in order to highlight innovative new understandings of the interaction between personal agency, scientific methods, and economic forecasting.

The intersection between divine and human conceptions of the will is also the focus of Charly Coleman's chapter, which explores what he calls the provocative similarities between eighteenth-century French mystics and materialists in their thinking about the self. Coleman shows how members of both factions participated in a far-ranging culture of anti-individualism predicated on divesting the human person of its possessive relationship to ideas and actions as an autonomous subject. The vehement polemics over the culture of personhood involved the great luminaries of the age – such as Fénelon, Voltaire, and d'Holbach – and centered on a fundamental question: the self's relationship to spiritual, material, and existential goods. Rather than assume, therefore, the conventional narrative of secularization, which links the loss of religious faith to the rise of individualism, Coleman points to a powerful counter-current that led to collectivism, interdependence, and a reliance on "resacralized nature." Coleman concludes by suggesting that the world was not only becoming disenchanted during the eighteenth century but also enchanted anew, as nature came to assume many of the attributes previously associated with persons.

This "transfer of sacrality" – from the divine to the civic and back – is the subject of Stephanie Frank's contribution. Van Kley has shown how the French Jansenists drew an analogy between the "whole church" and the "whole nation" in order to sacralize the notion of national sovereignty. Frank extends this point to consider a particular homology between the ecclesiology of Nicolas Malebranche and Sieyès' theory of political representation. This question of whether there is a structural analogy between theological and political concepts is, of course, long standing. It was most famously answered in the affirmative by Schmitt, and denied by Blumenberg who protested that secular concepts had their own legitimacy, irrespective of their vitiated theological origins. Like Schmitt, who attributed the idea of a sovereign will to the occasionalism of the seventeenth-century philosopher Malebranche, Frank also focuses on Malebranche's understanding of the relation between politics and theology. After showing the affinity between Malebranche's and Sieyès' arguments, her article considers the divergence between them. When deployed by Sieyès before the National Assembly, the *malebranchiste* argument ends precisely with what Malebranche could never have envisioned and certainly did *not* intend: political voluntarism.

Frank attributes this transformation to a new understanding of the relation between human and divine sovereignty, thus offering a fresh reinterpretation of Schmitt's secularization theory.

The role of political voluntarism in founding Europe's first secular state is likewise the focus of Sanja Perovic's contribution. This chapter also begins with an analogy: the French Revolution's adoption of a new Republican Calendar. Christianity may have been the first religion to be rooted in a concrete event dividing time into a before and after. However, it only became a universal religion once it mapped the story of Christ's life, death, and resurrection onto the cosmic time of the calendar. Similarly, the French Revolution also claimed to start time anew by establishing a new calendar that simultaneously vindicated secular time and reinforced the Revolution's structural affinity with Christianity. Nonetheless, it is one thing for religion to give time a new intentional structure in the form of a calendar, and quite another for an event as national and circumscribed as the French Revolution to warrant a change in calendar time. Perovic explores the conflicts between a horizon of expectation that remained Christological in orientation, allowing the French revolutionaries to transfer an expectation of closure to the future, and the open-ended nature of secular history in which the meaning of events can only be ascertained after the fact.

Part of the problem of assessing the continuities and discontinuities between past and future during the revolutionary period is of course the way in which this premise of a rupture in time was interpreted not just by the revolutionaries themselves but also by their adversaries. This is especially the case with counter-revolutionaries such as Joseph de Maistre who, as Francesco Manzini shows, opposed a "good" religious past to a secular and enlightened present that, according to Maistre, was directly responsible for the violence of the Revolution. Maistre famously vindicated the Inquisition as an act of clemency in which the Church sought to excuse the guilty and accept their repentance. He contrasted this with the Enlightenment's attempt to separate the religious and legal spheres, which led to the loss of sacrificial logic and the senseless killings of the Terror. Focusing on the French debates surrounding the execution in Lisbon of the Jesuit priest Gabriel Malagrida, condemned to death on charges of heresy in 1761, Manzini's chapter draws out broader relations between sovereignty and temporal justice implied in this secularization of punishment. In so doing, his chapter investigates the continuities and discontinuities between Maistre's reactionary and Catholic reconceptualization of capital punishment as sacrifice and a late-twentieth-century concern to account for an ever more efficient modern and secular use of execution inaugurated by the Terror that culminated in the Holocaust.

With the last two chapters, this volume returns full circle to its opening gambit: how are the various theoretical accounts of secularization subtended by the premise of a historical divide? It therefore makes sense to reconsider, as Craig Carson does in his chapter, the work of the nineteenth-century historian Jules Michelet, who, as Carson argues, was one of the first to insist on a theoretical understanding of the Revolution as both the fulfillment and contradiction of Christianity. The French Revolution is unique in French national history for many reasons – not least of which is that there is no monument capable of adequately commemorating it. For Michelet, the French Revolution occupies an empty space, both internally and externally: internally because the problematic division of Church and State has led to a self-divided individual; externally because words and historical discourse have had to replace the public monument. In his reading of Michelet, Carson ties this lack of embodiment to a new, specifically democratic problematic: how to write a history "of the people" when the people only ever appear as a voice and can never be directly embodied. Michelet, Carson concludes, represents a Revolutionary messianism without a messiah – a messianism based not on the coming of an individual, but of a people that can never itself be incarnated.

It is fitting that a book devoted to analyzing the fragments of religion that remain embedded in the secular should end with a postface on theories of the postsecular. Sophie Fuggle's chapter briefly considers how Giorgio Agamben's notion of a "signature" provides us with a new methodology for thinking the philosophy and history of secularization together – and without reproducing the very historical divide ostensibly problematized by this study. Unlike a concept, a signature reflects the process of interpretation whereby a given doctrine, discourse, or practice is transferred from one domain to another by way of displacements and substitutions. As Perovic, Frank, and Carson have all stressed, what is crucial in this idea of a transfer is that the theological leaves a mark on the political without ever being directly assimilable to it. Fuggle takes Agamben's example of economic theology as a case in point. Fuggle shows how Agamben's study of economic theology is not about finding the theological origin of Western modes of government or suggesting the way in which these origins have been concealed from us. In contrast to Schmitt, who bracketed questions about the economy from his discussions of political theology, Agamben seeks to unite these two strands together. His project thus casts new light on the economic aspects of political theology adumbrated by Thomson and Coleman.

A surprising and unexpected theme that has emerged from this volume is the importance of women as mediating influences in the process of secularization. Proponents of the secularization thesis have typically cast it as an entirely male debate, either emerging in theological arguments and monastic debates of the late medieval period (Blumenberg), in its concern with "origins" (Schmitt), or as leading up to a (male) modeled Protestant work ethic (Weber). It is male not just in its concern with provenance but also in its almost exclusive emphasis on conceptually rigorous explanations that largely depict secularization as a change in the history of ideas.

However, several of the chapters have emphasized not just important woman agents but also a female provenance of practices that were to prove extremely influential for subsequent thinking of the religious/secular divide. Catherine de Medici, as Crouzet reconstructs, modeled her understanding of *raison d'état* on maternal self-sacrifice; Marguerite de Navarre, as McClure shows, advocated a compassionate approach to humanity centered on uncertainty and ambiguity; Jeanne-Marie Guyon, the main instigator of Quietism in France, as Coleman explains, exerted enormous influence on Fénelon who, in turn, influenced an entire generation of thinking about the political and theological implications of the will. Even the relatively unknown Martine De Berteau, whose entrepreneurial energies Thomson uncovers, demonstrates the risks and potential rewards of a feminine pretension to superior access to divine wisdom.

Above all, what these chapters demonstrate is a world that is not empty of God or religion but still "full" – of God's Providence (Crouzet, Thomson), presence (McClure and, in nostalgic mode, Carson), and significance (Van Kley, Frank, and Perovic), as well as "full" of both material and spiritual goods (Thomson, Coleman). To be sure, this fullness is being everywhere fragmented. However, even the "emptiness" discussed by Manzini and Carson generates an extremely varied and polyvalent discourse that demonstrates the continuing intellectual, spiritual, and emotional appeal of age-old religious concepts. This polyvalent discourse is at the heart of this book, which attempts to chart the ways in which the "signature," the watermark of the religious in the secular, is not just generative of meaning but is, in fact, an ongoing process. It is hoped, finally, that this book will stimulate a far broader picture of human agency – political and otherwise – than that captured either by the rather rudimentary understanding of secularization as the separation of the Church and State or by all too facile assumptions about the "modernity" of our concepts.

Acknowledgements

The editor wishes to acknowledge the support of the University of Chicago for hosting the 2008 conference "Religion in French History and Literature," where some of these papers were presented for the first time.

Notes

[1] It would not be possible to provide a full bibliography on this vast literature except to briefly point to Giorgio Agamben, *Homo Sacer: Sovereign Power and Bare Life*, translated by Daniel Heller-Roazen (Stanford: Stanford University Press, 1998); Talal Asad, *Formations of the Secular: Christianity, Islam, Modernity* (Stanford: Stanford University Press, 2003); Jürgen Habermas, *Religion and Rationality: Essays on Reason, God, Modernity* edited by Eduardo Mendieta (Cambridge, MA: MIT Press, 2002), see also his dialogue with Ratzinger, *Dialectics of Secularization: On Reason and Religion*, Joseph Cardinal Ratzinger and Jürgen Habermas, translated by Brian McNeil (San Francisco: Ignatius Press, 2006); Mark Lilla, *The Still-Born God: Religions, Politics and the Modern West* (New York: Knopf, 2007); Tomoko Masuzawa, *The Invention of World Religions, or How European Universalism was Preserved in the Language of Pluralism* (Chicago: University of Chicago Press, 2005); Charles Taylor, *A Secular Age* (Cambridge, MA: Harvard Belknap Press, 2007); Hent de Vries, *Philosophy and the Turn to Religion* (Baltimore: Johns Hopkins University Press, 1999), *Religion and Violence: Philosophical Perspectives from Kant to Derrida* (Baltimore: Johns Hopkins University Press, 2001).

[2] See Marcel Gauchet, *The Disenchantment of the World: A Political History of Religion*, translated by Oscar Burge (Princeton: Princeton University Press, 1997); Dale Van Kley, *The Religious Origins of the French Revolution: From Calvin to the Civil Constitution* (New Haven: Yale University Press, 1996), *The Jansenists and the Expulsion of the Jesuits from France* (New Haven: Yale University Press, 1975); Denis Crouzet, *Dieu en ses royaumes: une histoire des guerres de la religion* (Seyssel: Champ Vallon, 2008), *La genèse de la réforme française vers 1520–1562* (Paris: Belin, 2008), *La nuit de la Saint-Barthélemy; un rêve perdu de la Renaissance* (Paris: Fayard, 1994); *Les guerriers de Dieu: la violence au temps des troubles de religion* (Seyssel: Champ Vallon, 1990), in addition to numerous other works; Thomas Kselman, *Death and the Afterlife in Modern France* (Princeton: Princeton University Press, 1993), *European Christian Democracy: Historical Legacies and Comparative Perspectives*, edited by Thomas Kselman and Joseph A. Buttigieg (Notre-Dame: University of Notre-Dame Press, 2003).

[3] Hans Blumenberg, *The Legitimacy of the Modern Age*, translated by Robert M. Wallace (Cambridge, MA: MIT Press, 1983).

[4] "What mainly occurred in the process that is interpreted as secularization, at least (so far) in all but a few recognizable and specific instances, should be described not as the *transposition* of authentically theological contents into secularized alienation from their origin but rather as the *reoccupation* of answer

positions that had become vacant and whose corresponding questions could not be eliminated." Blumenberg, 65.

[5] Kathleen Davis, *Periodization and Sovereignty: How Ideas of Feudalism and Secularization Govern the Politics of Time* (Philadelphia: University of Pennsylvania Press, 2008).

[6] See Dale K. Van Kley, Chapter 1 in this volume, for French historiography which, exceptionally, took its cue from literature in considering secularization.

[7] See *Rethinking Secularization: Philosophy and the Prophecy of a Secular Age*, edited by Gary Gabor and Herbert de Vriesse (Newcastle upon Tyne: Cambridge Scholars Press, 2009), x.

[8] Most notably in Karl Löwith, *Meaning in History: The Theological Implications of the Philosophy of History* (Chicago: University of Chicago Press, 1949).

[9] See Carl Schmitt, *Political Theology: Four Chapters on the Concept of Sovereignty*, translated George Schwab (Chicago: University of Chicago Press, 2005 [1922]), especially 36–52; these themes were reprised in his 1969 *Political Theology II: The Myth of the Closure of any Political Theology* (Cambridge: Polity Press, 2008).

[10] For the argument against Löwith, see Blumenberg 27–35; the argument against Schmitt can be found in 92–102.

[11] Blumenberg, 175–8, 196–8.

[12] Blumenberg, 188–98. Taylor claims 1500 as his theoretical departure point.

[13] Taylor, 572–3.

[14] See Van Kley, Chapter 1 in this volume.

Chapter 1

Robert R. Palmer's Catholics and Unbelievers in Eighteenth-Century France: An Overdue Tribute*

Dale K. Van Kley

For years, a rumor had been going around that Robert Palmer's mature opinion of his maiden book, *Catholics and Unbelievers in Eighteenth-Century France*, was that it was a "youthful indiscretion."[1] That rumor is untrue. If Palmer ever made any such judgment about his earlier work, it was about his doctoral dissertation on the reception of the American Revolution in France – more or less the subject of Durand Echeverria's *Mirage in the West*.[2] Parts of that dissertation undoubtedly later found their way into the first volume of Palmer's classic *The Age of the Democratic Revolution*.[3]

What he did say in my presence about *Catholics and Unbelievers in Eighteenth-Century France* was that he found it very difficult to re-read, and that he barely recognized himself in its pages. The occasion for this comment was our very first meeting when, shortly after joining the History Department at Yale University, Palmer found himself saddled with the task of presiding over the last stages of my doctoral dissertation that, years later, became my own first book on *The Jansenists and the Expulsion of the Jesuits from France*.[4] While hardly as damning a judgment as "a youthful indiscretion," Palmer's reaction to his experience of re-reading parts of his book caught me quite off-balance, because his *Catholics and Unbelievers* had been my "Bible" or at least my "New Testament" until then, with Carl Becker's *The Heavenly City of the Eighteenth-Century Philosophers* being my "Old Testament."[5] Well worn if not torn on my bookshelf today, my paperback copy of Palmer's *Catholics and Unbelievers* still bears the address of *6 rue de Quatrefages, Paris Ve* – handwritten testimony to the importance of a book I took pains to lug with me to Paris for my dissertation research there in 1966–7. Therefore, I regarded it as a rare privilege to be able to finish my degree under the direction of its author.

* This chapter was previously published in Robert R. Palmer's *Catholics and Unbelievers in Eighteenth-Century France: An Overdue Tribute* © Berghahn Books Inc. Reproduced by permission of Berghahn Books Inc

I might add parenthetically that this rare privilege came my way because my director, the late Stanley Mellon, a more authentic Palmer student than I am, had left Yale for the University of Illinois at Chicago. (Having deserted the eighteenth century for the Restoration and July Monarchy as one of Palmer's student at Princeton, Mellon thought it only fair for me to abandon his nineteenth century for Palmer's eighteenth at Yale.[6]) It was because Palmer was the author of *Catholics and Unbelievers* that, faced with a choice between Palmer and the recently arrived Peter Gay as Mellon's replacements around 1969, I gave this choice all of five seconds. Palmer's conception of the French Enlightenment was capacious enough to include not a few Catholics as Catholics. At that point in Gay's career, his conception of the Enlightenment as the "rise of Neo-Paganism" did not.[7] And, of course, by then Gay was also notorious for his critique of Carl Becker's *The Heavenly City* as a book possessed of every virtue "save one, the virtue of being right."[8]

The most probable reason for Palmer's discomfiture in trying to re-read his own first book is not the quality of its typically lucid prose style but the unfamiliarity of the subject, since he had long abandoned the subject of eighteenth-century French Catholic theology and philosophy for the study of the French Revolution. It was that change in direction, of course, that produced his translation of Georges Lefebvre's *The Coming of the French Revolution*, his book on the Terror titled *Twelve Who Ruled*, his two volumes on *The Age of the Democratic Revolution*, and later, *The Improvement of Humanity: Education and the French Revolution* and *The Two Tocquevilles: Father and Son*, and still others. If he had managed to finish the study of the abbé Henri Grégoire that failing eyesight and his death interrupted, that book would have represented his first return to the subject of religion since *Catholics and Unbelievers* in 1939.[9] In what follows, my remarks on the legacy of the work of Robert R. Palmer will be largely confined to that book, his very first book.

First published by Princeton in 1939 – and unfortunately out of print today after numerous reprintings – *Catholics and Unbelievers in Eighteenth Century France* still bears witness to the influence of Palmer's graduate director Carl Lotus Becker, whose seminar at Cornell University spawned one of the most illustrious generations of American historians of eighteenth-century France, including Leo Gershoy and Louis Gottschalk, among many others. While the thesis of Carl Becker's most famous book, *The Heavenly City of the Eighteenth-Century Philosophers*, is of course that the eighteenth-century *philosophes* or men of letters were far more indebted to deep assumptions peculiar to or at least conveyed by Christianity than they were aware,

Palmer in *Catholics and Unbelievers* turned Becker's thesis on its head by arguing that would-be defenders of Catholic Christianity against the *philosophes* in eighteenth-century France were far more "enlightened" in a philosophic way than they knew. The two theses are not contradictory; Palmer did not set out to refute his teacher. Rather, they illustrate the two sides of the notion of what Palmer's "modernist" mentor, borrowing the phrase from Alfred North Whitehead, famously called a period-specific "climate of opinion," or what Michel Foucault would later update in postmodern terms as an equally time-bound *episteme* or discursive "system of thought."[10] Fundamental to this approach to intellectual history is the thesis that the inhabitants of each time and space share certain basic assumptions and a language in which to express them. Revealed by key words so pervasive that those who deploy them feel no need to define them, it is these often half-consciously held assumptions that make debate – even meaningful disagreement – among contemporaries at all possible. *Philosophes* and their Catholic opponents therefore shared more in the way of a stock of concepts and words than they were aware of. In Becker's eighteenth century, such words were "nature, natural law, first cause, reason, sentiment, humanity, perfectibility," to which Palmer added "virtue."[11]

Although Robert Palmer is not commonly thought of as an intellectual historian, let alone one in the modernist mode, he employed the same tactic to good, if seldom noticed, effect in his treatment of eighteenth-century political thought in the first volume of *The Age of the Democratic Revolution*. There, both proto-liberal or "democratic" thought and proto-conservative or "aristocratic" thought emerge from the common matrix of enlightened thought, with the result that the baron de Montesquieu or even Edmund Burke is no less "enlightened" than, say, Jean-Jacques Rousseau.[12] As deployed more obviously in *Catholic and Unbelievers*, this tactic is a tour de force. In the long run, Palmer's evidence for the "enlightenment" of eighteenth-century French Catholic apologetics has been more convincing or at least less controversial than Becker's emphasis on the faith of the *philosophes*, although for the American academy the argument that *philosophes* were more Christian than they knew was admittedly the harder sell, beginning with Peter Gay. Thus, for example, did Palmer catch the Benedictine monk Dom Louis in the act of celebrating the pleasures of "virtue" in terms that might have made Diderot or Rousseau blush: "To embrace virtue, to die of pleasure in its arms, to be born again, to reproduce ourselves, to see our own image, a thing we have created, to caress our children," and so on. "This was strange language to come from a Benedictine monk" – thus Palmer's characteristically wry reaction – "and we hardly know whether to smile at such heated fancies, in which embracing virtue seems to be identical with falling on vermillion lips, or to take pity on a man who had shut himself off . . . from the licit enjoyment of the things he most valued."[13]

In his treatment of French Catholics and *philosophes*, Palmer's sensitivity to and exposure of shared assumptions between the two sides is more sophisticated than several recent visits to this contested site, including Darrin McMahon's book on the so-called French Counter-Enlightenment, which tends to conflate Jesuit and Jansenist responses to the Enlightenment that Palmer sharply distinguished. Far more flagrant is the case of Jonathan Israel's *Enlightenment Contested*, which simplistically writes off all French Catholic encounters with the Enlightenment as "Counter-Enlightenment," and then breathtakingly takes Palmer's *Catholics and Unbelievers* out of its bibliography, although it curiously includes *The Age of the Democratic Revolution*.[14]

Catholics came in many varieties, however, and it was not Benedictines such as Dom Louis but rather the Jesuits whom Palmer viewed as sharing the most philosophical ground with the French Enlightenment. Central to the Society of Jesus' preferred theological anthropology was the thought of its seventeenth-century Spanish theologian Luis Molina and his semi-Pelagian appropriation of the neo-scholastic notion of a hypothetical "state of pure nature" that lay between the created state of innocence and that of the "Fall." A condition in which God might have created human nature but chose not to, this hypothetical state came close to corresponding to the actual condition of mankind, minus the "supernatural" gifts of immortality and the immediate vision of God that mankind lost after the first couple's misuse of their free will and the resultant "Fall" into sin. But the result of limiting the consequences of the "Fall" to the loss of "gifts" extraneous to human nature, rather than to a vitiation of that nature itself, was tantamount to a defense of even un-baptized human nature, especially in contrast to Saint Augustine's far more tragic conception of a "Fall." For the Augustinian Fall resulted in nothing less than a total reversal in the direction of human will and love away from their source and rightful object in the creator, "concupiscently" binding them instead to the "fallen" self and other aspects of creation unless miraculously liberated by efficacious grace from God.

The result of the society's "Molinism" was, in Palmer's portrait, a group of Frenchmen quite committed to the eighteenth-century humanistic project of rehabilitating human nature. Palmer's French Jesuits thus regarded human "nature" as less than entirely corrupt, endowed human "reason" with the capacity to discern "nature's" moral laws, accorded the human will enough freedom to fulfill the main requirements of that law, and reserved whole swatches of human activity for the morally neutral or indifferent, that is, for actions neither sinful nor charitable in themselves. As Palmer himself put it, the Jesuits "marked out large areas of life for the autonomous operation of reason, natural law and free will," the better to communicate with Enlightenment that itself accepted "nature" and "reason" as its standards.[15] While trying to hold the *philosophes* to the duty to accept the dogmatic authority of the Catholic Church, the need to believe the "mysteries" of divine revelation along with "fallen" humanity's dependence on the sacraments for salvation, eighteenth-century Jesuits tended to free morality from these mysteries and therefore to find common ground with the *philosophes* and their attempt to elaborate a secular ethics.

To be sure, Palmer was not unaware of the differences between the paired concepts of "nature" and "reason" as used by Jesuits and *philosophes*. With a certain stake in neo-scholastic Aristotelianism, the Jesuits' concept of "nature" retained a normative and moral cast, their concept of reason quite active and distinct from the body. *Philosophes* in contrast thought of "nature" in more purely descriptive or behavioral ways and, while making "reason" ever more part of nature, reduced its role to a passive receptor of bodily sensations. No more than the French Enlightenment's "reason" did Catholic "reason" remain stationary during the eighteenth century, however. Palmer was therefore not insensitive to the subtle evolution of Catholic reason in an inductive and empirical direction, as evident in the apologetic appeal to the empirical "fact" of miracles and revelation as opposed to any attempt to demonstrate the truth of Christian doctrines. Rather less subtle and far more obvious was the increasing recourse to John Locke's sensational epistemology that burst upon Paris's scandalized attention in the affair of a Sorbonne thesis successfully defended by the abbé de Jean-Martin de Prades in 1751. Palmer was the first to call attention to this mid-century incident or *affaire* – about which more later – marking as it did a parting of the paths between French Catholicism on the one hand, however "enlightened," and the "party" of the *philosophes* on the other.

In the light of these and other common assumptions, Palmer proceeded to chart the degrees of overlap and difference in the debates between Catholics and *philosophes* in diverse areas such as traditional versus historically empirical thinking, the eternity presupposed by the notion of creation versus the kinds of temporal causation at work in history, and the normative character of traditional notions of nature as opposed to the *philosophes'* attempt to derive the concept of obligation from the mere description of "nature." Throughout these chapters, Palmer is careful to note not only the modernity of some of the defenders of Catholicism, but also the traditionalism of some of the *philosophes.*

It was Catholic truth as defined by the church's magisterium, for example, that the Jesuit pair Jean Hardouin and Isaac-Joseph Berruyer set out to defend by means of a textual criticism that, in the hands of Berruyer, was quite modern in its skepticism about the capacity of the "moderns" to think their way back into the mindset of the "ancients."[16] In paradoxical contrast stood Voltaire, who became everyman's own historian of the Bible in order to demolish this basis of Catholic tradition while never doubting that the "truth" as he understood it had always and everywhere been true, as though he himself had been an ongoing magisterium. It was again in defense of the orthodox doctrine of the existence of a spiritual and immortal soul that Catholic apologists such as Joseph-Adrien Lelarge de Lignac came to anticipate Kant's quite modern insistence on the mind's active contribution to knowledge. Meanwhile, however, the obvious modernity of Claude-Adrien Helvétius's deterministic and materialistic reduction of all ideation to sensation only imperfectly obscured the immutably true ideas in the name of which he proposed to reform France's state and society.[17] Similarly, it was in defending the traditional Christian doctrine of Creation against the modern restatement of the notion of the eternity of the world that Catholic apologists such as the abbé Gabriel Gauchat came to plead the case of reason and civilization against Rousseau's thesis of the brutish origins of mankind. As adumbrated by *philosophes* such as Diderot, however, the first modern attempt toward a theory of evolution came hitched to a notion of "progress" still visibly indebted to the Christian faith in divine purpose in the world.[18] It was moreover in fighting a rearguard defense of the doctrine of divinely imposed duties and obligations that Catholic apologists also tried to update Christianity's case in terms of social utility. Yet, the *philosophes'* quite modern use of the concept of "enlightened" utility in an effort to derive the ethical "ought" from a descriptive "is" did not prevent them from attributing normative ethical value to a quasi-deified "nature" and a universalized "humanity," lest their ethical project collapse into the relativism of individual pleasure, as it all but did in the case of Helvétius and d'Holbach.[19]

Evident in this brief summation is the influence of Carl Becker's thesis of the Enlightenment's indebtedness to Christianity. Just as obvious however, is Palmer's originality in insisting on the Enlightenment's imprint on the thought of the eighteenth-century defenders of the faith. For Palmer, the relation is reciprocal and the influence dialectical. Voltaire's refusal to believe Herodotus's account of ritual prostitution in ancient

Mesopotamia because it contradicted his conception of human "nature" is balanced by Nicolas Bergier's insistence on the social "utility" of Christianity.[20] In rereading these chapters, I cannot help but be struck by the degree to which my own conception of the limits of the modernity of the French Enlightenment remains influenced by Palmer's classic account of them.

Yet, for all its recognized brilliance – or its quality of "little short of brilliance," according to *The Christian Century* – Palmer's *Catholics and Unbelievers* cannot be said to have produced very much by way of a progeny after its publication in 1939.[21] The book "*n'a pas fait école.*" In the bibliography in my own *Jansenists and the Expulsion of the Jesuits*, only Albert Monod's *De Pascal à Chateaubriand* and Bernhard Groethuysen's *Die Entstehung der bürgerlichen Welt-und Lebensanschauung in Frankreich* figure as predecessors, and only John Pappas's *Berthier's Journal de Trévoux and the Jesuits* and John McManners' *French Ecclesiastical Society in the Eighteenth-Century* qualify as successors.[22] If, among Palmer's students, Norman Ravitch turned to eighteenth-century French ecclesiastical history, it was to social and institutional history rather than intellectual history.[23] The same may be said of John McManners's book on Angers – the other true classic on the subject. In studies of the Enlightenment, neither his book nor Palmer's was ever able to make a dent in Peter Gay's conception of the Enlightenment as "the rise of neo-Paganism." Although inspired by the book, my own initial interest in Jansenists and Jesuits fell more squarely into the domain of political than intellectual history. In France, however, Bernard Plongeron – Palmer's real successor – did not turn his attention to the subject of "Catholics and Unbelievers" until 1975 when he published his masterpiece, *Théologie et politique au siècle des lumières.*[24] Palmer himself left the subject for the French Revolution, never really to return to religion, while the inquiries into the origins of the Revolution in subsequent years remained fixated on socioeconomic rather than intellectual, to say nothing of religious ones. The genre of the social history of ideas as impressively practiced by Robert Darnton is an exception that proves the rule.[25]

Meanwhile interest in the ideas of the Enlightenment continued apace, but got decoupled from the French Revolution and tended to flourish in literary as much as historical studies, in France and in the United States alike.[26] Paul Hazard's *La crise de la conscience européenne* and *La pensée européenne au XVIIIe siècle,* George Havens's *The Age of Ideas,* Lester Crocker's *An Age of Crisis* and books on Diderot and Rousseau, Jean Ehrard's *L'idée de la nature en France,* and Ira Wade's *The Intellectual Origins of the Enlightenment* – these works all came from the field of French literature rather than that of history.[27] Kingsley Martin's *French Liberal Thought in the Eighteenth Century* managed to emerge from the field of journalism; while those historians of the French Revolution such as Alfred Cobban who also wrote about the Enlightenment tended to argue rather stoutly that the Enlightenment had nothing to do with the Revolution.[28] The few attempts, mainly French, to connect the Enlightenment to the French Revolution, ranging from Daniel Mornet's *Les origines intellectuelles de la Révolution française* to Henri Peyre's spirited essay on "The Influence of Ideas of the Enlightenment on the French Revolution," similarly emanated from French literature rather than from history.[29]

Apart from studies of the Jesuits as missionaries and the Chinese rites controversy, renewed interest in the eighteenth-century Jesuits' engagement with the Enlightenment had to wait until 1991 and Catherine Northeast's book on the *Parisian Jesuits and the Enlightenment*, which, like Palmer's, produced no very speedy sequel.[30] One of the major contributions of Northeast's book is to have highlighted the group of Parisian Jesuit "scriptores librorum" or writers of books who, housed in a special annex of the Jesuit College of Clermont-Louis-le-Grand in the rue Saint-Jacques, produced the bulk of polemics against Jansenists when they did not farm the task out to hack writers, as did Louis XIV's future confessor Michel Le Tellier. In the 1720's, this college cottage industry ran afoul of the disapproval of the Regency, which shut it down, redirecting the Jesuits' literary efforts to more civil exchanges with writers of the early Enlightenment, much as Palmer described them as doing.

For the rest, however, Northeast's picture of the Parisian Jesuits and their engagement with the French Enlightenment largely corroborates that of Palmer. If Northeast makes the skepticism of Jean Hardouin and Isaac-Joseph Berruyer a little more typical of the Jesuits' philosophical stance than Palmer did, she nonetheless concurs with him in pitting the empirical "fact" of miraculous revelation against any attempt to understand the Christian mysteries. If Northeast has the Jesuits more involved in textual criticism than Palmer allowed them to be, she concurs with him in stressing that the overall purpose was to bolster the authority of oral tradition and, by means of it, the authority of the church's magisterium. If, again, Northeast corrects Palmer a little in stressing that the "natural" religion whereby the Jesuits thought that all men might be saved included an "implicit" knowledge in humanity's need for divine redemption, she entirely agrees with Palmer in holding that the "universal possibility of salvation was the only conclusion consistent with the Jesuit insistence on divine mercy and human free will."[31] A kind of dim premonition of the need for revelation, mankind's "implicit" knowledge functioned in Jesuit theology as a way to maintain a connection between humanity's redemption and Christ. Above all, Northeast's study entirely confirms Palmer's picture of the society's continuing commitment to an anti-Jansenist or "Molinist" theological vindication of human nature that harmonized to a degree with the secular ethics of the *philosophes*.[32]

Nevertheless, Northeast's study was an isolated oasis in a desert of interest. What therefore would be Palmer's amazement if he could now see the sudden flowering of interest in publications about what is variously christened as the Catholic or Christian Enlightenment. Jeffrey Burson, Harm Kleuting, Ulrich Lehner, Michael Printy, Helena Rosenblatt, David Sorkin – these are only a few of the historians now active in what has begun to look like an industry on the subject.[33] Although the concept of a Catholic Enlightenment originally arose in the context of pre–World War I Germany, its most recent copyrights belong to Samuel J. Miller, who employed it in the context of the marqués de Pombal's Portugal, and Bernard Plongeron, who applied it to Catholic Europe as a whole.[34] Even greater would be his surprise if he could discern the shape of this Catholic Enlightenment and learn the identity of the enlighteners.

The Catholic enlighteners in question set out to enlist learning and historical erudition in an attempt to reform the liturgy, the devotional forms, the monastic establishment, and even the structures of the Catholic Church, in alliance with the secular but still Catholic confessional states in the second half of the eighteenth century. More puzzling, this movement for Catholic reform made the Society of Jesus one of its targets of choice and waxed most strongly in the wake of the mid-century international offensive against the Jesuits that, in France, resulted in the formal dissolution of the society in 1764. Outside of France, these efforts adopted heretofore mainly French or Gallican Catholic theses about the fallibility of the pope, the restoration of the usurped rights of bishops, the rehabilitation of the secular as opposed to the monastic clergy, and the extension of the jurisdiction of the state at the expense of the Tridentine Catholic Church. What makes these movements "enlightened" in a sense is the importance they attached to knowledge – for example, their attempts to purge popular piety of its "superstitious" veneration of apocryphal saints and inauthentic relics or to transform the performance of rote religious ritual into reasoned re-enactments of the Christian mysteries. If, as did French Jesuits, these movements also had recourse to the concepts of "nature" and "natural law," it was not in order to accommodate postlapsarian human nature, but rather in order to justify the extension of the jurisdiction of the state as an agent of religious reform into areas hitherto under the aegis of the church, often in open defiance of papal authority.

Aside from the enormous contribution of the Jesuit Bollandists to purge pious legends from the histories of the saints, this "enlightened" Catholicism in recent historiography had very little to do with the French Jesuits described in Palmer's *Catholics and Unbelievers*, and most especially reformist Catholic efforts to destroy the Jesuits! Far from wishing to transform the Catholic Church, much less their own society, French Jesuits were quite comfortable with its ever more monarchical or papal structure, the honored place of the religious orders in the clergy, the continued use of Latin in the liturgy – even with presence of "superstitious" elements in the belief system of the peasantry. Quite like such *philosophes* as Turgot in their own domains, the Jesuits were reasonably content with the ecclesiastical and doctrinal present, many of them willing to think that it represented "progress" in relation to the state of the primitive church.[35]

As for the French counterparts to those who figure as the most "enlightened" Catholics in recent historiography, it should be obvious enough that they are indeed the Jesuits' greatest and finally fatal nemeses, the Jansenists, whom Palmer regarded as eighteenth-century France's least "enlightened" Catholics, and at polar removes from the Jesuits' sometime student Voltaire.[36] The main reason that Palmer accorded them this dubious distinction is of course on account of their Augustinian theological anthropology. For, in comparison to Jesuits and *philosophes* alike, French Jansenists were least willing to grant any degree of autonomy to "nature," especially human nature. This "nature" they regarded as totally "fallen" and corrupt in its postlapsarian condition and totally dependent on special divine help or "grace," not only for any works "charitable" in the sight of God in the present state but also, more obviously, for "salvation" in the world beyond. Alone among members of the theologically Augustinian family in eighteenth-century Europe, French Jansenists defended the doctrine of divine predestination "without prevision of merits" against all comers, and deep into the century of light.

Far from being unaware of the proximity between the Jesuits' theological "Molinism" and the philosophical rehabilitation of human nature detected by Palmer, Jansenists roundly denounced it, after 1750 ever more stridently blaming the Jesuits and their "novel" theology for the rise of modern unbelief. To believe French Jansenists, the *philosophes* had no more determined enemies than they. It was in Molina's and the whole Jesuit Society's theory of a "state of pure nature" and its corollary of the possibility of a purely "natural," as opposed to a "supernatural" goodness and morality, that the century's new and ever more militant "unbelievers" had found the apology of their *"Morale,"* maintained the *Nouvelles ecclésiastiques* in January 1767.[37] That "lamentable opening" between natural and supernatural states – so the Jansenist argument continued – turned out to be the breach through which the "the enemies of Religion passed in order to set up their system of natural Religion on the ruins of Revelation," while the "fragile shelter" of a residual supernature proved unable to prevent the erection of a system of morality apart from "revealed Religion." Reviewing Claude-Adrien Helévetius's materialistic *De l'esprit* in 1758, the Jansenist journal argued that, where the precepts of "natural" morality were concerned, the Jesuits had already prepared the way by accommodating the moral demands of the Gospel to the weakness of human nature by means of a casuistry that excused individual sins if committed in "invincible ignorance" of the law or directed toward some intended good. It therefore only remained for Helvétius and his colleagues to define virtue as variable self-interest and, eliminating the soul as well as God, to justify everything from theft to sodomy in the name of a state-defined general good.[38]

Palmer's portrait of eighteenth-century French Jansenists is based on textual self-portraits such as these, and it is true insofar as it goes. The paradox is that, although perhaps in somewhat "softer" and less polemical form than in France, a certain theological Augustinianism accompanied the reformist activities of the reputedly "enlightened" Catholicism elsewhere in late-eighteenth century Europe – in the Italian states, the imperial German states, and even in Portugal and Spain – where it also bore the aspect of a Renaissance-style recovery of the literature of Christian antiquity and its rhetorical as opposed to "scholastic" style.[39] As for France itself, Monique Cottret has committed the ultimate heresy of opining that the eighteenth century witnessed many points of contact and "capillary" connections between Jansenism and the French Enlightenment – or rather French "Jansenisms" and "lights," because both ideological cities had many and overlapping boroughs and the argument works best in the plural.[40] At the national level, and as early as the 1750s, some Jansenists and some *philosophes*, not excluding Voltaire, found themselves making common cause in favor of civil toleration for Protestants and against the fiscal exemptions of the clergy.[41] At street level, the virtue of *bienfaisance*, or social beneficence as preached by *philosophes*, found one of its best exemplars in the "charity" of clandestine Jansenist schools and campaign for popular literacy presupposed by Jansenism's emphasis on theological or catechetical literacy.[42] What in part bound these agendas together was a common commitment to "enlightenment" by means of access to the printed word and a political appropriation of theories of natural law. Where Jesuits confined the use of natural law to their theological anthropology and sacramental practice, *philosophes* and Jansenists alike used it to extend the jurisdiction of the state at the expense of that of the church. Moreover, where Jesuits remained committed to their constitutional principle of "blind obedience" to their superiors – at least until after their society's final suppression – both Jansenists and *philosophes* used natural law in order to justify disobedience, not only to the church but, in the end, to the state in "absolute" monarchical form as well.

Aside, therefore, from the inspiration that late-eighteenth-century Catholic *Aufklärer* everywhere claimed to derive from the literature of Port-Royal, what best qualifies even French Jansenism for a place in the sun of the larger Catholic Enlightenment in recent historiography is, first of all, Jansenism's insistence on "rational" as opposed to the Jesuits' "blind" or unthinking obedience. Common throughout late-eighteenth-century European reformist Catholicism, the watchword of "rational" obedience was largely a French Jansenist invention that found its scriptural "proof text" in the first verse of Saint Paul's twelfth epistle to the Romans – "let your obedience be rational" – and application as a justification for disobedience to hierarchical ecclesiastical authority in an attempt to reform that hierarchy.[43] That this watchword justified bishops' attempts to reclaim rights usurped by the papacy goes more or less without saying. In combination, however, with a second maxim that even parish priests received their spiritual mission directly from Jesus Christ rather than indirectly via their bishops – the maxim of the "priesthood of all priests," as it were – the principle of Pauline "reasonable obedience" also justified attempts by parish priests to challenge the "despotism" of their bishops. This maxim held that ordination conferred a "radical" universal spiritual power to "bind and loose" on any and all priests qua priests that, the same in point of power as that possessed by Christ's apostles, came to be restricted to a given territory under the jurisdiction of bishops only by virtue of canon law, and for the sake of administrative good order.[44] Also of French Jansenist derivation, this maxim similarly gained widespread acceptance by reformers in all of Catholic Europe, whether Jansenist or not.[45]

What distinguished the French situation is that, while in most parts of Catholic Europe these forms of disobedient reformism often enjoyed the active support of "enlightened" if also Catholic absolute monarchies, in Gallican France itself, "Jansenist" reformist efforts ran up against the combined opposition of the monarchy and Gallican bishops largely chosen by the monarchy, not for their Gallicanism, but for their anti-Jansenism.

The resultant alignment of forces reinforced an already ideologically and socially "natural" alliance among Jansenists and priests and *parlements* versus both episcopacy and monarchy, making for a movement politically rather more radical than reformist Catholicism elsewhere in Europe. Another of the proximities between French Jansenism and even Jonathan Israel's "radical" materialist Enlightenment is therefore Jansenism's paradoxical combination of a politics of will with a denial of the freedom of the will, along with the sacralization of the notion of national sovereignty by way of transferring the Gallican conception of the "whole church" assembled as the locus of infallibility to the "whole nation" assembled as the locus of the nation's sovereignty. Opposition to a common enemy in ministerial "despotism" made Jansenists into allies of some *philosophes*, especially, as Monique Cottret has pointed out, after Chancellor Maupeou's brutal reform and purge of the parlements in 1771.[46]

In addition to the support of the *parlements*, a third point of contact between French Jansenists and the Enlightenment had to do with their massive recourse to print literature, making them pioneers in the politics of public opinion that facilitated the *philosophes'* exploitation of these politics later in the century. At the same time, the Jansenist faith in printed texts and access to them was part and parcel of a discursive religious sensibility that saw ignorance as itself a sin that excused no other sins and therefore literacy and the access to printed texts – catechisms, the Bible in vernacular translations – as mandatory antidotes to this sin. The Jansenist emphasis on biblical and catechetical literacy translated into a less-than-popular campaign to stamp out popular "superstition" and "ignorance," as well as an additional reason to despise Jesuits, tolerant as they notoriously were of sins committed in "invincible ignorance" and of even the most aberrant of cultic acts by reason of their value as evidence of a "natural" inclination to worship God.[47] Linking Jansenists with *philosophes* in France, this offensive against ignorance also proved to be among Jansenism's most exportable cultural commodities to the rest of Catholic Europe as enlightened or reformist Catholicism. The chief gravamen held against Jesuits by eighteenth-century Italian reformers such as the priest Daniele Concina was the society's lax or "probabilistic" penitential theology, while what most exercised enlightened reformers against the society in the Catholic German states was its perceived complicity in the popular "ignorance" thought to be implicit on the reliance on "mechanical" devotional helps and the gaudy externality of aspects of "baroque" Catholicism.[48]

If, therefore, I myself ever managed to "teach" anything to my mentor Robert Palmer in puny contrast with all he taught me, it is surely something about the radical nature of the political thought and activity of Jansenism during the French century of "light." Jansenists did not content themselves with debating with Jesuits and their allies in the Gallican Clergy on what for most of the century were unequal terms. They also contrived to dissolve the Society of Jesus, perforce taking on royal "despotism" at the same time. Truth be told, it was also Robert Palmer who persuaded me not to write off the importance of the Jansenist phenomenon after the suppression of the Jesuits in 1761–4, and to push on and specify the movement's long-term relation to the French Revolution. As I still remember Palmer reminding me, it is widely if not universally acknowledged that if anything in the expression of Denis Richet and François Furet "derailed" the Revolution, it was the religious issue. Moreover, the religious issue is in turn inseparable from the Jansenist controversy, even as late as in 1790.[49]

Should we at this late date take Robert R. Palmer and his *Catholics and Unbelievers* to task for minimizing Jansenism's relation to the French Enlightenment? Of course not, that would be silly. Palmer's *Catholics and Unbelievers* has stood the test of time far better than any book has any business doing. Even where the French Enlightenment is concerned, Palmer correctly pointed to Jansenism's crucial (and now neglected) role in prolonging the Cartesian dichotomy between the external body and the spiritual mind/soul, or *âme*, deep into the supposedly Lockean eighteenth century. Shored up by Jansenism – another bit of common ground shared by Jansenism and a certain French enlightenment – the Cartesian subsoil insured that the transplantation of Lockean empirical sensational epistemology via Voltaire and others in France would produce the radical materialist fruit that so distinguished the French from other European enlightenments. Another exception that may prove a rule, the only other Enlightenment quite so "radical" in Israel's and Margaret Jacob's sense was the Dutch Enlightenment of the late seventeenth and early eighteenth century that harbored a French Huguenot Diaspora of a heavily Cartesian persuasion.[50]

More important, at least on this side of the Atlantic, Palmer's *Catholics and Unbelievers* is arguably the long fuse that ignited the interest that resulted in so many studies of eighteenth-century Jansenism in distinction to its "classic" or Port-Royalist predecessor, studies that, in the nature of things, were bound to add to and modify what Palmer knew and was able to know. His book most certainly ignited my interest in the subject. But what, it may be finally asked, about the long-neglected Jesuits and their own very unique relation to the French Enlightenment – arguably the more central caste of protagonists in the plot of Palmer's book?

It now appears that Palmer and his book are at last getting their revenge in the form of Jeffrey Burson's *The Rise and Fall of Theological Enlightenment: Jean-Martin de Prades and Ideological Polarization in Eighteenth Century France*, now fresh from the University of Notre Dame Press.[51] The "theological enlightenment" that is the main theme of this book is not only a Catholic Enlightenment, but one that Burson calls as a "Jesuit synthesis" elaborated by such French Jesuits as Claude Buffier and René-Joseph Tournemine at the Parisian college of Louis-Le-Grand during the first half of the century of light. What makes the thought of these Jesuits a "synthesis" is that it reconciled the seemingly opposed epistemological empiricism of John Locke and the rationalistic epistemology of René Descartes as modified by Nicolas Malebranche. What makes this synthesis "enlightened" is its appropriation of Locke's sensate empiricism in an attempt to update the epistemology of Aristotelian Thomism in nonessentialist terms. By restating Descartes' "I think, therefore I am" as "I sense, therefore I am," and by eschewing all pretense of explaining the inner essence of either matter or thought or the efficient "cause" of their interaction, these Jesuits thought that they could demonstrate the existence of both the self and an external basis for the self's sensations, as well as the difference between the two. And by extending the individual or "intimate sense" to a communal "common sense" while typically interpreting humanity's "Fall" as its dependence on the senses, the Jesuits plotted an apologetic for Christianity based on the empirical "fact" of supernatural revelation and prophetic miracles. In the wake of the monarchy's anti-Jansenist purge of the Sorbonne in 1729, the "Jesuit synthesis," moreover, had a free field for influence in the University of Paris's philosophical and theological faculty and curricula, as attested to by the ever greater openness to Newtonian physics.

While granting more space for the Cartesian component in the Jesuit synthesis as well as for its acceptance of Newtonian physics, the picture of this Catholic enlightenment as sketched by Burson is again broadly consonant with the portrait of the Jesuits as drawn by Robert Palmer in *Catholics and Unbelievers*. On the cutting edge of Catholic apologetics against "unbelief" in eighteenth-century France, the Jesuits tried to get the better of the argument with the *philosophes* by using against them the largely shared assumptions of a more empirically observable nature, a more descriptive rather than rational natural law, and a more inductive rather than deductive reason. Quite compatible with Palmer's point of view as well is Burson's accent on the Jesuits' apologetic appeal to the empirical "fact" of revelation, as opposed to any effort to make the Christian mysteries seem accessible to intuitive reason. Burson's book hence restores a place for the Jesuits in a Catholic Enlightenment that Palmer had reserved for them thirty or forty years in advance of the historiographical designation of any such place.

One of the unique features of mid-eighteenth-century France in contrast to the rest of Catholic Europe at that time is the sharp tripartite division among Jansenists, the Jesuits and their allies, and a third self-consciously "philosophical" party that wished a pox on both of these Catholic houses. Burson's explanation for the emergence of this third party of philosophical "reason" takes the form of an analytical recounting of a French specialty – a scandalous but revelatory "*affaire*." The affair in question swirled around the Sorbonne's after-the-fact and shamefaced condemnation in 1751 of a thesis entitled *Jerusalem Coelesti*, successfully defended at the Sorbonne by a certain abbé Jean-Martin de Prades, a doctoral candidate in theology but also a minor contributor to Diderot and d'Alembert's new *Encyclopédie*. As it happened, the reason for the condemnation had less to do with the content of the thesis than with the pressure exerted by the *Parlement* of Paris and the Jansenist press on the anti-Jansenist Sorbonne to demonstrate its anti-Lockean orthodoxy, plus the desire of the Jesuits to make a scapegoat of Prades in order to wash their hands of Diderot's suspect *équipe* with whom they had their own bones to pick, not all of them very weighty.

As it also happens, however, the *affaire* of the abbé de Prades is the same affair that Palmer lingered over for nearly fifteen pages and saw as marking the decisive parting of the paths between the cause of Catholicism and that of the French Enlightenment, and for roughly the same reasons.[52] In condemning Prades's epistemology of sensate empiricism, the absence of justice in his account of humanity's pre-civil state of nature, and his questioning of miracles that failed to fulfill prophesy, both the Sorbonne and the archbishop of Paris condemned the entire "Jesuit synthesis" on which Prades was largely relying. These authorities thereby also destroyed the best and perhaps only bridge between eighteenth-century Catholicism and the emerging encyclopedic Enlightenment in France.

Palmer observed that "no satisfactory study" of the abbé de Prades and his affair had ever been done, and Burson has clearly done it, having picked up and put together the pieces of the story pretty much where Palmer had left them.[53] Prades was incontestably in contact with the coeditors of the *Encyclopédie*, Denis Diderot and Jean Le Rond d'Alembert; Prades himself was the author of an article on "certitude" for the new venture. While Palmer followed the then-current scholarly consensus that Prades had received literary and conceptual help from Diderot or d'Alembert, Burson convincingly corrects Palmer by proving beyond any doubt that Prades was the sole author of a thesis that reflected and further developed the "Jesuit synthesis" that had found widespread acceptance in the theological faculty of the University of Paris. In addition, although Palmer rather clearly regarded the Prades affair as revelatory rather than causal, as an event that threw a brief but brilliant light on a fissure between Catholics and unbelievers that was always already in the making, Burson introduces an element of uncertainty and real contingency into his history, regarding the story as an event without which relations between French Catholicism and the Enlightenment might very well have turned out differently.

For Burson as for Palmer, however, a crucial variable in comparison to the lay of the ideological land elsewhere in Catholic Europe was the presence of a second kind of Catholicism in the form of Jansenism that put intense pressure on both the Jesuits and the anti-Jansenist Sorbonne to demonstrate their anti-Lockean orthodoxy at a time of accumulating evidence of materialistic unbelief. For both, too, the affair hardened France's tripartite religious and political divisions on all sides. It hastened, if not caused, the transformation of a once negotiable French Enlightenment into a militant, embattled, and self-consciously anti-Catholic "party" of *philosophes*, while doing nothing to bring Jansenists and Jesuits any closer to each other. To the contrary, the Jansenist "party" was to use yet another scandalous *affaire* embroiling all three "parties" – this one over the publication of the philosophe Claude-Adrien Helvétius's *De l'esprit* in 1757 – to press home an offensive against the Society of Jesus that would end in its suppression by the *parlements* despite clear signs of royal disapproval between the years 1761 and 1764.

In addition to the affairs of Prades's thesis and Helvétius's *De l'esprit*, both of which of course Jansenists saw as evidence of the complicity between the Jesuits' Molinist theology and the rise of materialistic unbelief, what filled the Jansenist sails with additional anti-Jesuit wind was the publication of the second and third parts of Joseph-Isaac Berruyer's *Histoire du peuple de Dieu*, the second on the Gospels in 1753 and the third part on the Pauline epistles in 1756. With the appearance of these two additional parts that brought the total number of volumes up to 18, it became apparent not only that Berruyer persisted in "novelizing" Holy Writ – the main objection to his treatment of the Old Testament – but also that, by the "history of the people of God," Berruyer meant nothing less than the history of humanity. To that humanity, Berruyer was eager to vouchsafe salvation, if not by means of an entirely "natural" religion, then by means of an "implicit" belief in the need for a redeemer in the absence of any explicit revelation, and for the pagan gentiles no less than the "chosen" biblical Hebrews. In the sharpest imaginable contrast to the theology of Saint Augustine, it also became apparent, if it had not been so before, that for Berruyer the "Fall" had been in a sense a Fall upwards, in the long run providing God with "worshippers infinitely more perfect than those that [humankind's] first justice would have given Him in the calm of human passions and the serenity of the comely days of first innocence."[54] Berruyer's was an audacious theology, one that held out the prospect of progress in salvation and for which the eighteenth-century Catholic Church was already the "kingdom of God," and a vast improvement on the early church.[55]

Needless to say, the Jansenist press's cup of indignation ran over, again shaming the anti-Jansenist Sorbonne and the archbishop of Paris into condemnations and providing the *Nouvelles ecclésiastiques* with grist for three or four issues.[56] Needless to say as well, nobody has gone back to the case of Berruyer and his mentor Jean Hardouin since Palmer lingered fascinatingly in Jean Hardouin in *Catholics and Unbelievers* aside, it should be added, for a few well-chosen pages in Catherine Northeast's study of the Parisian Jesuits.[57] Or again until, after decades of fruitless efforts, I recently persuaded one of my own graduate students to take up the case where Palmer and Northeast left off.[58]

The return of Palmer's Jesuits to an enlightened terrain long surrendered to their philosophical and, more recently, even theological enemies, is nonetheless creating as many problems as it solves, not least of them that of two quite competitive Catholic enlightenments. That is one too many enlightenments for the good of the concept. The solution may be to jettison the whole concept of a Catholic Enlightenment in favor of seeing Augustinian "lights" as the religious side of the civic humanist or classical republican strain in the Enlightenment as personified by, say, Gabriel Bonnot de Mably, while regarding Molinist "lights" as the religious counterpart to the Enlightenment of "liberal" political economy as best represented in France by Turgot or André Morellet. Both were, perhaps not coincidentally, products of the post-Jansenist, quite Molinist Sorbonne of the 1750s. Nevertheless, Palmer's classic *Catholics and Unbelievers* will in any case have pointed toward a refraction of a single Enlightenment into spectrum of "lights," as well as toward a less adversarial conception of the relation of religion to these lights – that is, the directions in which the historiography of the Enlightenment now seems to be headed.

In view of that historiography, as well as of our civilization and its present discontents, one further thought may be in order. Indebted in part to the precociously disillusioned modernism of his mentor, Carl Becker, Robert Palmer's ability in *Catholics and Unbelievers* to maintain a certain critical distance from the French Enlightenment that he studied derived further fuel from viewing the *philosophes* through the eyes of some of their acutest contemporary Catholic critics, such as Le Large de Lignac and Nicolas Bergier, who discerned some of the inconsistencies in their impieties. Moreover, nowhere was Palmer harder on the *philosophes* than in regard to their attempt to replace Christian ethics with a system based on human nature and its sensations alone, and to derive the ethical "ought" from the empirical "is." The *philosophes* wished not only to have their sensate pleasures but to have them as "virtue" too. Or if, as Palmer put it, the *philosophes* agreed about "anything, it was in their belief that true virtue was pleasant, that what men ought to do was a form of what nature prompted them to do." And if, he added, "the religious apologists were successful in anything, defending as they were a losing cause, it was in exposing this notion as untenable by a rational mind."[59] By "rational" here, Palmer meant a "reason" that was somehow more than the sum of bodily sensations to which even a Diderot had tended to reduce it.

It is not immediately apparent after more than two centuries that the Enlightenment's ethical project has got much farther off the ground, or that the project has made much progress. When, in the pages of Israel's *Enlightenment Contested*, this project momentarily collapses into to the unabashed hedonism of Helvétius and his *De l'esprit*, it is curious to behold Israel's total identification with the moral indignation of his chosen band of truly "radical" *philosophes* in reaction to this "un-virtuous atheist" in their midst, who had only drawn moral conclusions from premises they could not disavow. The contrast could be hardly greater than to Palmer's attitude of critical and bemused detachment when, in the pages of *Catholics and Unbelievers*, the same Helvétius "shouted the praises of the passions" to the chagrin of the "discreet" Diderot, who preferred to remain unpublished.[60] Yet, Palmer's critical distance also extended to the relativistic implications of his mentor Carl Becker's pragmatic modernism, as would become apparent when he and other historians of the eighteenth century "revisited" Becker's *Heavenly City* in 1958. Beholden, on the one hand, for his critical distance vis-à-vis the Enlightenment to his mentor's skeptical historical relativism, Palmer maintained a critical distance from Becker's historical relativism as well. In all, Palmer's attitude toward the West's cultural inheritance from both Christianity and the Enlightenment resembles nothing quite so much as the discerning mix of gratitude and criticism characteristic of an Alasdair MacIntyre or a Charles Taylor.[61] Although this Palmer would not often reappear in his histories after the publication of *Catholics and Unbelievers*, this book's Palmer is a Palmer well worth the effort to remember.

Notes

[1] Robert R. Palmer, *Catholics and Unbelievers in Eighteenth Century France* (Princeton: Princeton University Press, 1939).

[2] Durand Echeverria, *Mirage in the West: A History of the French Image of America to 1815* (New York: Octagon Books, 1966).

[3] Robert R. Palmer, *The Age of the Democratic Revolution: A Political History of Europe and America, 1760–1800*, 2 vols. (Princeton: Princeton University Press, 1959–64).

[4] Dale Van Kley, *The Jansenists and the Expulsion of the Jesuits from France, 1757–1765* (New Haven: Yale University Press, 1975).

[5] Carl L. Becker, *The Heavenly City of the Eighteenth Century Philosophers* (New Haven: Yale University Press, 1932).

[6] Stanley Mellon, *The Political Uses of History: A Study of Historians in the French Revolution* (Stanford: Stanford University Press, 1958).

[7] Peter Gay, *The Enlightenment: An Interpretation*, 2 vols. (New York: Knopf, 1967–9). It was the first of the two volumes, published in 1967, that was subtitled "The Rise of Neo-Paganism." The subtitle of the second was "The Science of Freedom." For Palmer's own reaction to Gay's first volume, as well as for a defense of the basic point of Becker's *The Heavenly City*, see Palmer's review of the book in *The Journal of Modern History* 39 (1960): 164–6.

[8] Peter Gay, "Carl Becker's Heavenly City," in Raymond O. Rockwood, ed., *Carl Becker's Heavenly City Revisited* (Ithaca: Cornell University Press, 1958), 51.

[9] Isser Wolloch, "Robert R. Palmer, 11 January 1909–11 June 2002," Biographical Memoirs (*Proceedings of the American Philosophical Society*, 2002), 148 (2004): 393–8.

[10] For a spirited defense of Becker's *The Heavenly City* as an example of historiographical "modernism" anticipatory of post modernism, see Johnson Kent Wright, "The Pre-Postmodernism of Carl Becker," in Daniel Gordon, ed., *Post Modernism and the Enlightenment: New Perspectives in Eighteenth-Century French Intellectual History* (London: Routledge, 2001), 161–76.

[11] Becker, *The Heavenly City*, 47.

[12] Palmer, *The Age of the Democratic Revolution*, Vol. 1, *The Challenge* (1959), 56–66, 116–39, 308–17.

[13] Palmer, *Catholics and Unbelievers*, 108. Another example of Palmer as an intellectual historian is his still-valuable "The National Idea in France before the Revolution," *The Journal of the History of Ideas* 1 (1940): 95–111.

[14] Darrin M. McMahon, *The Enemies of Enlightenment: The French Counter-Revolution and the Making of Modernity* (Oxford: Oxford University Press, 2001); and Jonathan

Israel, *Enlightenment Contested: Philosophy, Modernity and the Emancipation of Man 1650–1752* (Oxford: Oxford University Press, 2006), 703–12, 774, 826–62, 934.

15 Palmer, *Catholics and Unbelievers*, 221.

16 Ibid., 65–76.

17 Ibid., 129–54.

18 Ibid., 155–77.

19 Ibid., 178–205.

20 Ibid., 210.

21 That phrase extracted from *The Christian Century*'s review graced the back of the paperback editions of *Catholics and Unbelievers*.

22 Bernhard Groethuysen, *Die Entstehung der bürgerlichen Welt-und Lebensanschauung in Frankreich*, 2 vols. (Halle/Saalle: M. Niemeyer, 1927–30); John McManners, *French Ecclesiastical Society under the Ancien Régime: A Study of Angers in the Eighteenth Century* (Manchester: Manchester University Press: 1960); Albert Monod, *De Pascal à Chateaubriand: Les défenseurs français du Christianisme de 1670 à 1802* (Paris: F. Alcan, 1916); John Nicholas Pappas, *Berthier's Journal de Trevoux* and the *Philosphes in Studies on Voltaire and the Eighteenth Century 3* (Geneva: Institut et musée Voltaire, 1957).

23 Norman Ravitch, *Sword and Mitre; Government and Episcopate in France and England in the Age of Aristocracy* (The Hague: Mouton, 1966).

24 Bernard Plongeron, *Théologie et politique au siècle des lumières (1770–1820)* (Geneva: Droz, 1973).

25 Robert Darnton, most notably in "The High Enlightenment and the Low Life of Literature in Pre-Revolutionary France," *Past and Present* 51 (1971): 81–115 and *The Forbidden Best-Sellers of Pre-Revolutionary France* (New York: W.W. Norton, 1995).

26 On this point, see Thomas E. Kaiser, "This Strange Offspring of Philosophie: Recent Historiographical Problems in Relating the Enlightenment to the French Revolution," *French Historical Studies* 15 (1988): 549–62, 551.

27 Lester Crocker, *An Age of Crisis: Man and World in Eighteenth Century French Thought* (Baltimore: Johns Hopkins University Press, 1959); Diderot, *The Embattled Philosopher* (New York: Free Press, 1966); *Jean-Jacques Rousseau*, 2 vols. (New York: Kennikat Press, 1968–73).

28 Jean Ehrard, *L'idée de la nature en France à l'aube des lumières* (Paris: Flammarion, 1970); George R. Havens, *The Age of Ideas: From Reaction to Revolution in Eighteenth-Century France* (New York: Holt, 1955); Paul Hazard, *La Crise de la conscience euopéenne* (Paris: Boivin, 1935); and *La pensée européenne au XVIIIe siècle de Montesquieu à Lessing* (Paris: Boivin, 1946); Ira O. Wade, *The Intellectual Origins of the French Enlightenment* (Princeton: Princeton University Press, 1971).

29 Kingsley Martin, *French Liberal Thought in the Eighteenth Century: A Study of Political Ideas from Bayle to Condorcet* (London: E. Benn, 1929). Alfred Cobban's main work on the Enlightenment is *In Search of Humanity: The Role of the Enlightenment in Modern History* (London: J. Cape, 1960). For Cobban's considered views on the relation between the Enlightenment and the French Revolution, see his "The Enlightenment and the French Revolution," in *Aspects of the French Revolution* (New York: George Braziller, 1968), 18–28.

30 Daniel Mornet, *Les origines intellectuelles de la Révolution française* (Paris, 1933); and Henri Peyre, "The Influence of Eighteenth-Century Ideas on the French

Revolution," in William Farr Church, *The Influence of the Enlightenment on the French Revolution*, 2nd ed. (Lexington, MA: Heath, 1974), 161–82.

[31] Catherine M. Northeast, *The Parisian Jesuits and the Enlightenment* (Oxford: Oxford University Press, 1991).

[32] Ibid., 160.

[33] Ibid., 179.

[34] Harm Kleuting, Norbert Hinske, and Karl Hengst, Katholische Aufklärung: Aufklärung in *Katholischen Deutschland* (Hamburg: Meiner, 1993): Ulrich Lehner and Michael Printy, eds., *A Companion to the Catholic Enlightenment in Europe* (Leiden: Brill, 2010); Michael Printy, *Enlightenment and the Creation of German Catholicism* (Cambridge: Cambridge University Press, 2009); Helena Rosenblatt, "The Christian Enlightenment," in Stewart J. Brown and Timothy Tackett, eds. *Christianity, Enlightenment, Reawakening and Revolution 1660–1815, The Cambridge History of Christianity* (Cambridge: Cambridge University Press, 2006), 283–301; and David Sorkin, *The Religious Enlightenment: Protestants, Jews, and Catholics from London to Vienna* (Princeton: Princeton University Press, 2008).

[35] Samuel J. Miller, "Enlightened Catholicism on a European Scale," in *Portugal and Rome, c. 1748–1830: An Aspect of Catholic Enlightenment* (Rome: Gregorian University Press, 1978), 1–27; and Bernard Plongeron, "Recherches sur l'`Aufkläring' catholique en Europe occidental, 1770–1830," *Revue d'histoire moderne et contemporaine* 16 (1969): 555–605.

[36] On Turgot on "progress," see Frank E. Manuel, *The Prophets of Paris* (Cambridge, MA: Harvard University Press, 1962), 13–51. Robert Palmer, too, wrote specifically about Turgot in "Turgot: Paragon of the Continental Enlightenment," *Journal of Law and Economics* 19 (1967): 607–19.

[37] Palmer, *Catholics and Unbelievers*, 23–30.

[38] *Nouvelles ecclésiastiques, ou Mémoires pour servir de l'histoire de la constitution Unigenitus*, 3rd ed. (Utrecht, 1728–1803), January 2, 1767, 4.

[39] Ibid., November 12, 1758, 184; and November 18, 1758, 185–6.

[40] On this presence, see in general Dale K. Van Kley, "Piety and Politics in the Century of Lights" in *New Cambridge History of Eighteenth-Century Political Thought* in Mark Goldie and Robert Wokler, eds. (Cambridge: Cambridge University Press, 2006), 110–43; as well as the essays on Austria, France, Italy, and Spain in James E. Bradley and Dale K. Van Kley, eds., *Religion and Politics in Enlightenment Europe* (Notre-Dame, IN: University of Notre Dame Press, 2001).

[41] Monique Cottret, *Jansénismes et lumières: Pour un autre XVIIIe siècle* (Paris: Michel Albin, 1998). See my review of this and other recent books on eighteenth-century Jansenism in "The Rejuvenation and Rejection of Jansenism in History and Historiography: Recent Literature on Eighteenth-Century Jansenism in French," *French Historical Studies* 29 (2006): 649–84.

[42] Ibid., 179–214.

[43] Ibid., 241–69.

[44] The watchword in question comes from a Jansenist interpretation of the phrase "rationabile obsequium" in the Vulgate's version of Saint Paul's advice to the Romans in Romans 12:1. The passage reads, "Obsecro itaque vos fraters per misericordiam Dei ut exhibeatis corpora vestra hostiam viventum sanctam. Deo placentem rationabile obsequium vestrum" *Biblia sacra vulgatam versionem*, eds.

Bonifatio Fischer, Johannae Gribomont, H. D. F. Sparks, W. Thiele, 2 vols., 3rd ed. (Stuttgart, 1983), 2: 1764. Most English Bibles translate "obsequium" as "service" or acts of "worship."

[45] For an example of a Jansenist articulation of this ecclesiology chosen more or less from my notes at random, see Nicolas Travers, *Pouvoirs légitimes du premier et du deuxième ordre dans l'administration des sacremens et le gouverenment de l'église* (n.p., 1744), 22–5. On the "despotism" of the bishops, see 552–3.

[46] Bernard Plongeron, "Recherches sur l''Aufklāring' catholique en Europe occidental, 1770–1830," *Revue d'histoire moderne et contemporaine* 16 (1969): 555–605.

[47] Cottret, *Jansénismes et lumières*, 270–301.

[48] Northeast, *The Parisian Jesuits and the Enlightenment*, 157–8.

[49] Daniele Concina, *Della storia del probabilismo e del rigorismo: dissertazioni teologiche, morali,e critiche* (Venice, 1748); and Mario Rosa, "Jésuitisme et anti-jésuitisme dans l'Italie du XVIIIe siècle," in Pierre-Antoine Fabre et Catherine Maire, eds., *Les anti-jésuites: Discours, figures et lieux de l'antijésuitisme à l'époque moderne* (Rennes: Presse universitaire, 2010): 603. On anti-Jesuitism in the Catholic German states, see Printy, *Enlightenment and the Creation of German Catholicism*, 131–8.

[50] Denis Richet and François Furet, *La Révolution* (Paris: Hachette, 1965).

[51] Margaret C. Jacob, *The Radical Enlightenment: Pantheists, Freemasons, and Republicans*, 2nd ed. (Lafayette, LA: Cornerstone, 2006).

[52] Jeffrey D. Burson, *The Rise and Fall of Theological Enlightenment: Jean-Martin de Prades and Ideological Polarization in Eighteenth Century France* (Notre Dame, IN: University of Notre Dame Press , 2010).

[53] Palmer, *Catholics and Unbelievers*, 117–31.

[54] The closest things to any such study are Thomas O'Connor, "Théologie et lumières chez Luke Joseph Hooke" (thèse de doctorat, Sciences des religions, Paris IV and l'Institut catholique, 1993); and John Spink's "L'affaire de J.-M. de Prades" in *Dix-huitième siècle* 3 (1971): 150–80.

[55] Isaac-Joseph Berruyer, première partie, Histoire du Peuple de Dieu depuis son origine jusqu'à la naissance du Messie, tirée des seuls livres saints, ou le texte sacré des livres de l'ancien Testament, réduit en un corps d'histoire. Nouvelle édition. 10 vols. (Paris, 1753), 1: "preface," xii–xiii.

[56] Isaac-Joseph Berruyer, *Histoire du peuple de Dieu, depuis la naissance du Messie jusqu'à la fin du Synogogue, deuxième partie* (La Haye, 1753), 8 vols. 2: 7, 240–5.

[57] *Nouvelles ecclésiastiques*, March 19, 1760, 49–64; November 16–23, 1762, 181–7; May 2, 1763, 73–6; June 13–20, 1763, 97–101. For the Sorbonne's condemnation, Vota deputatorum sacrae facultatis parisiensis, super opere cui titulus, Histoire du Peuple de Dieu, &c In comitiis generalibus ejusdem Sacrae Facultatis discutendia. Pars secunda. Parisiis (Paris, 1763). See the *Nouvelles ecclésiastiques* less than glowing review of the second part of the Sorbonne's judgment on January 16, 1765, pp. 13–17.

[58] Northeast, *The Parisian Jesuits and the Enlightenment*, 103–5, 129–34; 143–8, 151–6, 160–5, 180–1.

[59] The student in question is Daniel Watkins, now in his fourth year of graduate study at Ohio State University.

[60] Palmer, *Catholics and Unbelievers*, 188.

[61] Israel, *Enlightenment Contested*, 794–813; and Palmer, *Catholics and Unbelievers*, 187.

[62] Alasdair MacIntyre, *After Virtue: A Study in Moral Theory* (London: Duckworth, 1981); and Charles Taylor, *Sources of the Self: The Making of the Modern Identity* (Cambridge, MA: Harvard University Press, 1989). Palmer's distance from Becker's modernist historical relativism, even as applied to the Enlightenment, would certainly have held a fortiori for the relativism of the postmodern critique of the Enlightenment as well. On that critique, see Daniel Gordon, ed., *Post-Modernism and the Enlightenment* (London: Routledge, 2001) and Keith M. Baker and Peter H. Reill, eds., *What's Left of the Enlightenment? A Postmodern Question* (Stanford: Stanford University Press, 2001).

Chapter 2

The Regency of Catherine de Medici: Political Reason during the Wars of Religion

Denis Crouzet

From 1559 onwards, but most notably following her accession to the title of ruler and then regent of the kingdom, Catherine de Medici cast her relationship to power in dramatic terms. This dramatic self-image was one she would cultivate to the end of her life as she returned again and again to its founding moment: the death of her husband, King Henry II. Henceforth, all her actions were defined in terms of her unstinting service and loyalty to the dead king's memory. For instance, on September 26, 1575, when she wrote to Henry III demanding to be informed of the kingdom's affairs while away from court, she justified her interest by citing her complete devotion to the kingdom. "You are everything to me," she wrote, claiming that if he should ever cease loving and trusting her service she would be "unable to live any longer." Life would lose all meaning, "because, since the death of the King your father, I have never wanted to live except to serve you and God; and you know it, I am sure."[1] Self-sacrifice and complete dispossession – these were the key terms that informed Catherine de Medici's engagement to the king and characterized her political activity on behalf of the monarchy.

My aim in this chapter is to demonstrate the importance of the regency period for the construction of Catherine de Medici as a figure so devoted to both king and God that she ceased to live for herself. The regency period itself is relatively short. It began in March 1561, when Catherine de Medici obtained the position of regent for Charles IX, and lasted until the proclamation of Charles IX's coming of age on August 17, 1563. However, it also reflects a larger context crucial for understanding Catherine's will to sacrifice, namely the double crisis of royal authority, which was faced with desacralizing discourses and practices from both Protestant and Catholics. In addition to the Conspiracy of Amboise in March 1560, trouble was brewing throughout the kingdom. Catholics and Protestants alike defied royal ordinances and edicts proclaiming civil peace, despite the threat of judicial punishment for those who infringed them. Throughout the spring of 1561, Huguenots committed increasingly numerous acts of iconoclasm and occupied religious buildings with the aim of turning them into Protestant places of worship. Royal officers either opted to stand by passively on the sidelines or, on the occasions they did intervene, proved powerless to stop these public actions. Catholics, meanwhile, were also causing civil discord; groups of militants organized themselves in *confréries* to attack and even sometimes ritualistically massacre Huguenots at Holy Communion.

It is worth noting that, while the king's evil councilors were denounced, official discourse on both sides never advocated violence against the person of the king, who remained shielded from attack. However, when considered on a more symbolic or "unconscious" level, this violence contained a radicalizing potential. In 1562, while destroying wooden and stone images in churches in towns under their control, Calvinists sometimes went further. At the Hôtel de Ville in Orleans, sculptures of kings, as well as saints, were thrown down and destroyed. At Notre-Dame de Cléry, the statue of Louis XI was broken. Blaise de Montluc reported that one iconoclast who refused to obey the king's law called Charles IX a "petit reyot de merde" ("a shitty little king"). Such desacralizing actions and speech indicated that a certain violence against royal authority was at work, even if only in exceptional circumstances and of a largely symbolic nature. By treating the royal person as a human being like any other, this violence denied the sacred nature of royalty. To be sure, it was mostly confined to the margins of official Calvinist discourse, which otherwise remained faithful to Calvin's teaching that submission to the magistrate was the will of God, even when the magistrate was unjust. Nonetheless, it shared something in common with the Catholic faction, which made no qualms about comparing Catherine de Medici and Antoine of Bourbon to Jezebel and Ahab for their refusal to take sides.

Catherine de Medici's role as a mediating figure was constructed at this time, partly as an ideological rejoinder to this escalating religious violence and partly also to express what was probably her own subjective self-understanding. The regency justified itself by invoking several complimentary claims to authority. First, it invoked a power driven by motherly love, in which Catherine was represented as attached as much to her son, Charles IX, as to her subjects. The regency was thus identified with a power exercised in the name of wisdom's virtue. Second, the regency associated itself with a power founded upon *logos*, upon the speech originally given by

God to men so that they might live in harmony, far removed from barbarity. In such a way, discourse, the order of words, came to be opposed to the chaos of violence. Finally, and most crucially, was Catherine's claim about the superiority of woman as mother. Her entire policy should be reassessed in light of the maternal imaginary through which she legitimized her authority as regent. This superiority enabled her to assume sweeping powers, both to oppose religious sectarianism and to restore peace among the king's subjects. As a minor, Charles IX was kept from public view by the figure of his mother who assumed full control over all areas of political activity, occupying, as it were, the entire stage upon which she now projected her love, her speech, and her identity as a woman.

The Regency as the Duty of Motherly Love

To better understand how this image was constructed, we need to return to the period before 1559 and consider the manner in which Catherine of Medici justified and vindicated her presence and role in the kingdom. As Nicolas Houel later claimed in his *Histoire françoyse de nostre temps*, from the moment Catherine disembarked at Marseilles with her great uncle Pope Clement VII, she was hailed as "the wise Catherine." Her marriage to Francis I's son was to create a peace "as durable as it is divine."[2] The wise Catherine and her husband Henry II were depicted as holding a horn from which flickered a divine fire – a symbol of fertility – and which represented the new queen as the hope and future joy for the kingdom and earth.[3] She was compared with the queen of Olympus, "the Juno of France," the "pronube Juno."[4] She had been called by Providence to conceive "sons who would inherit the world."[5]

An important aspect of this self-image was her decision to adopt the rainbow of the Greek Goddess Iris as her emblem. The rainbow signified the return of sunlight to the human world after a dark period of tempests and storms. In his *Premier livre des Odes*, the poet Ronsard celebrated her as a woman unrivalled by those who possessed the highest achievements in learning and virtue. "*Quelle Dame a la pratique / De tant de Mathematique? / Quelle Princesse entend mieux / Du grand Monde la peinture, / Les chemins de la nature, / Et la musique des Cieux?*" [What lady has such extensive knowledge of mathematics? / What princess better understands the world of painting / the paths and byways of nature / and the music of the Heavens?]. The poet added that Heaven had granted "us" a princess from Florence, favored by the stars, "who shall be our light," and whose children were predestined to ensure that France ruled the world. In referring to this light, Ronsard merely reiterated Catherine de Medici's own chosen symbolism. As soon as she had arrived in France, she had claimed for herself the mission of mediating between God and men. Her motto was: "she brings light and serenity." This motto offers up several interpretations. The most obvious relates the motto to the learning that Catherine de Medici claimed to possess and thanks to which she was predestined to chart a new history for France. Sunlight also symbolized the truth of *bonae litterae*, which had been revived in Italy. She thus had arrived in France in order to fight ignorance, which kept human beings in the lower sphere of opinions and passions. Committed to this struggle of light against darkness and illusion, her work was to be one of conversion (in the sense that this word had in Plato's *Republic*, meaning the conversion of souls to wisdom, the transition from darkness to light).

This motto was later revised in various interesting ways. Catherine's new motto became: "she brings hope and joy before her." This second motto identified her with the divine messenger whose coming was necessary for the establishment of a reign of peace and fecundity for the kingdom. Catherine's presence in France thus announced a golden age, which prefigured peace in Europe. Her motto connected her with the image of a mother giving birth to children, whom Providence had called upon to reign over a united and peaceful Christendom. From 1555 onwards, and even after the wars of religion had begun, Ronsard continued to celebrate this theme of Catherine's presence as a springtime of renewal for the world, a return to the golden age.

All this would change after the death of Henry II, and especially during the regency. Although the mission of mediating between God and men was maintained, it was re-centered upon the sacrificial identity assumed by the queen mother after her husband's death. Court poets were commissioned to promulgate this change in identity throughout the regency's two crucial years. Catherine de Medici remained the force that gave life to the Kingdom, but she was now depicted as having sacrificed her own self in the continuing battle against the passions, which threatened to overwhelm mankind's God-given reason. The regency was thus represented as a period of labor and sorrow. In a 1563 sonnet dedicated to the queen, Estienne Jodelle described these two crucial years as a period of time in which peace was threatened by "holy or sham enthusiasms."[6] Identifying Catherine with the giant Atlas who supported France, he recalled how the regent had dedicated herself ceaselessly to the revival of reason, the ardor for which was in danger of being extinguished. Ronsard represented the queen mother in a similar vein, as someone who had devoted herself to suffering, to questioning, to voyaging, to planning and, in the last instance, to speaking.[7] This dramatic and painful labor made the regency a special period, during which time the life of the French people revolved around the work of salvation and sacrifice prepared by the queen mother.

The poets Melin de Saint-Gelays and Estienne Jodelle represented this tireless work with a play on her namesake, as did the Neo-Platonic poet Amadis Jamyn, who compared her name to the mother of the gods, she who was able to purge and purify France.[8] Just like the saint whose name she bore, and who was tortured on the wheel before being beheaded, the "mother of France" too had suffered a great many evils, anxieties, and dangers. In the manner of a true apologist for the monarchy, Brantôme described how Catherine de Medici transformed her emblems after the death of Henry II in order to symbolically reflect this need for self-sacrifice. Broken mirrors, fans, chairs, and feathered pens were pictured around her motto, with her jewels and pearls scattered upon the ground. This visual imagery signified her intent to give up all worldly pleasures after her husband's death, which she would never cease to mourn. Brantôme explained that without God's gift of peace and the constancy of her love, Catherine would have sunk under the weight of her immense sadness and anxiety.[9] However, she could see that her children needed her, as experience would indeed prove. Brantôme depicted the queen mother as someone who fought on, like a Semiramis or an Athalia, to protect those children and their realm from the various conspiracies that had already been in the making since their youth, and which were averted due to her prudence and industry.[10]

Poets did not restrain themselves from singing her glory. They stressed the homophony of her Christian name, which had by now become an allegory of her life's work as one long study in patience and prudence. Under the influence of fate, she had been called upon to liberate the senseless French from their civil struggles. Fate had made her the purifier who cleansed France. "By a great, good and wise medicine" she extinguished the "ardeur" that was burning the Kingdom: Catherine became Catharsis.[11]

In this exuberant series of identifications, everything was done to portray the queen regent as a mother.[12] This was in accordance with the Christocentric viewpoint that the love that she devoted to the kingdom, and through which she was fighting France's destructive passions, reflected an energy that derived from and belonged to her faith in Christ, who had died on the cross. This led to a further permutation of her identity. In contrast to her previous association with Juno, Catherine was now identified with Pallas, becoming the very incarnation of reason, virtue, justice, and wisdom. In the apothecary Nicholas Houel's *Histoire françoyse de nostre temps*, she is described as being "like a Pallas" who has driven discord out of France, a Pallas who loves piety and justice and guides reason away from vice. Inspired by a poem that Houel wrote which had allegorically linked her to Artemisa II, Catherine commissioned the painter Antoine Caron to depict her as a new Artemisia of Caria, a princess who had devoted her entire life to protecting royal power. This eternal devotion to her deceased husband was depicted in a sequence of illustrations representing the new motto of the widowed queen: *ardorem extincta testantur vivere flamma*. This time the image accompanying the motto featured a pile of quick-lime with drops of water falling from the sky. It signified that her love was like a fire that continued to burn in the absence of any flame. This image recalled the strength of a light, which, even when barely visible, nonetheless remained powerfully regenerative, like a spring or source of life. "She was thus stating that the flames of the true and sincere love she had for the King were still throwing sparks, after the life of this good prince, who used to light them, had been extinguished."[13] Artemisia, who was full of love for her late husband, had also devoted herself to peace and to the survival of the Kingdom. She built the mausoleum of Halicarnassus, she defended the realm against internal and external threats; moreover, she gave her son Lygdamis an exemplary education that made him a prince full of wisdom. Artemisia's life-story was like a scene-by-scene transcription of the same dream that guided Catherine de Medici throughout her regency: that of complete devotion to civic duty, which she conveyed to her son's subjects through poetry and painting. This dream reflected the Neo-Platonist belief that simply recalling and re-enacting the deeds of historically important individuals was enough to renew past historical cycles. Like Artemisia, Catherine appeared to herself as dead. As Loys Dorleans would sing in his own poems, she was remembered as the one who had drunk her husband's ashes, thereby absorbing his death.[14] This suggests a view of politics in which history was not linear. On the contrary, both history and politics shared the same mythological understanding of human intervention in which words, by giving order to time, were also imagined as capable of reactivating the cycles of the past.

The Regency: A Utopia of Pacifying Discourse

As indicated at length in the preceding section, during the regency, Catherine de Medici sought to appear as a wise ruler, who used discourse – the first instrument of wisdom – to ward off the forces of evil. One significant example of this reorientation occurs in Ronsard's hymn "On Winter," which appeared in the collection "The Four Seasons of the Year," first published in 1563. The poem narrates the story of Hephaistos, god of winter, who, born lame and ugly, was rejected by the Gods. Taking refuge in Thracia, he meets Boreas, the god of wind, who urges him to use warfare to claim the title of "king of snow and ice and cold." War is prepared, but Mercury imprisons Hephaistos by putting him to sleep. Jupiter would have struck him by lightning but Juno intervenes. Once more, speech is depicted as the condition of peace and harmony. Having achieved his release, Juno gives a banquet to all the Gods, with copious amounts of food, music, dancing, and singing. Reconciliation is achieved, and Hephaistos is given the earth for three months each year, enabling the world to live in friendship and harmony. In the original story, Mercury, messenger and god of eloquence, is depicted as occupying the middle seat during the banquet, indicating the superiority of logos over violence and passion.

Ronsard developed the same theme in his allegory about Catherine de Medici. Like Juno, now Catherine de Medici was depicted as presiding over the winter ballet, thereby confirming the primacy she granted to discourse when threatened with violence. Nevertheless, there is a further meaning in this allegory. In the mythological story, Juno is the sister of Jupiter: "as from the same seeds sky and air have been created; and she is his spouse, as air is subject to sky." Through this double connection, Juno has "power in the sky and if, authorized by Jupiter, power over mankind as well."[15] Winter represents, therefore, the allegory of the earthly world and of mankind, constantly attracted by war, but ready for a peace that reflects the will of God. Once commissioned to represent royal power, poetic discourse too became part of this incantational, "magical" kind of thinking.[16] Singing of the life of man under the guidance of myths, poetry activated a kind of cosmic "sympathy," an incantatory struggle against the forces of evil, which replicated the regent's own struggle. Discourse was represented as the weapon of choice in the fight for peace and for God, whether poetically, through mythology, or practically, through politics. By opposing words to the gestures of violent people, Catherine too aspired to dispense a fair and pious order.

If poetry represented one kind of discourse, speech and letter writing were another. In 1563, the Venetian Barbaro recorded his observations of a queen who stood out for her ability to speak as well as listen. He related the "patience" of Catherine in obtaining other people's esteem and "the tireless constancy" with which she received all kinds of people; "she listened to their speeches and showed them as much politeness as one could have wished." As the author of the *Vie des dames illustres françoises et étrangères* put it, although Italian born, the queen mother "spoke French very well." She was a princess "who displayed her fine speech to Great Lords, to foreigners and to ambassadors," displaying a gracious and majestic discourse in both speech and writing.[17] Brantôme recounted how he had once seen the queen, after dinner, writing "twenty pairs of long letters" by herself.[18] We know that, as early as December 6, 1560, during the first King's council of Charles IX's reign, she ordered that all correspondence be sent to her in the first instance.[19] In this constant stream of oral and written communication, power was wielded through the flow and counterflow of words, a plenitude of words, at once both centrifugal and centripetal. In addition, whenever Catherine wrote during this period of transition, she insisted on repeating to her correspondents that she was fully involved, fully conscious of the immense difficulties facing the kingdom but also committed to peace to her dying breath. For instance, on May 18, 1563, she wrote to the Lord of Lansac: "I am incessantly trying to establish everything that belongs to and depends upon reaching peace. As you can well imagine, after all the calamities, ruins and damages which the people have suffered, this is hardly one day's work. So many angry minds cannot be reconciled at one stroke."[20] Clearly, Catherine was doing full time work in the service of peace.

Whenever a critical point was reached – for example, when relations with some great lord of the kingdom had broken off because he had deliberately absented himself from court, sending off signals of mistrust – a letter became the instrument of last resort, even if, at times, only indirectly. Letters symbolized the force that pacified tensions. For example, at the end of 1561, the Guises, through the intermediary of the Duke of Nemours, had tried to persuade the Duke of Anjou to flee the court and seek refuge outside the kingdom. After Catherine was informed and their ruse revealed, the Guises retired to their castle in Joinville, communicating an attitude of simultaneous trust and mistrust toward the royal power and its policy of tolerance and pacification. Although extremely nervous at this point, Catherine tried to extend a hand to the Guises once more, this time using female friendship as an intermediary. Around mid-December, she wrote to Anne d'Este, ostensibly to assure her that her goodwill and friendship had in no way been damaged by the recent developments. However, the letter also implicitly induced its recipient to inform the Duke of Guise and his clan that the monarchy was expecting a gesture of reconciliation.

The Colloquy of Poissy, in particular, represented a high point in this reliance on speech to reconcile religious differences. Its aim was to create a temporary space for Catholic and Protestant theologians to engage in discussion, thereby demonstrating that their differences, which were leading the faithful into an escalating spiral of violence, were not irreconcilable. Although this project of concord was doomed to fail, Catherine de Medici played an important and decisive role in its preparation.[21] The idea for the Colloquy was most likely inspired by Nicholas of Cusa's *De pace fidei*, which concluded that the differences opposing the representatives of different religions related more to rites than to the underlying truths of faith. Despite the Colloquy's eventual failure, Estienne Jodelle was able to write that it had provisionally fulfilled its aim, as peace had become stronger at the very moment when the threat of civil conflict loomed greatest.[22] Toward the end of December 1561, the queen regent summoned an Assembly of Notables in another attempt at resolution through dialogue. The outcome of this meeting was the drawing up of the Edict of January 1562, which granted freedom of worship and conscience to the Huguenots. This was incredible progress. From the monarchy's point of view, the Edict was proof of the conviction that the mere fact of living together in peace gave Catholics and Calvinists time to speak together. In other words, it allowed the time necessary to realize that reconciliation was possible both in the short and medium terms, especially if God forgave a kingdom that was able to resolve its differences peacefully. During the assembly held in St. Germain-en-Laye, some participants expressed serious reservations about religious coexistence but their objections were overturned when, at the conclusion of all the speeches, the monarchy resorted to a vote. This vote was intended to demonstrate that a certain kind of wisdom had indeed emerged out of all the verbal confrontations.

The period following the massacre of Vassy (Wassy) on March 1, 1562, was undoubtedly the most tense in Catherine's struggle against the passions. Caught between the Huguenots who, under the Prince of Condé, were exercising their "duty to revolt," and the royalist party, to which she herself belonged and whose bellicose appetites she wanted to refrain, the regent committed herself utterly to the work of negotiation. Negotiators were sent to Orleans; meetings with Condé, such as those on June 28–29, were arranged in the countryside; talks were held again near Paris on December 2–4. Even after the failure of these negotiations, and when Catherine openly rallied to the party of warfare, she still hoped that the threat of war would bring the Huguenots back to the negotiating table. In a letter dated April 11, 1562, the Queen stated that she had done everything to disarm those who now refused peace. However, when dealing with "harshness" and an all-powerful "hidden venom," even mildness had its limits. She wrote that when tensions reached such a boiling point, a clear-cut decision had to be made and everything possible done to make people understand that henceforth the queen would privilege the defense of royal authority above all else, relying on the lords who surrounded her and were ready to shed their last drop of blood for their king.[23] Nevertheless, even here, the language of war was instrumentalized as a means to exert pressure. As the regent herself would say, the peace of Amboise was still intended as a work of kindness and humanity, even if it took the form of a battle fought with masterly stratagems.

The Regency: Struggle of a Feminine Ideal

It is at this point during the regency that Catherine de Medici's personal mythology was explicitly marshaled in support of her political program of mediation. In April 1563, Catherine, openly and without hesitation, proclaimed that the pacifying role of women alone had the power to stop the continuing threat of violence. She wrote to Artus Cossé that she "was working" to stop the plunders and murders, and that her incessant letter writing was an attempt to persuade the king's subjects to be obedient. In this letter, she expressed regret that the unfortunate quarrels during March and April 1562 had prevented the completion of the work begun at St. Germain in January of that same year. Had men not imposed their will, all the disasters that had befallen the kingdom could have been avoided. She wrote:

> For this, there is no remedy. To be sure, if this war has made things worse than they had to be, it is easiest to lay blame on a monarchy ruled by a single woman. But in all honesty what should be blamed and calomnied is the rule of men who all want to act as kings. Henceforth, if I am not prevented again, I hope that people will understand that women have more will to preserve the kingdom than those who have brought about the current situation. I ask that you try to persuade all those who speak to you of this essential truth, as told by the King's mother who only loves him and who desires the preservation of his kingdom and subjects.[24]

For Catherine, to be humane was, above all, to be feminine. Lines such as these went much further than the usual sixteenth-century discourses on the excellence of women that proclaimed not so much the superiority of women as such, but rather their equal abilities to accede to knowledge. Here we find Catherine de Medici taking up the same antitheses that had structured Marguerite de Navarre's novel *Heptaméron*, which opposed the brutal and violent honor of men – who conquered women only to glory in the act of possession – to the prudent and dignified honor of women.[25] In their ability to love more readily than men, women enabled a glimpse of a truly sustainable peace.

As this confidential letter by Catherine de Medici makes clear, it is thanks to women that mankind was able to move away from its negative tendency toward destruction. This was not solely because women dispensed and protected life but also because only women were sufficiently capable of promoting and defending a new era of human quiet, of "humanity." Catherine de Medici never doubted this, and throughout her regency, she used her identity as a woman to give added weight to the policy of reconciliation. In a letter sent to the Lord of Limoges, during the crucial days of April 1562, Catherine expressed her commitment to stalling for time in the march toward war in the hope that "Our Lord would bring some improvement" to the great fires burning throughout the kingdom. Even while resorting to any available means to gain time and forestall war, she claimed to have always made her decisions as "a woman," as "the mother of a King in ward."[26] These two attributes, she claimed, led her to consider "gentleness more suitable in curing that disease than any other remedy."

The power that she assumed both as woman and as regent consisted in taking back the kingdom's future from the hands of men in order to return it to God. It was in the name of this love that she had offered herself up in self-sacrifice. We can of course question the originality of this emphasis on feminine virtue, which gave the regent such a sense of purpose. *Il Cortegiano*, Castiglione's famous book, had already expressed similar views when the character Guiliano de' Medici attacked Ottaviano, who had denigrated women as incapable of virtuous action, by arguing that although physical weakness made women less bold than men, it also made them more capable of prudence.[27] Lorenzo the Magnificent had similarly pointed to numerous historical examples of women with the strength to appease the most bellicose of men. In all these discourses on female virtue, sweetness was synonymous with courage and courage with love. These virtues were exemplified by the story of the Sabine women who, clad in black and crying, some of them holding small children in their arms, came between their fathers and husbands. In this legendary story about the foundations of Rome, female love and wisdom succeeded in ending the struggle between the Sabian tribe and the Romans, creating an "indissociable friendship and confederation" between the two peoples. The excellence of women was exalted in both the recent female figures of Margaret of Austria and Isabella of Castile, as well as in the numerous references to queens of antiquity, among them Zenobia, Cleopatra, Semiramis, Thomiris, and, naturally, Artemisia of Caria.[28]

It was vital that this sweetness be taught to the king who, although still a minor, was soon to reign over his subjects. Catherine shared this conviction with Michel de l'Hosptial, the Chancellor of France, with whom she collaborated very closely during the two years of the regency. Both shared a similar view of the relationship between the civil crisis and God's almighty power, a view that led them to formulate a policy of reconciliation focused on the sacred figure of the king. For l'Hospital, if there was religious division in the kingdom, it was because the French people had increasingly neglected their virtues and abandoned themselves to vice – to luxury, ambition, greed, and lust. God, according to the Chancellor de l'Hospital, had punished the French by sending religious division, which was less a cause than a result of division. The violence between Catholics and Huguenots, in which both parties sought to defeat each other and conquer the kingdom for their own religion, only plunged the state and the people deeper into evil. To imagine that violence and the incitement of cruel and wicked passions could reduce religious divisions was to make use of evil and therefore persist in evil. Men could not by their own means put an end to God's punishment, for violence was the very figure of evil through which they had incurred divine wrath. Violence was sin. What was needed was prayer and God's pardon for the sins that had caused rival faiths to appear in the kingdom. Only God could put an end to religious division, and no one could know when that would happen.

However, despite this rhetoric of providential justice, or perhaps because of it, l'Hospital, like Catherine, privileged the role played by the king in averting further violence. For l'Hospital, the king was chosen by God not to make war, but to ensure that justice reigned and that passions were suppressed. It was, therefore, the king's responsibility to do everything possible to prevent war by imposing peace on all parties concerned. The model of the exemplary prince was that of a Stoic emperor ruling in full control of his passions, and against the passions of his subjects. L'Hospital, who was influenced by Erasmus, sought to impose a vision of political order in which the state followed the doctrines of Christ, teaching and demonstrating to all that peace should unite men for eternity.

War and violence were evils. The only acceptable wars were those between nations whose aim was to defend the king's subjects against the aggression of greedy and ambitious sovereigns. In the sphere of domestic politics, the king's law should always be used to prevent civil troubles. The model of the good king was Solomon, not David. In other words, the king was to be both judge and arbiter. He could not seek to use violence against the wicked and unjust, for they were wicked and unjust only on account of blindness. The king's role was best exercised through the use of pardon, which was not a defeat of absolute power but its finest expression. By preventing his subjects from tearing each other apart, the king appeared as a model of justice, showing that love prevailed over hate. For l'Hospital, as for Catherine, violence began when the sacred character of kingship was denied.

This should make clear the extent to which the regency was intended as a period of apprenticeship for Charles IX. Even though the king was completely overshadowed by his mother, who assumed sweeping powers, her actions were nonetheless intended as a type of pedagogy for the future king. By way of conclusion, therefore, we can draw a parallel between Catherine de Medici's political program of reconciliation and her pedagogical program that was inspired by the Neo-Platonic Florentine philosophy of the late fifteenth century, popularized in France during the second half of the sixteenth century by the poet Pierre de Ronsard and the philosopher Loys Le Roy. This philosophy stressed that the king's role was to do everything possible to prevent the violence that was pitting his subjects against each other. When Catherine entrusted the education of her sons to the Bishop Jacques Amyot, she hoped to inculcate them with the Platonic model of the philosopher–king. Such a king had to gain familiarity with all the sciences in order to penetrate the mysteries of the universe. Knowledge, in this case, was synonymous with access to the divine, because wisdom's virtue lay in its power to unveil creation as a divinely ordered harmony. Knowledge, in other words, substituted for violence. On the one hand, this meant that the duty of the king was to contemplate this divine harmony. On the other hand, it also meant that his duty was to elevate the base human world, divided and corrupted by human passions, closer toward that divine harmony. In either case, violence was represented as standing at the opposite extreme of good statesmanship. The king had to do everything possible to avoid violence. He had to show love toward his subjects, governing them with prudence as well as cunning in order to bring them into the union and concord demanded by God. In other words, the king had to govern just like his mother.

Notes

1 *Lettres de Catherine de Médicis*, edited by Hector de la Ferrière and Gustave Baguenault de Puchesse (Paris: Imprimerie nationale, 1880–1943), Vol. V, 141–2. Hereafter *Lettres de Catherine de Médicis*.

2 Jean Ehrmann, *Antoine Caron, peintre des fêtes et des massacres* (Paris: Flammarion, 1986), 90. On Nicolas Houel, see S. E. Lepinois, *Nicolas Houel. Apothicaire et bourgeois parisien fondateur du jardin de l'Ecole des apothicaires de Paris. Notes biographiques d'après des documents inédits* (Dijon: Therèse Jacquet, 1911).

3 On this motif of love, see Geneviève Monnier and William Mac Allister-Johnson, "Caron antiquaire: à propos de quelques dessins du Louvre" in *Revue de l'Art*, n. 14 (1971): 23–30. The horn of fire recalls an emblem from the *Hecatomgraphie* (1540) by Gilles Corrozet: surrounded by a woman whose heart is pierced by an arrow and a gentleman, Cupid holds in his right hand his bow, and in his left a cornucopia in which love's fire burns. For a list of French Neo-Platonist publications, see *Marsile Ficin, Sur le banquet de Platon ou de l'Amour*, edited by Raymond Marcel (Paris: Les Belles Lettres, 1956), 124–31. This list includes Gilles Corrozet's *La diffinition et perfection d'Amour* (1542) and Jehan de La Haye, *Le sophologe d'Amour* (1546). It also notes that Pontus du Tyard dedicated his translation of *Philosophie d'Amour de Léon l'Hébreu* (1552) to Catherine of Medici.

4 Pierre de Ronsard, "A la royne Catherine de Médicis, mere du roy, Ode II" in *Œuvres complètes* (Paris: P. Jannet, 1857–67), Vol. III, 171.

5 Ronsard, "Mascarades, Les sereines représentées au Canal de Fontainebleau" in *Œuvres complètes*, Vol. IV, 145.

6 *Les œuvres et meslanges poétiques d'Estienne Jodelle*, edited by Marty-Laveaux (Paris: LeMarre, 1868–70), Vol. 2, 156–7.

7 Ronsard, *Œuvres complètes*, Vol. IV, 204–6.

8 Amadis Jamyn, *Œuvres poétiques d'Amadis Jamyn. Avec sa vie par Guillaume Colletet*, edited by Charles Brunet (Paris: Léon Willem, 1878), 36.

9 *Œuvres complètes de Pierre de Bourdeille, Seigneur de Brantôme*, edited by Ludovic Lalande (Paris: Société de l'histoire de France, 1864–82), Vol. VII, 351.

10 See also Amadis Jamyn, "Pour la Junon nopcière à la même entrée" in *Œuvres poétiques*, 46.

11 "C'est par destin qu'avez nom Catherine/Qui grande, bonne et sage médecine/ Avez purgé la France de l'ardeur," Amadis Jamyn, *Œuvres poétiques*, 37.

12 On the opposing myth of Medea at the end of the early French Renaissance, see Jean de La Péruse, "Médée" in *Théâtre français de la Renaissance: La tragédie à l'époque d'Henri II et de Charles IX*, Vol. I (Florence: Leo S. Olschki; Paris: Presses universitaires de France, 1989), 120–73.

13 Brantôme, *Œuvres complètes*, Vol. VII, 349; also cited in Anna Franchi, *Caterina de' Medici, regina di Francia* (Milan: Casa Editrice Ceschina, 1933), 81: "par ainsi dire notre Reyne monstroit son ardeur et son affection par ses larmes, encore que sa flamme, qui estoit le Roy son mary, fust esteinte; qui estoit autant à dire que, tout mort qu'il estoit, elle faisoit bien paroistre par ses larmes qu'elle ne le pouvoit oublier, et qu'elle l'aymoit toujours." Another image that circulated was that of a broken lance with the motto: *Hinc dolor, Hinc lacryma.*

14 See "A la Reine mere du roi Caterine de Medicis" in Ingrid Lamur, *L'Œuvre manuscrite de Louis Dorleans: Histoire de l'origine de la Ligue et Poezies*, Mémoire de maîtrise under the direction of Denis Crouzet, 1999–2000, Université de Paris IV-Sorbonne, 112–13.

15 Quoted in Jean Céard, "'Au travers du voile': *L'Hymne de l'Hyver* de Ronsard," in *Les fruits de la Saison. Mélanges de littérature des XVIe et XVIIe siècles offerts au professeur André Gendre*, edited by Philippe Tessier, Loris Petris, and Marie-Jeanne Liengme Bessire (Neuchâtel-Genève: Droz, 2000): 209–22.

16 On the mythological garb that clothes the *poeta philosophus*, see Jean Céard, "Les mythes dans les Hymnes de Ronsard," in *Les mythes poétiques au temps de la Renaissance*, edited by Marie-Thérèse Jones-Davies (Paris: J. Touzot, 1985), 21–34: "le mythe raconte un lointain passé pour nous aider à entendre notre présent et soutenir l'espoir de l'avenir qui nous est promis de Dieu" (30). In a manner typical of fables, myth functions like a lesson but it is also a history insofar as it seeks to influence both present and future.

17 Brantôme, *Œuvres complètes*, Vol. VII, 375.

18 Brantôme, Vol. VII, 374.

19 See Jean Boutier, Alain Dewerpe, and Daniel Nordman, *Un tour de France royal. Le voyage de Charles IX* (1564–66) (Paris: Éditions Aubier, 1984), 214.

20 *Lettres de Catherine de Médicis*, Vol. II, 42.

21 See Alain Tallon, *Conscience nationale et sentiment religieux en France au XVIe siècle. Essai sur la vision gallicane du monde* (Paris: Presses Universitaires de France, 2002), 102–5 and Denis Crouzet, *La sagesse et le malheur. Michel de l'Hospital chancelier de France* (Paris: Seyssel, 1998).

22 Estienne Jodelle, *Œuvres complètes*, 2 Vols, edited by Eneas Balmas (Paris: Gallimard, 1965), Vol. I, 294–6.

23 *Lettres de Catherine de Médicis*, Vol. I, 294–6.

24 *Lettres de Catherine de Médicis*, Vol. II, 16–17.

25 See, for example, Catherine des Roches and Marie de Romieu, cited by Madeleine Lazard, *Les aventures de Fémynie. Les femmes à la Renaissance* (Paris: Fayard, 2001), 228–30.

26 *Lettres de Catherine de Médicis*, Vol. I, 293–4.

27 Casteglione, *Il Cortegiano* (Paris: Garnier-Flammarion, 1991), 240.

28 Casteglione, *Il Cortegiano*, 272.

Chapter 3

Religion and Representation in Marguerite de Navarre's *Heptaméron*

Ellen McClure

It may seem strange to find a discussion of Marguerite de Navarre in the context of the present volume. King François I's sister was a protector, defender, and friend of the early French reformers as well as the author of a series of devotional poems and plays.[1] Although her best-known literary work, the posthumously published *Heptaméron*, was long viewed as a purely secular diversion, recent scholarship has rightly, and often brilliantly, pointed to the importance of religious themes in that work.[2] Yet, a closer look at the scholarship surrounding the *Heptaméron* raises the question of the place of religion in a French literary canon that has played an integral role in shaping French secular national identity. More than their American counterparts, French critics tend to view the undeniable religious themes of the *Heptaméron* as vestiges of an ideology that the modernism of her prose seeks, quite successfully, to surpass, allowing Marguerite to be considered alongside those less obviously religious members of the French literary canon, Rabelais and Montaigne. In this essay, I reread the thirty-second story in the *Heptaméron* in order to problematize this opposition between religion and secular modernity, and to show that the plea that Marguerite articulates in that story, for more flexible models of human agency and of representation, is representative of, rather than opposed to, her theological views. By demonstrating the tight relation between theories of representation and religious debate in the *Heptaméron*, I hope to point the way toward a new French literary history, one that would integrate religious themes and discourse rather than casting them out as evidence of a totalizing ideology relegated to the historical, unenlightened past.

The *Heptaméron* consists of 72 short stories told by a group of ten characters who find themselves stranded at an abbey due to a catastrophic rainstorm and ensuing flood. To pass the time while a nearby bridge is being rebuilt, they decide to take up a project first mentioned by members of the French court and modeled after Boccaccio's *Decameron*.[3] The most striking difference between Marguerite's text and that of her Italian predecessor (aside from the proclamation that all of the stories will be "true" [*véritable*], a statement to which I will return) is the discussion that follows each story, where the storytellers attempt to interpret the preceding tale and apply it to their lives. The inevitable failure of this process to end in consensus appears to celebrate the tireless human search for an always-elusive final meaning in narrative and the world. The thirty-second story is narrated by the oldest and most religious of the characters, a woman named Oisille. Proclaiming to have proof that death is not, in fact, the worst fate that one can encounter, she proceeds to recount the grim story of a woman forced to contemplate her sinfulness in penitent silence.

The story begins when Bernage, an envoy of Charles VIII whom the French king has sent to Germany on unspecified business, stops at a castle and asks for hospitality. After some resistance from the castle servants, Bernage explains the purpose of his travels, and the chatelain agrees to host him out of respect for his royal master. At dinnertime, Bernage is presented with a strange spectacle. A beautiful woman dressed in black and with a shaved head appears from behind a tapestry and proceeds, in silence, to share the men's meal. After eating, she drinks from a cup that is in fact a skull. She then disappears, still silent, behind the tapestry. Bernage is understandably confused and fascinated by the scene, and the master of the house proceeds to explain that, upon discovering a young nobleman in the bedroom of his wife, he killed him. To provide his wife with a punishment worse than death, the master of the castle then decided to hang the gentleman's bones in an armoire in the bedroom and to make his wife drink out of her lover's skull during meals. The husband then asks Bernage if he would like to speak to his wife, and Bernage eagerly agrees. The wife expresses her conviction that her punishment is just, given the extent of her sinfulness. The next day, before leaving, Bernage exhorts the gentleman to forgive his wife, pointing out that prolonged silence and punishment only serves to deprive him of children, and, therefore of his home. Upon returning to court from his mission, Bernage relates the story to the king, who sends his painter, Jean de Paris, to paint a portrait of this beautiful woman. We learn that the husband did, in fact, forgive his wife, and that the couple went on to have many beautiful children.

The critical reception of this particular story marks an increased receptivity to religious themes in *Heptaméron* scholarship over the past decade, a receptivity facilitated by the fact that the story is narrated by the deeply devout Oisille. François Rigolot's compelling reading of story thirty-two views it in light of sixteenth-century France's captivation with the Magdalene story.[4] This Biblical example of a beautiful penitent woman held great sway over Catholics and Protestants alike during this period. As Rigolot points out, Marguerite de Navarre had herself visited the relics of the Magdalene on a pilgrimage to the south of France with her mother and brother in 1516, and most likely remained fascinated with the relic of her skull, "adorned with a golden crown and supported by four kneeling angels" (67–8). Further strengthening Rigolot's argument for the relevance of the Magdalene is the identity of the royal artist named in the text, Jean de Paris, otherwise known as Jean Perréal and quite possibly the painter of a well-known, yet misattributed, Saint Mary Magdalene (60). Moreover, during the conversation that follows the story, Ennasuitte, one of the story-tellers, explicitly mentions the Magdalene, confirming the association that any reader of the time who considered the skull-cup, the beautiful woman, and the theme of penitence would have already made.[5]

Having established the relevance of the Magdalene model for the story, however, Rigolot goes on to note the many ways in which the story escapes and problematizes any kind of neat religious allegory. In the story, of course, the skull does not belong to the woman herself; rather, as Rigolot states, "It has been displaced both literally and figuratively" (68). It belongs, instead, to the woman's lover, and thereby attains significance as a marker of human, rather than divine, love. As a result, the story loses its exemplarity and becomes open to a variety of interpretations, of which Ennasuite's overt reference to the Magdalene is just one. As Rigolot concludes, "One no longer knows if the *Heptaméron* story should be read solely on the literal level as a realistic tale, removed from any brand of apologetic intentionality, or if it should retain some higher figurative meaning, some *altior sensus*" (70). This rather disingenuous suggestion that the only ways in which to read the story are either naïve literalism or theologically informed allegorization opens the way for a third method of reading, one that heralds the openness of a nascent French literature. Indeed, the conclusion of Rigolot's essay draws the following stark opposition: "Contrary to Counter-Reformation ideology, in Marguerite de Navarre's hermeneutics Magdalen's skull is never a finality. It is always meant to emerge toward new beginnings . . ." (72). In other words, Marguerite engages with religion in order, ultimately, to move beyond it through the ambiguity and ambivalence of literature.

It should be noted that Rigolot's critique of storytelling in service to religious allegory, and his praise of Marguerite's success in escaping this model, is not without foundation. Although Rigolot does not mention it, a possible source for the thirty-second story can be found in the fifty-fourth chapter of the *Violier des histoires romaines*, a French translation of the *Gesta Romanorum* that appeared in 1521 and which would have been familiar to the French princess. In this iteration of the story, a merchant is struck with admiration for a prince while hunting, and the prince invites him to his palace. At dinnertime, the prince's beautiful wife joins the pair, and begins eating from a human skull. As the prince later recounts, the skull belongs to the princess's lover, whom the prince killed upon discovering their infidelity. The prince also has two dead bodies strung up by their arms in his own room; these bodies belong to two children who had been killed by the son of the lady's lover, and their continued presence in the prince's room excites him to avenge their deaths and perpetuates his hatred of his wife's lover. Having told these stories, the prince exhorts the merchant to leave, which he does.

The similarities between the two stories are striking, but equally notable are the differences. The most notable difference between the two, however, resides not in the actual details of the story itself, but rather in the interpretative framework surrounding it. The *Violier* ends the tale not with a playful discussion of the story's meaning among several interlocutors, each with a valid point of view, but rather with a religious lesson that recasts the surprising story as religious allegory. In this "*moralisation,*" the prince is identified as "the good Christian, rich by virtue of his baptism, and who should have a beautiful family." The merchant, in turn, is the priest or confessor who is called upon to visit "the house of his heart in order to plant good virtue there." The skull represents sin, vanquished and amputated through "good and decent operations, instructions, and examples"; and the two dead bodies are, quite simply, "the affection towards God and your neighbor, which the sin of our first parents killed, but which should be kept in your bedroom so that you remember to persecute he who committed that murder, by loving God and your neighbor with all of your thoughts."[6]

Although the *Violier* predates the Reformation, and thereby also the Counter-Reformation, it exhibits precisely the ideological totalizing decried by Rigolot. The surprise or even revulsion experienced by the reader or by the visiting merchant is almost completely recuperated by the moralizing allegory that accompanies the tale. From the dead children to the prince's wife, the characters are stripped of their independence and interest and instead reduced to quasi-transparent signifiers of moral values and virtues. The reading process suggested by the *Violier* is meant to translate the good Christian's ideal experience of the world, in which events and people who might prove interesting or distracting in and of themselves are regarded through the corrective lens of godly ideals. Against such a backdrop, the innovations in storytelling and embrace of incertitude that scholars such as François Rigolot and Maurice Tetel celebrate in Marguerite de Navarre's collection of stories are indeed truly revolutionary.[7]

However, are they therefore representative of a literary turn from religion and toward modernity? If we read the thirty-second story attuned to its internal thematics and details, a sophisticated reflection on the possibility and role of representation in service to the divine emerges, a theme that will remain central to Protestant–Catholic debate and polemic over the next century. The story's deep engagement with the subject of representation is chiefly conveyed through its deployment of the theme of sight and seeing.[8] The scene where Bernage beholds the beautiful woman for the first time is particularly laden with verbs of vision:

> Bernage *saw* (*veit*) a woman emerge from behind a tapestry, the most beautiful woman that it was possible to *look at* (*regarder*), but her head was completely shaved, and the rest of her body was clothed in black, *à l'Allemande*. After the gentleman and Bernage had washed their hands, water was brought to the lady, who washed her hands and went to sit at the end of the table without speaking to anyone, nor anyone speaking to her. Bernage *looked at her* (*la regarda*) closely, and she seemed to him to be one of the most beautiful women that he had ever seen (*veuë*), although her face was quite pale, and her demeanor very sad.[9] (Emphasis added)

The emphasis on visuality in this passage is reinforced by a linguistic frame that mirrors the narrative framing of each story by the storytellers' interventions and which ingeniously anticipates the painted portrait that will play a central role later in the story. This linguistic framing takes place not merely in the repetition of the superlative ("the most beautiful woman") but also in the choice and placement of verbs of seeing, as the "voir/regarder" ("see/look") pair in the first sentence is counterbalanced by "regarder/voir" ("look/see") in the last sentence. At the center of these pairs lies the presence of the sad woman herself, who silently takes her place at the table. This tableau stuns Bernage and reduces this envoy, whose job for the king requires both speech and swift movement, to sadness and thoughtful silence: "Bernage was so stricken to see such a strange thing that he became quite sad and thoughtful" (354).[10]

The proprietor of the castle breaks this silence by underscoring the importance of sight in his domain: "I see clearly that you are astonished by what you have seen at this table . . . The lady whom you have seen is my wife . . ." (354).[11] He continues by narrating the story that has led to such a spectacle, and here again, the visual dominates. He says that his love for her blinded him to the possibility of her infidelity: "The love which I had for her was so great that I could not suspect her until experience opened my eyes, and I saw what I feared more than death" (355). He spies on her until he receives visual proof of her betrayal, and, unsurprisingly, decides to punish her through the sense of sight:

> And so that she never forgets this, I have her food and drink served in front of me, with, instead of a cup, the head of this rogue so that she can see, alive, the person that she has made her mortal enemy through her sin, and, dead from her love, the man whose friendship she preferred to my own: and therefore she sees during supper and dinner the two things that should displease her the most . . . (355)[12]

Sight continues to dominate the gentleman's tale, until even the verbal is described in its terms; when the gentleman takes Bernage to see his wife, he suggests that speech can be rendered, or at least admired, only through the language of sight: "If you would like to say something to her, you *will see* how graciously she speaks" (356).[13] This repeated and intense deployment of visual language is, however, restricted to the world inside of the gentleman's castle, a world characterized by a frozen stasis that exists in sharp contrast to the movement and speech of Bernage, the king's envoy. This enclosed and motionless space is marked by death – not merely through the bones and skull of the dead lover that are the object of the lady's near-constant contemplation, but also, as Bernage himself points out, through the lack of offspring. The castle's mortal stillness is further accentuated by the silence that has reigned there until the arrival of the royal envoy; as we are told at the end of the story, the gentleman had vowed "to never speak to his wife" (257).[14]

In placing such a clear emphasis on looking and seeing in a story narrated by Oisille, the storyteller most closely identified with the study and commentary of Scripture, Marguerite de Navarre is intervening in a debate that would lie at the center of religious debate for at least the next century: are memory, meaning, and, ultimately the presence of the divine best accessed through visually striking physical objects, such as icons or relics, or through the relative abstraction of language? This question had already begun to divide the Reformers. Karlstadt's categorical and violent denunciation of images, and the iconoclastic riots that his writings and sermons provoked, led Luther to articulate a theory of images that categorized them as *adiaphora*, or indifferent to religious practice.[15] Despite Luther's efforts at moderation, the issue of idolatry continued to mobilize European Protestants and Catholics, who hotly debated the question of whether images were inherently seductive and dangerous.[16] Special scorn was reserved for relics, the use of which Jean Calvin equated with superstition and idolatry.[17]

Bernage's reaction to the gruesome objects in the castle and to the strange silence that reigns there can be viewed as representative of the early reformers' increasing discomfort with the carnal literality of Catholicism, whose emphasis on the real presence of Christ in the Eucharist and on the martyred bodies of the saints had led to a reaction that Frank Lestringant calls "a holy terror."[18] In forcing his wife to contemplate the actual bodily remnants of her dead lover, to drink from his skull and to contemplate the crucifix-like skeleton in her bedroom, the gentleman is applying the lessons of Catholic faith, in which representational abstraction can only serve to mitigate the immediacy of divine presence.[19] The husband's refusal to engage his wife through the relative abstraction of verbal speech reflects his stubborn literality, and as a result, the couple is frozen into a narcissistic stasis from which time and life have been removed.

Ironically, however, it is just this belief in the perfect adequacy of signifier and signified that provides the means through which the spell over the castle is eventually broken. Although the gentleman refuses, on principle, to allow strangers into his autonomous domain, he makes an exception for Bernage once the envoy explains his identity and the purpose of his trip. As the story relates, "Bernage told him the reason for his embassy, after which the gentleman offered to do everything possible to serve the king his master, and brought him inside of his house, where he lodged and fed him honourably" (353).[20] In the terms of the gentleman's economy of signification, which does not admit of any slippage or inadequacy between the instrument of representation and that which is represented, the king's ambassador *is* the king, and needs to be honored accordingly. Bernage is therefore admitted to the house, where he observes the strange practices that prevail there, and, before taking his leave, advises the gentleman to pity his wife, if only to keep the house through the production of heirs. The gentleman reflects upon this advice, and vows to follow it if his wife persists in her humility.

The gentleman may or may not have learned his lesson; as Bernage leaves, we are unsure whether the ambassador's intervention sufficiently altered his reluctance to admit representational flexibility and abstraction into his relations with his wife and her actions. Yet, the story does not end here, and the coda which follows Bernage's departure from the castle strongly suggests that the subject of the story reaches beyond the happiness or fate of this particular and strange couple. Instead, it touches directly upon the puzzle of how and whether to convey presence through various representational vehicles, and points to a solution that seeks to accommodate both the Catholic literalists in thrall to the visual and the more extreme Reformers, who would do without images entirely.[21] Once Bernage completes his mission and returns to the king, he tells him about the castle and its inhabitants. This discursive report is necessary, it should be noted, precisely because, contrary to the belief of the gentleman, he is *not* the king, but rather his representative. The king, upon hearing of the strange events but also of the lady's exceptional beauty, sends his painter, Jean de Paris, "to bring him this woman 'alive', which he did, after the husband gave his consent" (357).[22]

Here, the relation between vision and speech is reversed. If, inside the castle, vision dominates to an extent that speech represents a brief interlude in the frozen silence and is, indeed, likened to vision (we should recall the gentleman's exhortation to Bernage to speak to his wife, in order to *see* "how gracefully she speaks"), outside of the castle, speech precedes and conveys physical beauty. Real presence – skulls, bones, literal remnants of the body – is not necessary in order to manifest the essence of what is; rather, this can be translated and carried through the abstraction, the non-physicality, of speech. Bernage's ability to represent his experiences to his king would therefore seem to be an unqualified endorsement of the verbal over the physical, of Scripture over relics. Yet, it would seem that Marguerite, wary of over-reliance on the visual, is equally sensitive to the dangers inherent in privileging the verbal to the extent that the specificity of the physical completely disappears. The king's decision, upon hearing of the lady's beauty and extraordinary story, to commission a portrait of her represents a compromise between the verbal sign and the literality of physical presence. In stark contrast to the gruesome reliquary presence of his wife's dead lover, pictorial representation allows the monarch to enjoy the lady's exceptional beauty without entailing the death or the frozen physical presence of its subject. This continued *life* of the painting's subject is conveyed in the final words of the story; referring to the husband who granted permission for the portrait to be made, it states that "after a long penitence, and because of his desire to have children, and because of the pity he took upon his wife who had received her penitence with such great humility, the husband took her back and had many beautiful children with her" (257).[23] The spell of literal representation has been broken; the stasis of the king's portrait exists alongside her continued penitent existence as wife and mother, and time and life have once again begun to flow through the castle.

Marguerite's effort to articulate a world in which representation is simultaneously imperfect and faithful represents her compassionate and tolerant approach to human frailty; the status of men and women as images of their divine creator is obscured, but not abolished, by the inevitability of their falling short of the divine ideal. This well-considered and deliberate representational argument, founded in Marguerite's theology, has, however, encountered resistance from critical readings of the *Heptaméron* that seek to categorize religion as an ideological totality against which literature, with its celebration of ambiguity and complexity, is imagined to stand in opposition.

This critical resistance appears in a series of curious misreadings of the texts that work to collapse the distance between signifier and signified that Marguerite so carefully cultivates. François Rigolot, for example, attributes the gentleman's forgiveness of his wife to the prince's commissioned portrait: "Following up on the advice of the King's messenger and moved by the art of the King's painter, the husband will finally show compassion for his wife" (61). In the text, however, the relationship between the two is unclear, represented only by a colon; the reader is unsure whether these words are a tribute to the power of the royal painting or whether they are instead the painter's account of affairs at the castle during his visit, reported back to the king. Rigolot's eagerness to attribute the husband's forgiveness to the painting exemplifies, in miniature, critics' haste to attribute the positive and progressive elements of Marguerite's collection to artistic and literary prowess rather than religious reflection, or, more accurately, her complex account of how literature and religion are as interrelated as life and faith. Elevating the painting's power runs the risk, averted by Marguerite's clever use of ambiguous punctuation, of attributing a power to the created and the creature that is the creator's alone. In short, collapsing Marguerite's carefully constructed indeterminacy is tantamount to idolatry.

Curiously, the same scene is misread by Marcel Tetel, who summarizes the final lines of the thirty-second story as follows: "At the end the visual theme takes on a pictorial dimension when the husband, as a further sign of reconciliation, has her portrait painted in order to immortalize her newly acquired beauty, a counterpart to what Marguerite herself does through the creation of the story" (90–1). Whereas Rigolot hastens to attribute power and agency to the artistic work, Tetel emphasizes the intent and importance of the portrait's creator, which he misidentifies as the husband. The complex representational layering between king, Bernage, and painter is completely obscured in order to elevate the creative act accomplished first by the husband, and then, neatly, by Marguerite herself. Tetel's praise of the new and the creative runs against both our knowledge of the woman's beauty (she was beautiful even before the portrait was painted) and of the story itself (which, as we have seen, was not completely original). Yet, this emphasis is in keeping with Tetel's larger ambition of inserting Marguerite de Navarre into the French literary canon. Having identified ambiguity as the dominant characteristic of the *Heptaméron*, Tetel works to move it away from its religious foundations and connotations and toward a literary modernity that he sees emerging in the French Renaissance. His study concludes as follows: "The search for a constant produces ambiguity because it creates an acute realization of the insufficiency of human judgment. The modernity of this concept, starting with its all-pervading presence in the three major prose writers of the sixteenth century, manifests itself later in Diderot and then in this century with Proust, Pirandello, and Sartre" (108). In other words, although Tetel, like Rigolot, grants a fundamental indeterminacy to the content of the literary work, he fails to extend this ambiguity to authorship itself, neatly represented through the proper names signaling the unproblematic and masterly intentionality of France's greatest writers.

Tetel's misreading, however, is valuable in that it inadvertently points out the close link between the questions of idolatry and authorship. Idolatry is not merely the inappropriate worship or attribution of power to the image; it is also, essentially, about the misattribution of creation to the creature, humans, rather than to the divine Creator. Marguerite's sensitivity to this issue and its theological implications complicate efforts to elevate her originality and creative autonomy. Nowhere is this more apparent than in the prologue to the *Heptaméron*, which recounts the genesis of the storytelling project all while subjecting the very concepts of authorship, originality, and origin to a sustained and subtle critique. The storytellers are brought together by the natural calamity of the rainstorm and ensuing flood; chance encounters and close escapes from danger bring the ten together at the abbey at Notre Dame de Serrance.[24] There, the exhausted travelers search for a project to occupy them while they wait for a nearby bridge to be rebuilt. Oisille, the oldest and most devout of the storytellers, complains that she is unable to furnish such a diversion, since she finds the reading and study of Scripture to be the only pastime that provides true joy and repose to the soul. To this, Hircan, who generally represents the voice of physical pleasure throughout the collection, objects that such devotion is unrealistic for the imperfect and embodied members of the party, and suggests a rather salacious pastime that may or may not include his wife.[25] This wife, Parlamente, is another of the storytellers present, and her proposal of the storytelling project is a successful and significant attempt to mediate between the verbally based devotion of Oisille and the carnality of her husband – a mediation that anticipates the work done by the king's portrait in the thirty-second story. Moreover, the idea that each member of the party should tell a story a day for ten days stands in strong opposition to monologism or authorial control.[26]

Yet, it is also vital to note that Parlamente's solution is, professedly and emphatically, not original. In fact, the source of the project is impossible to locate with certainty within the complex play of relative and non-original authorship that Marguerite establishes in order to better maintain and emphasize the sole creative power of the divine. On one level, of course, it is Marguerite de Navarre herself. On another, it is Boccaccio, whose *Decameron* had so impressed and seduced the French court that its members, including King François I, the Dauphine, or crown princess, and "my lady Marguerite,"[27] decide to emulate the Italian collection, but with the important vow "not to write any tale that was not a true story" (65).[28] The crown prince joins the project, and this illustrious group agrees to assemble a group of ten people to tell the stories, with the exception of "those who have studied and who are literary figures, since the crown prince feared that their art would be mixed in with the stories and that the beauty of their rhetoric would somehow damage the truth of the story" (65–6).[29] Unfortunately, important events, such as the peace with England and the birth of the crown prince's child, derailed this worthy project, which Parlamente suggests that the ten stranded storytellers finish.

The impossibility of firmly establishing the origin and authorship of the project appears, against the backdrop of the theme of idolatry, as an implicit critique of the human pretense to creative powers (evident in Boccaccio) and concomitant praise of authorial humility. Yet, once again, Marguerite's critique of idolatry stops well short of endorsing a wholesale elimination of artistry that would embrace the opposite extreme. It is significant that it is the Dauphin, the impossible embodiment of royal potentiality whose self-effacement must be absolute so as not to threaten his father's sovereignty, who stipulates that literary artists should be excluded from the project. The stylistic neutrality that the Dauphin advocates is as appropriate to his position as neutral and faithful verbal representation was to that of Bernage, and represents an effort to erase the voices of the storytellers from the tales. The suggested reworking of Boccaccio is aimed at achieving a level of authorial anonymity that approaches complete transparency, wherein the stories themselves, and their truth, shine forth unclouded by the identities or stylistic preferences of those that tell them. The Dauphin's rigor ironically comes to resemble the gentleman's refusal to admit any representational deviation from the truth of his wife's affair and the real bodily presence of her lover; both the elimination of representational vehicles and the inappropriate clinging to literality demonstrate a refusal of the humble flexibility that is both recommended and exemplified in the actual *Heptaméron.*

Indeed, Parlamente modifies the courtly project in important ways. She suggests not that the participants write true stories bereft of stylistic interference, but rather that they each "tell some story that he has seen or else heard from a man worthy of trust." Implicitly acknowledging the distance between her and the rigidity of image-oriented Catholic practice, she adds that "if God finds that our work is worthy of the eyes of the ladies and gentlemen previously named, we will give this to them as a present after our return, instead of images or paternosters, and I assure you that they will like this better" (66).[30] The presentation of the project to the court lends the text an instrumentality and utility that prevent it from being considered as a vainglorious display of artistry for its own sake, but, as Margaret Ferguson has noted, it also marks a mysterious and anonymous passage of the text from word to page.[31] Once again, authorship is occluded; the hand that will write the text of the *Heptaméron* is invisible, and of no importance. However, unlike the Dauphin's proposed text, whose intended rigid faithfulness to truth cannot withstand or represent events brought about by the passage of time (the royal birth and international peace), Parlamente's project demonstrates the fluidity of imperfection, as it shimmers between the witnessed and the heard, the told and the written, to produce a text that is quite conscious of its distance and difference from its inaccessible royal model, but at the same time bears its image and influence, just as humanity itself simultaneously and continuously represents and betrays the perfection of its divine origin.[32]

The *Heptaméron*'s deep ambiguity is indeed a sophisticated attempt to navigate between the ever-present dangers of idolatry and abstraction. Yet, the theological charge surrounding these perils does not necessarily imply the participation of Marguerite's text in a literary, secular modernity *avant la lettre.* Marguerite's deep suspicion of authorship, combined with her compassionate view of humanity's seemingly inevitable search for impossible certainty, is tied to her advocacy of a different approach to truth, one that eschews a transparency and stability that can lead to deadening narcissism and instead posits truth as fundamentally relational, less object than movement. Recognizing this movement, which is not random but anchored in a divinity whose existence and goodness are never placed in doubt, requires the reader to suspend his or her urge to reject the religious and remain open to the middle way that Marguerite herself embraced.

Notes

[1] For a recent, and thorough, discussion and reassessment of Marguerite's relationship to the early Reform, see Jonathan A. Reid, *King's Sister, Queen of Dissent: Marguerite de Navarre (1492–1549) and her Evangelical Network*, 2 vols. (Leiden: Brill, 2009). For a reading of Marguerite's devotional poetry, see Paula Sommers, *Celestial Ladders: Readings in Marguerite de Navarre's Poetry of Spiritual Ascent* (Geneva: Droz, 1989).

[2] See, most notably, Carol Thysell, *The Pleasures of Discernment: Marguerite de Navarre as Theologian* (New York: Oxford University Press, 2000), as well as Paula Sommers, "Marguerite de Navarre's *Heptaméron*: The Case for the Cornice," *French Review* 57:6 (1984), 786–93. See also George Hoffman, "Doubles, Crosses: *Heptameron*, Story 71," and Jan Miernowksi, "Fiction and Ritual in the *Heptameron*," in *Approaches to Teaching Marguerite de Navarre's Heptaméron*, edited by Colette Winn (New York: Modern Language Association of America: 2007), 102–5 and 106–12, respectively.

[3] The *Heptaméron* was published, and named, after Marguerite de Navarre's death, in 1558 and 1559, respectively; the text was most probably not completed, and was intended to contain 100 stories, like its Italian model.

[4] François Rigolot, "Magdalen's Skull: Allegory and Iconography in Heptameron 32," *Renaissance Quarterly* 47:1 (1994), 57–73.

[5] "Even without Ennasuite's explicit clue, the reader was expected to know the meaning of specific codes and read the sinister suppertime scene in a symbolic mode. The skull was to be interpreted as a *Speculum Poenitentiae*." See Rigolot, 64.

[6] M. G. Brunet, ed., *Le violier des histoires romaines* (Paris: P. Jannet, 1858), 125–8. The translation of the moralization, the original French version of which follows, is mine: "Cestuy prince tant enrichy est le bon chrestien, riche par la vertu du baptesme, qui doit avoir belle famille: ce sont les sens intereux et exterieux sans maculle de peché, et doivent administrer à l'homme, le menant chasser, c'est assavoir prendre bonnes œuvres meritoires. Ce marchant est le bon prelat ou discret confesseur qui est tenu tel accompaigner, visiter la maison de son cueur et les bonnes vertus y planter. L'ame tant belle doit estre mise de costé; le prelat ou confesseur à la table de l'Escripture saincte pour apprendre ce qui est de salut. La teste morte qui est devant le confesseur est l'amputation de peché occis par bonnes et decentes operations, instructions et bons exemples. Les deux pendus sont la dilection de Dieu et de ton prochain, que le peché des premiers parents tua, et pourtant tu les dois tenir en ta chambre cordialle, si

que tu ayes mémoire de persecuter celluy qui a ce meurtre commis, en aymant Dieu et ton proesme de toute ta pensée" (128).

7 See Maurice Tetel, *Marguerite de Navarre's Heptameron: Themes, Language and Structure* (Durham, NC: Duke University Press, 1973), especially 104–204.

8 The preponderance of the gaze in this story has not gone unnoticed by scholars; see Tetel, 90, and Catherine Randall, *Earthly Treasures: Material Culture and Metaphysics in the "Heptaméron" and Evangelical Narrative* (West Lafayette, IN: Purdue University Press, 2007), 28–37.

9 Bernage "*veit* sortir de derriere la tapisserie une femme, la plus belle qu'il estoit possible de *regarder*, mais elle avoit la teste toute tonduë, le demeurant du corps habillé de noir à l'Allemande. Après que le gentil-homme eut lavé avec ledict Bernage, l'on apporta l'eau à ceste dame, qui lava, et s'en alla seoir au bout de la table, sans parler à nul, ny nul à elle. Le seigneur de Bernage la *regarda* bien fort, et luy sembla l'une des plus belles dames qu'il eust jamais *veuë*, sinon qu'elle avoit le visage bien pale, et la contenance bien triste." Marguerite de Navarre, *L'Heptaméron des nouvelles*, edited by Nicole Cazauran (Paris: Gallimard, 2000), 354. Translation and emphasis mine.

10 "Bernage fut tant esbahy, de veoir chose si estrange, qu'il en devint tout triste et pensif."

11 "Je voy bien, que vous vous estonnez de ce qu'avez veu en ceste table (…) Ceste dame, que vous avez veue, est ma femme…"

12 "Et à fin qu'elle n'en oublie la memoire, en beuvant et mangeant luy fais servir à table tout devant moy, en lieu de coupe, la teste de ce meschant à ce qu'elle voye vivant celuy qu'elle a faict son mortel enemy par sa faulte, et mort pour l'amour d'elle celuy duquel elle avoit preferé l'amitié à la mienne: et ainsi elle voit à disner et soupper les deux choses qui plus luy doivent desplaire…."

13 "S'il vous plaist luy dire quelque chose, vous verrez quelle grace de parolle elle a."

14 "de ne parler jamais à sa femme."

15 See Andreas Karlstadt, "On the Removal of Images," in *A Reformation Debate: Three Treatises in Translation*, translated by Bryan D. Mangrum and Giuseppe Scavizzi (Ottawa: Dovehouse Editions, 1991), 19–39. Luther's views on images are developed most notably in the Invocavit sermons, delivered in 1522, the year of Karlstadt's treatise and the iconoclastic violence in Wittenberg.

16 As Olivier Christin reminds us in his excellent account of iconoclasm in France, 1549, the year of Marguerite de Navarre's death, also saw Jean du Tillet's publication of the *Libri Carolini*, in which Charlemagne's bishops registered their disapproval of the decisions regarding sacred images that were taken at the second Council of Nicea, in 787. The *Libri Carolini* would remain an influential source for those attempting to argue for a French skepticism concerning religious imagery, and Marguerite de Navarre would almost certainly have known about their discovery and impending publication. Olivier Christin, *Une Révolution symbolique: l'iconoclasme huguenot et la reconstruction catholique* (Paris: Editions de minuit, 1991), 49.

17 Jean Calvin, *Traitté des reliques* (Geneva: Pierre de la Rouiere, 1599), 3.

18 Frank Lestringant, *Une sainte horreur, ou le voyage en Eucharistie XVIe-XVIIe siècle* (Paris: Presses Universitaires de France, 1996).

19 Frank Lestringant characterizes the differing religious approaches to representation in the following manner: "Pour les zwingliens et les calvinistes, il y a dans l'Eucharistie relation de contiguïté, c'est-à-dire de pure extériorité, entre le signe et la chose signifiée; en revanche, luthériens et catholiques affirment l'identité partielle ou totale de l'un et de l'autre, puisque telle est la vertu du sacrement qu'il transporte instantanément au significant les qualities du signifié. A un procès sémantique de marquage s'oppose une fusion instantanée de type magique ou poétique" (19).

20 "Ledict Bernage luy dist l'occasion de sa legation, en quoy le gentilhomme s'offroit de faire tout service à luy possible au roy son maistre: et le mena dedans sa maison, où il le logea et festoya honorablement."

21 As Lestringant notes, "La sainte horreur pour la chair sanguinolente de l'hostie repousse le croyant réformé vers l'hypothèse contraire, tout aussi inacceptable, à vrai dire, que serait le pur néant de toute présence. La vérité du sacrament, selon Calvin et son interprète Viret, se situe dans l'intervalle de la surabondance charnelle que prône le catholicisme, et du déficit du signe qu'établit le zwinglianisme" (29).

22 "pour luy rapporter au vif cest dame, ce qu'il feit, après le consentement de son mary."

23 "lequel après longue penitence, pour le desir qu'il avoit d'avoir enfans, et par la pitié qu'il eut de sa femme, qui en si grande humilité recevoit ceste penitence, la reprint avec soy, et en eut depuis beaucoup de beaux enfans."

24 Paula Sommers's article, cited earlier, provides a provocative and nuanced reading of the prologue that demonstrates the ways in which Marguerite de Navarre opposes human pretention to knowledge to the positive force of spiritual faith.

25 Margaret Ferguson seizes upon the ambiguity of Hircan's statement to note that although Parlamente views his remark as directed at her, he may not have her in mind as a partner for his amusement. Margaret Ferguson, "Recreating the Rules of the Games: Marguerite de Navarre's *Heptaméron*," in *Creative Imitation: New Essays on Renaissance Literature in Honor of Thomas M. Greene*, edited by David Quint, Margaret Ferguson, G.W. Pigman III, and Wayne A. Rebhorn (Binghamton: Medieval, & Renaissance Texts & Studies, 1992), 152–87: 175–6.

26 For Philippe de Lajarte, this playful openness is constructed in opposition to Oisille's scriptural model of devotion; Parlamente's project represents a literary modernity, based in ambiguity and ambivalence, that is only possible once the universe has been freed from the totalizing grip of religion and the divine. Philippe de Lajarte, "Le prologue de l'*Heptaméron* et le processus de production de l'oeuvre" *La nouvelle française à la Renaissance*, edited by Lionello Sozzi (Geneva: Slatkine, 1981), 397–423, 421.

27 Nicole Casaubon, in her edition of the text I use here, argues that "Madame Marguerite" is not, in fact, a reference to the author, but rather to her niece, Marguerite de France (628).

28 "de n'escrire nouvelle, qui ne fust veritable histoire."

29 "sauf ceux qui auroient estudié, et seroient gens de lettres: car Monseigneur le Daulphin ne vouloit que leur art y fust meslé: et aussi de peur que la beauté de rhetoricque feist tort en quelque partie à la vérité de l'histoire."

30 "chacun dira quelque histoire qu'il aura veuë ou bien ouy dire à quelque homme digne de foy. Au bout des dix jours aurons parachevé la centeine. Et si Dieu faict que nostre labeur soit trouvé digne des yeux des seigneurs et dames dessus nommées, nous leur en ferons present au retour de ce voyage, en lieu d'images ou de paternostres, vous asseurant qu'ils auront ce present ici plus agreable."

31 "This passage, which ends with a witty assertion of the book's superiority to objects of 'superstitious' religious purchase and veneration—objects, that is, of Catholic idolatry—dramatizes Parlamente's status as an author-figure who *mediates* between various realms, among them those of oral and written modes of discourse, with their different ontologies and temporalities: she straddles the boundary between a 'present' of story-telling and a future when some less-ephemeral representation will memorialize that now past 'present'." Ferguson, 182.

32 This reading is borne out by an intervention of Oisille's during the conclusion to the 48th story, during the fifth day. Hircan hesitates to tell a story of an infamous great lady, and Oisille reminds him that everyone had sworn to tell the truth, and therefore to listen to it as well. "Parquoy vous pouvez parler en liberté: car les maux, que nous disons des hommes ou des femmes, ne sont point pour la honte particuliere de ceux desquels est faict le compte: mais pour oster l'estime et la confiance des creatures, en monstrant les misères où elles sont subjectes, afin que nostre espoir s'arreste et s'appuye à celuy seul qui est parfaict, et sans lequel tout homme n'est qu'imperfection" (455).

Chapter 4

The Gallican Mines: Martine de Bertereau's *Restitution de Pluton*, Astrology, Providence, and Empire during the Reign of Louis XIII

Erik Thomson

This chapter analyzes a forgotten author, a forgotten text, and a forgotten manner of understanding the French nation as a providential space. While the author did attract some attention in her own day, that attention ultimately would be fatal. Yet, I think that both author and text, apart from their inherent interest, provide a glimpse into a crucial but neglected aspect of the French political imaginary.[1] Martine de Bertereau's *La Restitution de Pluton* of 1640 reveals the depth of trust in God's providential care for France, even in a moment when that very belief had brought the kingdom near bankruptcy. I hope here to enrich the way we understand discourses that might be labeled "proto-political economy" or even "proto-mercantilism" in the late Renaissance, by showing how these discourses should not be understood as prefiguring a secular science of wealth, but are rather deeply enmeshed in debates about the working of providence. Historians, most notably Pamela H. Smith in her rich *The Business of Alchemy*, have elucidated some of the connections between alchemical knowledge and proto-economic discourses.[2] Yet, scholars have not discussed how works such as Bertereau's helped naturalize the idea of the nation as a divine territory, provided by God's foresight with natural goods suitable and sufficient to allow it to carry out a preordained mission. Bertereau's project offered to use her skills and secret expertise in order to unearth these divine treasures and resolve the fiscal constraints to France's natural empire. Such projects drew upon human expertise to reveal and perfect the goods that God provided for human use, and thus might seem to prefigure a science, like economics, that proposes to delineate the most efficient use of scarce resources. However, Bertereau – like other early-seventeenth-century authors – also thought that such resources also gave knowledge to human ends, for the nature of a kingdom's goods indicated their role in God's providential plans.

Many early modern people imagined the earth as a providential space created for the needs and delectation of mankind, as inheritors of the Latin Church's anthropocentric view of nature, described by Lynn White Jr. in a classic article.[3] The precise disposition of goods was fraught with meaning, for it served to indicate God's intention for mankind. Of course, God's providence often seemed to puzzle and provoke early modern thinkers, for his intentions were murky. On the one hand, writers praised God for distributing his blessings throughout the world, making commerce necessary and creating sociability and even friendship among people otherwise divided into nations. The Dutch polymath Hugo Grotius echoed a common trope when, in his 1609 book *Mare Liberum*, he defended the proposition that "every nation is free to travel to every other nation and to trade with it," with the argument that "God himself says this speaking through the voice of nature, for it is his will that all the necessities of life shall be supplied to every region by nature."[4] Yet, on the other hand, authors celebrated divine favors with consequences that were less pacific, praising God for endowing a particular polity with goods so that it could realize its divine mission. It is not surprising that the Calabrian astrologer, philosopher, and polymath Tommaso Campanella, a thinker given to provocative and dangerous speculations about the working of providence, insisted that God had been working through Christopher Columbus to give the wealth of the New World to the king of Spain, at least until he reconsidered and thought that God had shaped Spain to be a weak polity.[5] However, in this matter, it is more surprising to see Campanella mouthing a commonplace, for many other writers of the time also thought that the king of Spain, by Columbus's discovery and conquest of the gold and silver mines of the New World, had received a sure sign of God's favor, a clear support not only to his kingdom's mission to covert the world but perhaps also an impetus and means to aspire to a Universal Christian Empire.[6]

French authors usually admitted that the king of France had no mines that resembled those of Spain or even of the Holy Roman Emperor. They consoled themselves quickly, by noting that God had given France different and ultimately more valuable resources. Jean Bodin, for instance, noted that France possessed three mines of "salt, of wine, and of grain." These French mines were inexhaustible, "while the foreign mines are emptied in a few short years, and cannot be reborn but in many centuries."[7] Bodin drew upon a view of France's nature formulated by writers devoted to the cause of the Valois kings, as historians such as Colette Beaune and David Potter have argued, as a response to the existential threat the kingdom faced during the Hundred Years War.[8] By the end of the fifteenth century, Gallican statesmen and humanists routinely used fragments from Strabo and Pliny the Elder to consolidate a vision of France as not merely the sort of autarky recommended by Aristotle, but as a kingdom destined to exercise Empire over its neighbors because of its fertility in goods that all of its neighbors needed.

Chancellor Guillaume de Rochefort, giving the royal speech of Convocation at the Estates General of 1484, noted that France was the most glorious kingdom one could imagine, as it had lovely and navigable rivers. He continued:

> Where can you find better forests for hunting, for construction and for every other use? Who else possesses such fertile pastures, such fish of all species, of small and great herds? Who can compare his wine and grains to ours? Where else would you find a country better provided with all the riches necessary to men?[9]

This package of ideas became common both in royal speeches and ordinances, and in broader works of panegyric, chorography, and jurisprudence. Thus, an Ordonnance of 1498 could declare that "this kingdom, by the grace of God, is the first and the best provided in all things, more than any other."[10] Chancellor Antoine du Prat repeated such sentiments in a speech of 1519.[11]

Concepts of benediction and providence shaped one important strand of early modern French discourse about the kingdom's nature and power. Statesmen, projectors, jurists, and theologians argued that France was a kingdom endowed with a natural empire over its neighbors, because of the fertility with which God had blessed the kingdom. One way in which early modern French thinkers imagined "France" was as a providential space, which God had endowed with a certain nature, and, if you like, with natural resources. Interestingly, such a providential space seems to posit a France destined to exist in its seventeenth-century form from creation, a view that rarely intersected with and is difficult to reconcile with historical accounts of France's origins whether in Troy, Gaul, or among the Franks.[12] This vision of France as endowed by God with the goods that assured its empire over its neighbors served a number of ideological functions. Artists and writers could use this vision of fertile empire as a part of royal iconography, for example, as Rebecca Zorach has shown, in the iconography of the Palace of Fontainebleau.[13] Beyond representation, however, the interpretation of France's nature was invoked rhetorically to support reforms so as to make the best use of God's gifts. Many pamphlets of the late sixteenth and early seventeenth century proposed the more attentive and more assiduous application of labor to nature's gifts, hoping to make perfect use of benediction. If the realm could only be placed in its right order, the argument often went, God's gifts would secure the realm riches and the power that would surely follow them.[14]

Although the trope of France's natural fertility and benediction of goods was common, it was not unchallenged. For example, during a debate about coinage under Henri IV's reign, Denis Godefroy challenged those who thought that France was an autarky, not to speak of those who thought that France's goods gave it sway over its neighbors. He argued that Spain did not depend upon French grain, for he maintained that "I have enquired among merchants who trade [in the Baltic] and who have had grains from Gdansk and Poland brought to this kingdom, and according to them the grains of Gdansk and Poland could be and often have been transported to Spain, Italy and Barbary."[15] While surely Poland offered no competition for French wine, alternatives for French goods challenged counsels that were based on French ideals of natural empire.

These denials of the reality of the French benediction of goods gained little purchase. Authors continued to espouse the idea in books, and perhaps more importantly, statesmen continued to use the idea as a point of departure for their counsels. Among them was Louis XIII's principal minister, Armand Jean du Plessis, the Cardinal of Richelieu. As Françoise Hildesheimer has argued, the Cardinal's politics were deeply marked by his interest in Thomas Aquinas, whose scheme of causation invited speculation and attempts to know God's providential plans.[16] Once conflicts with the Spanish and English forced commercial jurisdiction into his counsels, Richelieu rapidly combined Grotius's notion of free trade and the French concept of natural empire. He affirmed this belief in his *Testament politique*, a book of political advice intended for Louis XIII, commenting that:

France is so fertile in grains, so abundant in wines, and so filed with flax and hemp for making the sails and ropes needed for shipping, that Spain, England and all of our other neighbors need to have recourse to us for them, and, given we knew how to assist those advantages that nature has procured for us, we would draw money from those who want our goods which are so necessary to them, and we would not take on many of their goods which are of so little use to us.[17]

Nature, in short, provided France with goods essential to life, whereas nature gave foreigners only vain trivialities. The French could give assistance to nature by rejecting vain and foolish expenditure, but also by forcing others to recognize justice. Rather than focusing on the skillful and diligent use of labor to improve the goods God had given France, the Cardinal adopted Hugo Grotius's idea of the free and equitable nature of trade, to argue that the unfair and unjust exercise of sovereignty on the part of other powers – and above all the Spanish – was the primary obstacle to France exercising its natural predominance, as I have argued elsewhere.[18] If international relations, so to speak, were rooted in justice, France's goods would procure the kingdom the precedence over all other kingdoms, as God intended.

While the articulation of this belief took many forms, one form had great consequences. When Louis XIII declared open war on the king of Spain in 1635, Richelieu attempted to prohibit trade with Spain generally, and particularly of those goods commonly represented that Spain absolutely required. What is more, he was willing to completely stop French exports of such goods – grain, wine, and sail-cloth – in order to deny them to the Spanish. Perhaps this was all a part of Richelieu's belief that French participation in the war would cause Spain's rapid defeat. As early as 1635, though, the superintendents of Finance began to complain of a real shortage of coinage and precious metals in the kingdom. These complaints only grew more acute as the war dragged on, as monetary problems combined with the stoppage of trade made it difficult to attract new coinage to France while the war still required the export of large amounts of coin. France's fertility might provide it with inexhaustible mines, but these mines failed to provide the gold and silver needed to win the war.

Authors responded to this problem with some creativity. Isaac Loppin, the superintendent of the king's chambers, devised one typical solution in his 1638 work *Les Mines Gallicanes, ou thresor du Royaume de France, Ou sont monstrés Les Droits du Roy, & les moyens justes & legitimes, par lesquels sans foulle ny oppression d'aucun de ses subiects, Sa Majesté peut avoir & perpetuellement posseder les richesses & les utilitez. . . .*[19] Loppin argued that the mismanagement of the royal finances had overwhelmed the people, who allowed the true mines of France to flourish through their labor. The work attracted some ministerial attention, as notes on the work survive amongst Richelieu's papers. Yet, while financial reform might have been part of Richelieu's hopes for after the war, it was not possible during it; Isaac Loppin would reiterate many of his proposals a decade later as Mazarinades during the *Fronde*.[20] Loppin, in any case, did not answer the problem of how to gain coin and precious metals while trade was prohibited.

Another solution was proposed by Martine de Bertereau, in her remarkable *La Restitution de Pluton* – dedicated to Richelieu – or *the Mines and Minerals of France, hidden and detained in the stomach of the earth, by the means of which his Majesty's finances will become much more great than those of other Christian Princes and his subjects the most happy of all peoples.*[21] The political importance of her project was underlined by the book's significant sub-title, "with the reason why the said mines and minerals have remained to the present moment almost completely useless and without profit to Sovereignty and the Royal Majesty" (*RP*, 115). Bertereau has received some attention from historians of science, as well as some from New-Agers who think she made great strides in using a divining rod.[22] She had published in 1632 another pamphlet, the *True Declaration of the discovery of mines and minerals in France*, and promised in both the *True Declaration* and the *Restitution of Pluto* a long treatise on the science of mines, which alas, never seems to have appeared.[23] Yet, her work has not been seriously scrutinized – as it deserves – nor has it been used by historians of politics and the political imaginary.

Bertereau begins her work with a dedicatory epistle to Richelieu, which starts by affirming stridently France's natural empire. She notes that "One has the custom to draw Europe with a crown on her head, as being the Queen of the other parts of the world." Not only that, "if one wants to figure France suitably, one must crown her as the Queen of other parts of Europe. Because one must count among the particular favors which she has received from Heaven, both that she is rich in grains, wines, fruit and other things necessary for human life." According to Bertereau, the French as a people are superior to all other Europeans, "which makes them not only more estimable than those of other nations, but also because in these things Nature speaks, seeming tacitly to say by these marks, that [the French] are born to command the entire world and to rule the Universe" (*RP*, 117). Her rhetoric not only echoes the generic Gallican tropes of France's chauvinism, but placed it in a form to suit Richelieu's particular aims, widely circulated in pamphlets, of establishing France's pre-eminence.

Unfortunately, Bertereau notes, there was "one sole point which makes one believe that other kingdoms have precedence over ours" – the lack of gold and silver – which "constrains us to go to our neighbors and gain from them the nerves of war and the spirit of commerce" (*RP*, 117–18). Happily, she informs the Cardinal, "Today God will open your eyes and teach your most august Eminence, by me, who is nothing but a woman, but perhaps one whom it has pleased the divine Goodness to serve himself, to the ends of giving advice about the treasures and riches enclosed in the mines and minerals of France, as he wished on another occasion to serve himself of Joan of Arc to repulse the English from the inheritance which his ancestors left his majesty" (*RP*, 118). The reference to Joan of Arc – while forming part of her broader effort to legitimate female political counsel and her own advice – appears in retrospect both deeply apropos and most unfortunate.

God's care for France was so great that the precious metals that the kingdom lacked merely needed to be found; Bertereau offered technical expertise to find them, promising at the end of a sonnet also addressed to Richelieu:

> La France et les Français vous demandent les mines,
> L'or, l'argent et l'azur, l'aimant, les calamines,
> Sont des trésors cachés de par l'esprit de Dieu.
> Si vous autorisez ce que l'on vous propose,
> Vous verrez, Monseigneur, que sans Métamorphose,
> La France deviendra bientôt un Riche-Lieu. (*RP*, 120)

> (France and the French demand mines from you,
> Gold, silver, and azure, lodestones and calamine,
> Are treasures hidden by the spirit of God.
> If you authorize that which one proposes to you,
> You will see, My Lord, that without Metaphorphosis,
> France will soon become a Rich-Place.)

Apart from providing an opportunity for the crashing pun on the Cardinal's name to conclude the sonnet, worthy of attracting patronage on its own, the sonnet begins to suggest some of Bertereau's distinctive concerns and methods. The list of minerals described as "secret treasures hidden by the spirit of God," as well as the note that she can find the riches without metamorphosis, were not mere throw away pieces of rhetoric, but rather precise clues to the "scientific" methodology, if you will, that would allow her to recover the favor of Pluto for the Cardinal and his employer, Louis the Just.

One cannot – or at least, I cannot – describe the innermost workings, the arcane of Bertereau's methods, for she was careful to protect her value by being discrete about the exact nature of her secrets.[24] Yet, for her own reasons, she does reveal enough about her methods that we can begin to place her methodological assumptions within the contexts of early-seventeenth-century science. Nevertheless, I think it is important to emphasize the "without metamorphosis" line of this sonnet, for she explicitly denies that she used magic to transform other goods into precious metals or relied upon the aid of demons to find France's hidden mines. The denial was in the first instance designed to remove suspicions of a woman who not only quoted Latin and Hebrew – suspicious in itself – but who was also deeply engaged in arts which could too easily seem a manner of sorcery and witchcraft. However, her denial was also designed to emphasize God's providential care for France, by discovering mines that God had created. Rather than claiming the status of a magician, she compared herself repeatedly to Christopher Columbus, who had after all discovered those mines which the Spanish used to claim empire (*RP*, 152–3). Columbus may imply many things to us, but she most liked intended to invoke an image of a man whom God had made an instrument of providential favor by a grant of human knowledge and courage.

Even the use of human knowledge was controversial enough, for the nexus of alchemy, astrology, metallurgy, and natural philosophy had become deeply contested in France during the first half of the seventeenth century. She had proposed finding the French mines earlier in the 1630s, and even seemingly had some success attracting privileges from the Superintendent of Finances Antoine de Coeffier de Ruzé, marquis D'Effiat, before his death, as well as for German princes, the Prince of Orange, and the Holy Roman Emperor (*RP*, 177–88). Despite this experience and previous elite support, each of her moves into alchemical politics placed her in dangerous territory, inhabited by political pitfalls, rival scientific enterprisers, and suspicions of sorcery.

Bertereau, by all appearances, did not adhere to a single school of natural philosophy, but had forged an idiosyncratic mixture from a group of pan-European influences. God had created all things in the universe in the form of a sort of seed, whether animal, vegetable, or mineral, and had a "principle of growth" that made all things grow. Depending upon the amount the metal had grown, it could appear to be a moist, vaporous oily substance, or a powder. Fire liberated the "core" or "matrix" of metal from other surrounding material. The matrix otherwise would grow from a powder to an oily liquid, to a butter-like substance, to the pure metal, all the while emitting the vapors that otherwise burned off in the fire. The growth of metals and minerals from stage to stage was affected by a variety of influences, ranging from the conjunction of planets and stars and different aspects of the sun and stars, which controlled the principle of growth, to the quantity of vapor in the earth, the ambient temperatures, and the veins within the earth in which the liquids and vapors flowed. The growth of minerals and gems was generally favored by cold and dry vapors, where metals were favored by cold and wet humors, affirmed and consolidated by the earth (*RP*, 134–7). Her language for the earth is deeply organic and bodily, referring to metals as lying in its entrails, or even in its womb.

Her technique for finding the metals, as far as one can tell, began with an astrological examination of particular locations, and how they related to particular conjunctions of planets. Some of the stars and planets had particular affinity for a metal; "Gold," she declared, "king of metals, is a Child of the Sun, not admitting any more rust in itself, than his Father permits shadows" (*RP*, 138). Others had more general effects:

> The Moon conjoins with all the stars and all the signs of the zodiac, according to its diverse aspects and movements. She is a common spouse, which being the medium between the celestial world above and the inferior terrestrial world, communicates with all. Silver receives her influence from her and generates according to her, for just as the tides in the seas and rivers follow her movements, so do all the other cold and humid objects. (*RP*, 139)

The movement of the planets thus influenced the flow of humors in the terrestrial world, providing the necessary nourishment for the metals to grow.

Having calculated where minerals were likely to be found using astrological tables, it then was necessary to proceed to the place, and examine the territory first hand for signs of the metals and minerals growing within the earth. These included scrutiny of the local rocks, sand, and plants. Careful consideration of the smell of the air was sometimes profitable, as occasionally one could sniff the vapors released by the growing metals. Central to her efforts was locating water, and testing whether it was sufficient and cold enough to support the formation of noble metals. The water itself could be scrutinized, to see whether it was properly metallic; once found, metallic waters, containing traces of metal but more importantly the humors necessary for growing the matrix, would not only reveal likely sources for mining precious metals, but also had wonderful medical properties in itself (*RP*, 166–76).

Her general approach, if not some specific details, recalls aspects of the theories propounded by the early-sixteenth-century Swiss natural philosopher, doctor and magi Theophrastus Bombastus von Hohenheim, better known as Paracelsus.[25] These include the metaphor of the microcosm and macrocosm joined by the stars, the vegetative nature of minerals and metals, and the idea of a common matrix. Yet, these ideas seem to be general tropes, found widely in a range of early modern metallurgical, alchemical, astrological, and natural philosophical texts. Some of Paracelsus's most distinctive and widely imitated ideas, such as his vaguely Trinitarian conception of the elements, are not to be found in Bertereau's book. Yet Bertereau, nonetheless, takes some pains to assure her readers of the orthodoxy of her approach. Perhaps she was aware of the controversy over Paracelsus's work in France, particularly the scare in 1623–5 that had associated his doctrines with the Rosicrucian order and atheism. French historian of science Didier Kahn has recently revealed that this scare was a student prank gone so seriously wrong that a few people including the philosopher–poet Théophile de Viau were executed as a consequence.[26] Maybe, too, she was aware that, as Hugh Trevor-Roper astutely noted, Paracelsism had been co-opted by the Calvinist international, and was viewed by many Catholic scholars as "an ill-defined Protestant heresy."[27] Perhaps this is why Bertereau was so careful to justify her use of astrology by references to St. Thomas Aquinas, collecting statements from the *Summa Theologica* to justify the stars ruling over the earth, as superiors govern inferiors (*RP*, 141–2).[28]

Her invoking of the Angelic Doctor, however, certainly connected her scientific efforts, the workings of providence, and France's empire. She assured Richelieu that "one must not doubt that at the creation of the world, God placed [Gold and Silver] in this Empire, in this marvelous climate, in this noble kingdom, just as well as . . . in Peru, so that his Majesty could serve himself of them for his needs and necessity to defeat his enemies and relieve his people" (*RP*, 155). Interestingly, though, while insisting that France could produce nearly everything that one sought from strangers, she found it necessary to list those that could not be found – "spices from the Levant, monsters from Africa, elephants, lions and other animals of Asia, and beavers from Canada" – seemingly to point out that they could easily be done without as they were not necessary to human life (*RP*, 146). Once the mines were found, she maintained that everyone would know that "France is the sole and unique jewel of the world, opulent in goods, in fruits and other things necessary to the life of men and in addition so well filled and fecund in treasure that she is sufficient to make her king equal to Solomon, both in glory and in riches, because God visibly blesses him both in war and in peace" (*RP*, 155).

Once supplied with revenues worthy of Solomon, Louis XIII with Richelieu's guidance would have the means not only to win the war, but also the whole almost routine panoply of benefits for the kingdom normally enumerated by authors of pamphlets and others *donneurs d'advis*. He would be able to lower taxes. He could maintain an army of 100,000 men, and a naval fleet powerful enough to repulse the pirates of the Barbary Coast. At the same time, a crusade would be a distinct possibility. What is more, with such funds, one could finally give work to those people who contributed no labor to society, whether through beggary or aristocratic indolence (*RP*, 150–1). In a moment when fiscal chaos, revolt, and military reverses called into question France's natural blessings and providential empire, Bertereau expressed a powerful faith in God's mission for France, arguing that France had in itself positively Peruvian wealth, which could render Louis the Just, rather than those other kings living in that most Solomonic of palaces, the Escorial, God's chosen instrument.

Rather than being celebrated as the French Columbus, though, Bertereau and her daughter were confined in the Castle of Vincennes, though it is unclear whether she was suspected of sorcery or of treachery, because her husbands' family might have been caught up in a plot against Richelieu known as the Conspiracy of Cinq-Mars. Although she avoided Joan of Arc's place on a pyre, she died in prison.[29] Women who proclaimed themselves to be providential solutions to France's political problems were playing a distinctly risky game. This was true whether they were Queens such as Catherine de Medici, or more humble alchemists such as Martine de Bertereau.

The Gallican mines remained the grains, wine, and fruit produced by Nature, France's marvelous climate, and the labor of the king's subjects. Richelieu, though, abandoned his idea that prohibiting commerce would force the Spanish to recognize the French empire. Instead, faced with a crisis in finance and following the revolt of the *Nu Pieds* in Normandy, which was (so the syndics of the town of Rouen claimed) motivated by people angered by the prohibition of commerce, Richelieu instead ended the prohibition of trade. This did not, however, mean that the minister no longer believed that the Gallican mines were a sign of divine favor. The Edict itself declared that the king knew no more "prompt and just route" to relieve his subjects from suffering than "in re-establishing the liberty of commerce which we have prohibited in all foreign countries, knowing well that they will receive much commodity and profit from the sale of their grain, wine and other goods that by divine providence are found in great abundance in our kingdom."[30] In the absence of Bertereau's mines of gold and silver, Louis XIII would have to trust to the traditional Gallican mines of grain and wine to realize France's providential mission. Yet, these mines would not work, in this case, by merely depriving France's neighbors of essential goods. Instead, when the subjects of the king of France enjoyed the liberty of commerce, they could trade these goods and not only support themselves, but provide the king with the coin necessary to wage war, and thus prove France's divine rank above the other kingdoms.

Fertile fields, good wine, and the other fruits of nature continued to play an important role in the French political imaginary as signs of God's unique favor for the kingdom. (Indeed, one could suggest that perhaps a secularized ideal of the blessings of French fertility in good wine and food continues to convince many that the French live in a marvelous climate.) However, the role of the Gallican mines was never clear, as God worked in mysterious ways, his wonders to perform. The Imperial implications of the providential benediction of goods shifted radically under the pressures of a pan-European war. Despite the remarkable claims made for France's nature by Richelieu and by Martine Bertereau, France was not a perfect autarky, filled with the precious metals that would allow it to exercise empire over its neighbors. France's benediction of the traditional mines of grain and wine could only work when France allowed peasants and artisans to harvest and refine such goods, and procured merchants the liberty to answer the diverse needs of human society through commerce. In a world where Grotius's doctrine of free trade as a natural right was a polemical attack on Habsburg Empire rather than a plea for economic efficiency, God's justice could only be procured through the exercise of arms, not realized as an emanation of nature or by the direct working of providence. Historians hoping to understand the ways in which early modern French people understood the place of commerce in the polity should emphasize the connections between the polity and the Divine economy, for not only does it more accurately recover the past but might also hint at remnants of the providential lurking among the riches of the dismal science. Economists make few claims to practice a science that discerns the moral and just ends of life from the providential perfection of polities. Yet, their emphasis on the necessity of circulation and commerce in a world of scarce resources may suggest an effort to replace the dark glass of divine intention with the face-to-face meetings of mercantile sociability.

Notes

1   For example, providential space receives only a brief mention in the excellent book by David Bitterling, *L'invention du Pré Carré: Construction de l'espace français sous l'Ancien Régime* (Paris: Albin Michel, 2009).

2   Pamella H. Smith, *The Business of Alchemy: Science and Culture in the Holy Roman Empire* (Princeton: Princeton University Press, 1994).

3   Lynn White, Jr. "The Historical Roots of Our Ecologic Crisis" (1967) *Science*, 155, 1203–7. I thank Bert Hall for pointing this out to me.

4   *Hugo Grotius: Mare Liberum 1609–2009*, edited and translated by Robert Fennstra (Leiden: Brill, 2009), 25. More generally, see Istvan Hont, *Jealousy of Trade: International Competition and the Nation-State in Historical Perspective* (Cambridge, MA: The Belknap Press, 2005).

5   Tommaso Campanella, *Monarchie d'Espagne et Monarchie de France*, edited by G. Ernst (Paris: Presses Universitaires de France, 1997), 36–43.

6   John M. Headley, *The Emperor and his Chancellor: A Study of the Imperial Chancellery under Gattinara* (Cambridge: Cambridge University Press, 1984), 86–112.

7   Jean Bodin, *Les Six Livres de la République* (Paris: Fayard, 1986), Vol. VI, 64–5.

8   Colette Beaune, *The Birth of an Ideology: Myths and Symbols of Nation in Late-Medieval France*, edited by Fredric Cheyette and translated by Susan Ross Huston (Berkeley, CA: University of California Press, 1991), and David Potter, *A History of France, 1460–1560: The Emergence of a Nation State* (New York: St. Martin's Press, 1995), 17–28.

9   Jehan Masselin, *Journal des États Généraux de France tenus à Tours en 1484*, edited by A. Bernier (Paris: Imprimerie Royale, 1835), 38.

10 Ordinance of March 1498, in *Recueil general des anciennes lois françaises*, edited by François-André Isambert *et al* (Paris: Plon, 1821–33), Vol. 11, 332.

11 Lionel Rothkrug, *Opposition to Louis XIV: The Political and Social Origins of the French Enlightenment* (Princeton: Princeton University Press, 1965), 20.

12 Donald R. Kelley, *Foundations of Modern Historical Scholarship: Language, law and history in the French Renaissance* (New York: Columbia University Press, 1970).

13 Rebecca Zorach, *Blood, milk, ink, gold: Abundance and excess in the French Renaissance* (Chicago: University of Chicago Press, 2005), 88–93.

14 Henry Heller, *Labour, Science and Technology in France, 1500–1620* (Cambridge: Cambridge University Press, 1996) and Mark Greengrass, *Governing Passions: Peace and Reform in the French Kingdom, 1576–1585* (Oxford: Oxford University Press, 2007).

15 Denys Godefroy, *Advis presenté à la Royne, Pour reduire les Monnoies à leur juste prix & valeur, empescher le surhaussement & empirance d'icelle* (Paris: Pierre Chevalier, 1611), 148–9.

16 Françoise Hildesheimer, *Relectures de Richelieu* (Paris: Publisud, 2007).

17 Françoise Hildesheimer, ed. *Testament Politique de Richelieu* (Paris: Société de l'histoire de France, 1995), 335.

18 Erik Thomson, "France's Grotian Moment? Hugo Grotius and Cardinal Richelieu's commercial statecraft," *French History*, 21:4 (2007), 377–94, and for a broader context Erik Thomson, "The Dutch Miracle, Modified: Hugo Grotius's *Mare Liberum*,

Commercial Governance and Imperial War in the Early Seventeenth Century," *Grotiana*, 30 (2009), 88–106, and Martine van Ittersum, "The Long Goodbye: Hugo Grotius' Justification of Dutch expansion overseas, 1615–1645," *History of European Ideas*, 36:4 (2010): 386–411.

[19] Isaac Loppin, Les Mines gallicanes, ou le Thrésor du royaume de France, où sont montrez les droicts du Roy et les moyens justes et légitimes par lesquels ... Sa Majesté peut avoir... les richesses et les utilitez suivantes: I. Mettre par chacun mois, dans ses coffres, neuf millions de livres ... II. Dresser promptement et entretenir, à peu de frais, une milice de cinquante mil hommes de guerre ... III. Et ... l'establissement d'une juste, saincte et chrestienne police (Paris, 1638).

[20] Isaac Loppin, Advis très juste et légitime au Roy Très Chrétien, pour le repos et soulagement des III Ordres de son Estat et le moyen de dresser une milice de cinquante mil hommes. Ensemble une police exemplaire à tous les Estats, Empires et Républiques de l'Univers, pour la descharges de toutes tailles, taillons, aydes, gabelles et générallement tous subsides et imposts . . ., Paris,1648 with similar pamphlets printed during the next three years.

[21] I consulted a copy in the Newberry Library, Chicago: Martine Bertereau, La restitution de Pluton a Monseigneur l'Eminentissime cardinal duc de Richelieu: des mines & minieres de France, cachées & detenuës jusques à present au ventre de la terre: par le moyen desquelles les finances de sa majesté seront beaucoup plus grandes que cells de tous les princes chrestiens ... : ensemble la raison pourquoy les ditesmines ... ont estè iusques à present presque inutiles & sans profit (Paris: Hervé du Mesnil,1640) Case R, 339.093. Bertereau's texts are reproduced in Michel Vallet, *L'aventure Magique de Martine de Bertereau* (Nice: Collection Belisane, 1976); references to *RP* are to this edition.

[22] Bertereau is mentioned frequently in histories of science and biographical dictionaries. Short entries aside, the most extended treatments are Nicholas Gobet, *Les anciens minéralogistes du royaume de France* (Paris: Rualt, 1779) Vol. 1, 261–452, with re-editions of Bertereau's works, Louis Figuier *Histoire du merveilleux dans les temps modernes* (Paris: Hachette, 1860, 2nd edn.) Vol. 2, 269–304, *RP*, and Martina Kölbl-Ebert, "How to find water: the state of the art in the early Seventeenth Century, deduced from writings of Martine de Bertereau (1632 and 1640)," *Earth Sciences History*, 28:2 (2009), 204–18.

[23] Martine de Bertereau, Veritable declaration de la descouverte des mines et minières en France (1632) as reproduced in *RP*, 91.

[24] The closest technical analysis is by Kölbl-Ebert, but she plays down the role of astrology.

[25] On Paracelsus, see most recently Charles Webster, *Paracelsus: Medicine, Magic and Mission at the End of Time* (New Haven: Yale University Press, 2009).

[26] See Didier Kahn, *Alchimie et Paracelsisme en France (1567–1625* (Geneva: Droz 2007), 413–99 and Didier Kahn, "The Rosicrucian Hoax in France (1623–24)," in *Secrets of Nature: Astrology and Alchemy in Early Modern Europe* edited by W.R. Newman and A. Grafton (Cambridge, MA: The MIT Press, 2001), 235–344.

[27] Hugh Trevor-Roper, "Paracelsianism made Political, 1600–1650," in *Paracelsus: The Man and his Reputation, his Ideas and their Transformation*, edited by O. P. Grell (Leiden: Brill, 1998), 119–33, quote 121.

28 She also mentions Albert the Great in passing, as an authority for the orthodoxy of her practice: *RP*, 161.

29 The most detailed account of the imprisonment is in Figuier.

30 "Declaration du Roy pour le Restablissement du commerce par Mer et par Terre," (registered by the Parlement of Paris, November 22, 1639), Paris: Archives des Affaires Etrangères, Mémoires et Documents France, 834, f. 142 r. "Nous avons estimé ne le pouvoir faire une meilleure, plus prompte & juste voye, qu'en restablissant la liberté du commerce que nous avons interdit en tous païs estrangers: sachant bien qu'ils recevront beaucoup de commmodité & profit de leurs bleds, vins & autres denrées, dont par la providence Divine il se trouve grande abondance en nostre Royaume."

Chapter 5

Resacralizing the Self: Mysticism, Materialism, and Personhood in Eighteenth-Century France

Charly Coleman

In eighteenth-century France, secularization had a more precise range of meanings than it does today. Its usage related not to an abstract transformation in worldview or *mentalité*, but to a concrete, verifiable change in social status: the conversion of members of the regular clergy (that is, those belonging to a religious order and bound by its rule) or the benefices under their control into members or properties of the secular clergy (diocesan priests, who were not so bound). The other definition applied to the transfer of ecclesiastical property to temporal authorities – for instance, the confiscations made by Protestant rulers during Luther's Reformation, or by the National Assembly during the French Revolution.[1]

Despite its institutional grounding, secularization and its cognates also retained a telling ambiguity. The *Encyclopédie* entry for *séculier* noted a particular source of confusion: the term could describe either a class of clerics (secular as opposed to regular clergy), or the lay authorities responsible for civil administration.[2] This potential slippage in meaning corresponded to the interpenetration of the sacred and the profane under the *ancien régime*. For instance, in absolutist theory and practice, the monarch's person was regarded as sacrosanct, and his realm considered part of a celestial hierarchy that descended from the heavens to the earth. At the coronation, the king was anointed with oil and received communion, as did members of the clergy, in both bread and wine. He was believed to draw his power directly from divine sources, which endowed him with the miraculous ability to cure scrofula with a touch of his hand. It was also his prerogative to name bishops to their posts in the Gallican church and even dictate terms of the use of ecclesiastical property if the need arose.[3] More generally, the crown was charged with the task of maintaining doctrinal order, and as recent scholarship has made clear, when the reigning Bourbon dynasty's intransigent stance first toward Protestantism and then Jansenism cast doubt on its ability to fulfill this mission, it gradually lost not only credibility, but also its sacrality.[4]

Eighteenth-century formulations of the relationship between the sacred and the profane thus operated along a continuum, so that a person, institution, or movement could pass back and forth between one domain and the other. The mutability of these categories stands in sharp contrast to the binary oppositions that have tended to structure their latter-day counterparts. After all, modernity has long been defined by its opposition to religion. One need only consider Weber's famous pronouncement regarding the "disenchantment of the world": for better or for worse, he predicted, the spirit of rationality would become ever more pervasive, and the space allotted to belief ever more curtailed.[5]

Historians, philosophers, and literary scholars specializing in the eighteenth century have long accepted this view as dogma. Past luminaries of the field such as Peter Gay and Paul Hazard heralded the Enlightenment as an intellectual and cultural watershed that opened an unbridgeable gulf between the ages of faith and reason.[6] More recent scholarship continues to affirm this interpretation in novel ways. For instance, Jonathan Israel has endeavored to remap the intellectual history of the period, with the Dutch Republic of Spinoza, rather than Voltaire's France, at its center. The new *dramatis personae* retain the same *modus operandi*, however, which is to serve as the vanguard in an unprecedented drive toward "rationalization and secularization."[7]

This master narrative of the Enlightenment, for all its weight, has begun to shift in new directions. A wealth of research undertaken during the past several years has turned increasingly to the role of religion in the development of what were once regarded as unambiguously modern ideas, institutions, and events.[8] In French historical studies, Dale Van Kley has demonstrated the central relevance of Catholic theology, and especially the explosive debates between Jesuits and Jansenists during the eighteenth century, to the political struggles that precipitated the collapse of the *ancien régime* and contributed to the chronic instability of the Revolution.[9] To cite another, still more recent, example, David Bell has marshaled compelling evidence in support of the view that nationalism in France "arose simultaneously out of, and in opposition to, Christian systems of belief." Adapting the theoretical insights of the political philosopher Marcel Gauchet, his account holds that the modern nation's dual provenance stemmed from the need to bridge the perceived distance between a transcendent God and the terrestrial sphere through the invention of new concepts and institutions regarded as autonomous from divine oversight or legitimation.[10]

For Van Kley, Bell, and a host of likeminded scholars, secularization no longer indicates a one-sided departure from religion, or the collapse of traditional beliefs and forms of observance in the face of modern standards of rational inquiry. Their approaches recall instead the elastic, polyvalent usage of the term in eighteenth-century French, which referred to the reclassification of places and persons within the religious domain as well as to their passage outside it. With both meanings, at stake was the status of physical objects or personal attributes that informed the identity of the possessor.[11] It is the problem of secularization as it pertains to property, broadly defined as the relationship of the self to spiritual and physical belongings, that this chapter aims to explore.

In the following pages, I will show how eighteenth-century polemics surrounding the self, especially in controversies over mysticism and materialism, coalesced around two related but opposing positions. On one side, orthodox theologians and mainstream *philosophes* joined forces to support a *culture of self-ownership* that valorized the individual's accumulation of spiritual and intellectual goods – and by extension, as we shall see, of material possessions. In contrast, heretical mystics and atheistic materialists sought to undermine the grounds on which the human person could appropriate or subjugate either its internal functions or external objects. According to the anti-individualist *culture of dispossession* that they advocated, personhood was characterized instead by its passivity, dependence, and resignation to totality – situated alternatively in the God of the mystics, or in materialist conceptions of nature.

I will then make the case that the cultures of personhood that clashed during debates over Quietism, an illicit form of mysticism that flourished in the late seventeenth and early eighteenth centuries, also informed polemics over Spinozism and materialism in Enlightenment-era France. I have two overarching aims in doing so, both of which relate to this volume's central themes. The first is to uncover the striking affinities between two movements – mysticism and materialism – which have gone almost entirely unnoticed among scholars. Yet eighteenth-century commentators recognized the ways in which partisans of radical spirituality and radical philosophy (heretical Quietists and atheistic materialists, respectively) both called into question the human person's capacity for independent, self-possessed thought and action. Accounting for what brought together these oddest of bedfellows will go some way in establishing the crucial interactions between eighteenth-century religious culture and Enlightenment thought.

Second, I will argue for the ways in which the cultures of self-ownership and dispossession inculcated distinct understandings of the relationship not only between the self and its possessions, but also between the sacred and the profane. The longstanding theological problem posed by a transcendent, remote, and seemingly hidden god gave rise to an array of conflicting responses that have until now received only scant scholarly attention. For mainstream clerics and lay authors committed to the ideal of self-ownership, it gave credence to their belief that the human person, like God, exerted transcendent powers in and on the world. Their views corresponded most closely to the mechanics of secularization elaborated in current revisionist histories. In schematic terms, the remoteness of the divine allowed the self and its world to assume an exalted status that was seen as distinct from God and increasingly secular in orientation. The ensuing "transfer of sacrality" – to adopt Mona Ozouf's evocative phrase – ultimately conferred upon the self, nation, and society the paramount, authoritative status once monopolized by the Church and the king, though progressively divested of most (though not all) of its explicitly Christian referents.[12]

Partisans of dispossession on both sides of the religious divide pursued a drastically different course. Radical mystics sought ways to span the chasm between the individual soul and eternal divinity by annihilating the former before the terrestrial presence of the latter. Radical materialists, for their part, contended that it was not God, but nature alone that imperiously imposed itself on the human person's every thought and deed. In both instances, one can identify the workings of what I call *resacralization* – a process by which first the divine, and then nature, came to be endowed with an immanent power and totalizing force to neutralize personal autonomy.[13] The term denotes not so much the reversal of a prior move toward desacralization, but rather an alternative means of configuring the sacred in the first place – not only in relation to God, but to purely physical beings and powers as well. I will explore this dynamic in the writings of mystics and materialists during the long eighteenth century, before concluding with an outline of the directions in which it might lead future work on the role of the sacred in Enlightenment-era theology and philosophy.

Quietism and the Vicissitudes of Self-Annihilation

The first major clash between the cultures of self-ownership and dispossession took place during the Quietist Affair of the 1690s – a prolonged controversy involving King Louis XIV, Pope Innocent XII, and much of the

Gallican ecclesiastical establishment. Its doctrinal origins can be traced to certain contradictions within post-Tridentine Catholicism. The Church taught that salvation depended on the accumulation of a range of spiritual goods extending from the sacraments to the theological virtues to salvation itself. The Council of Trent (1545–63) reaffirmed this stance, with its catechism instructing pastors and spiritual directors to "apply themselves to explicate (. . .) that which they deem appropriate to ignite in the heart of the faithful the desire to acquire this sovereign bliss."[14] At the same time, the halting enactment of the Council's reforms in France was accompanied by a resurgence in highly charged devotions – a "mystic invasion," according to Henri Bremond – featuring extreme practices of physical as well as spiritual self-denial.[15] Although the mystic tradition had a history as long as Christianity itself, those who took its ideals of abandon and annihilation too much to heart now found themselves derelict in their religious duty to approach salvation as a good that the soul had a clear and active interest in pursuing.

Dire consequences awaited those who defied this imperative. Jeanne-Marie Guyon, a widow of aristocratic origins whose teachings provided the original impetus for the Quietist Affair, spent nearly a decade held captive in various convents, prisons, and asylums for professing sentiments deemed heretical by Jacques Bénigne Bossuet, the Bishop of Meaux, who would emerge as one of the most powerful prelates of the age. Guyon had already made a name for herself as an adept at mystic theology. Her writings – especially *Le Moyen court et très facile de faire oraison*, first published in 1685 – captivated readers with methodical descriptions of how to purge from the soul all vestiges of "self-ownership (*propriété*)," along with "all that is human and of one's own industry."[16] In this state of abandon, she reported from personal experience, "the soul is left without distinctions: God is the soul, and the self (*moi*) is no longer me."[17] These teachings attracted disciples around France, including at the Maison royale de Saint-Louis in Saint-Cyr, an establishment founded by Louis XIV's morganatic wife Madame de Maintenon to educate daughters of the threadbare nobility.[18] In 1688, she met François de Fénelon – then the school's spiritual director, shortly to be named tutor to the Duke of Burgundy and Archbishop of Cambrai – who placed himself under her tutelage as well.[19] When he persisted in asserting her fundamental orthodoxy, he himself fell victim to a scandal that would end in his public censure and exile from court.

Guyon's activities at Saint-Cyr aroused the suspicion of ecclesiastical authorities, and Maintenon turned to Bossuet for advice. He soon became convinced that her position, and Fénelon's defense of it, amounted to an assault on the soul's necessary desire for eternal beatitude. Their views lent support to a dangerous heresy – what Bossuet referred to in his *Instruction sur les états d'oraison* (1695) as the "new" mysticism for which the Spanish priest Miguel de Molinos and others had recently been condemned.[20] To succumb to a state in which one rejected all hope for recompense as self-interested, and therefore corrupt, was to oppose divine intentions as well as human aspirations. "God wants to give all these gifts," Bossuet contended, and "one cannot love oneself as is necessary, without procuring, or at least desiring, all the goods that God has proposed for our faith" (*Instruction*, 107–8). It followed that the soul's striving for salvation transcends its particular interests in conformity with divine will. Likewise, "the excessive abandon of the new mystics," which also applied to the faculties of reflection and action, threatened to render practitioners powerless in the face of temptation, and thus more susceptible to lapses in morality (115). Even the hope for earthly belongings could be justified, since without it "many of the faithful would succumb to the temptations of impatience and despair" (195). Bossuet and his allies vehemently upheld the soul's rightful possession not only of spiritual riches promised by God, but also of existential goods (i.e., its thoughts and actions) and material objects. To their minds, any and all efforts to mitigate the prerogatives of self-ownership contravened the moral economy of the Chruch, which depended for its operation on the exercise of accountability and the hope for remuneration.

Bossuet made a point of insisting that the personal desire for salvation remained perfectly compatible with charity, and therefore should be considered apart from self-interest in monetary gains or bodily pleasures (*Instruction*, 82–4). Not all his supporters, however, had the same time or talents for theological demonstration. For instance, a priest commenting on the Quietist Affair from Bourges, one père Loire, described to a correspondent how the immediately gratifying effects of self-ownership were inseparable from the desire for salvation. As he put it, "I could not love it if it were not for me a true or apparent good, a thing that did not promise me or had not given me pleasure. The pleasure that a thing is capable of producing is the essence of the good in it."[21] While this priest by no means went so far as to advocate a laissez-faire approach to the desires of the flesh (a charge reserved, on different grounds, for heretical mystics), he seemed content to discuss the virtues of spiritual and economic possession on the same discursive and conceptual plane. Indeed, his remarks in certain respects anticipate, by more than a half century, the stance taken by "Enlightened" proponents of luxury consumption such as Georges-Marie Butel-Dumont, who argued for its utility in terms of sensationalist psychology.[22]

Fénelon, for his part, rejected all such efforts to reconcile self-interest and charity. In a series of writings published during the 1690s, he staunchly defended Guyon while compiling a list of doctrinal errors made by their mutual adversaries. His *Explication des maximes des saints sur la vie intérieure* (1697) asserted that her beliefs belonged to "the general tradition of Christianity" on the basis of the long-acknowledged distinction between an exalted love of God that no longer takes into account the "precise motive of our *own* happiness and our *own* reward" and the less perfect degrees in which some measure of interest still figures.[23] Writing of the nearness of the divine during the highest forms of devotion, he observed, in the letters and tracts later collected in his *Oeuvres spirituelles* of 1718, how "this *self* (*moi*), of which I am so sensitive, and that I have loved so much, must be foreign to me."[24] Where one's particular person once stood, "God places himself," as if "between myself and me," thereby becoming "closer to me by his pure love than I am to myself" (*OS* I, 12). The soul should accept divine gifts when offered, but "not for the love of them" in themselves, but merely as "a remedy, without connivance, without attachment, without ownership" (I, 102). Even the state of abandon granted by God as a means of purification must itself be abandoned in "this real sacrifice of all of oneself after having lost every interior resource" (I, 171).

Yet, the soul's cultivation of total dispossession yielded a paradoxical harvest. According to Fénelon, God only deprives us of something in order to "return it without the impurity of this evil appropriation that we make without perceiving it" (*OS* I, 172). Once the self and its acquisitiveness have been removed as obstacles, one no longer thinks or feels through the mediation of gifts or other objects, but in the immediate presence of God alone, who, "without being possessed by the soul," "possesses entirely as he wishes" (I, 172). From this perspective, one remains obliged to love the divine for divinity itself, not for the promise of salvation or any other reward. The soul that wavers for an instant, even if damned to hell, admits a modicum of self-interest that has not yet been expunged (I, 248–59).

For Fénelon, pure love cast a revealing light on the nature of both self and God. The former was a mere figment to be annihilated, the latter a totalizing, immanent force that subsumed the existence of all individual beings in itself. This view formed the basis of his attempts to articulate a mystic metaphysics in the *Traité de l'existence et des attributs de Dieu*, a work he began in the late 1680s.[25] There, Fénelon confronted the challenge of reconciling two contradictory tenets. God, as a perfect being, must be a "simple and indivisible infinity, immutable and without modification" (*Traité*, 63). Yet there also seem to be in the natural world defective human creatures made up of two distinct substances – mind and matter, the soul and the body. In an effort to resolve this difficulty, he returned to the clarifying dictates of spiritual abandon that guided his understanding of devotion. "There is nothing but unity," he professed, "it alone is all" (76). The physical universe, like the individual human person, projected "a misleading image of being" (76). A truly infinite God must in reality encompass "all the being of the body" as well as "all the being of the spirit" (69). Before its sublime presence, Fénelon could regard himself only as a passing shadow, a "*je ne sais quoi* (. . .) who cannot for a single moment find myself fixed and present to myself" (79).

Once again, his convictions clashed sharply with those of his peers in the Gallican church. Louis-Antoine de Noailles, the Archbishop of Paris, firmly supported Bossuet in the dispute over Guyon's theology. He took specific aim at the implication that a mind in the throes of mystic abandon might lose sight of God as depicted in scripture – the creator of the world, the Word made flesh in the person of Jesus Christ, the crucified savior who rose from the dead and paved the way for the redemption of humankind.[26] Bossuet's philosophical inclinations – set forth in his treatise *De la Connaissance de Dieu et de soi-même*, first drafted before the Quietist Affair – led him to emphasize the autonomy and agency of the soul.[27] He noted with particular admiration how the "empire" that the mind exercised over the body evoked "the absolute power of God, who turns the entire Universe by his will" (*Connaissance*, 203). According to these formidable critics, Fénelon had shown himself guilty of impugning the sacred character of personhood on at least two counts. His deviant understanding of mystic theology, they alleged, not only diminished the scope of divine transcendence by failing to distinguish sufficiently between God and the natural world, but also tarnished the splendors of the human self created in the image of the perfectly supreme being.

Fénelon would pay dearly for his recalcitrance. The publication of his *Maximes des saints* set off a volley of damaging works likening his views to those of Molinos and other condemned Quietists. Bossuet also employed *ad hominem* tactics in his *Relation sur le Quiétisme* of 1698, which indulged in tawdry speculation that Guyon's doctrines had seduced Fénelon in body as well as in spirit.[28] Increasingly isolated, the archbishop appealed to the judgment of the Vatican, but Pope Innocent XII, under pressure from Louis XIV and the pro-Bossuet faction in Rome, handed down a sentence denouncing him.[29] Fénelon duly submitted to the papal brief *Cum alias*, issued in March 1699, which condemned 23 propositions from *Maximes des saints*, and he retreated to his diocese in Cambrai. From there, he attempted to influence events behind the scenes, most notably through the intimate ties he maintained with his former pupil, the Duke of Burgundy, who became heir to the throne. His hopes for political reform, however, were dashed with the young prince's premature death in 1712.[30] Guyon, who had been held in custody since the start of the Quietist Affair, remained imprisoned in the Bastille until 1703.

Between Mysticism and Materialism

For Bossuet and his supporters, the victory against heretical mysticism appeared to have been decisively won. Yet the theology of abandon elaborated by Guyon and Fénelon lived on in their writings, which were reprinted in numerous new editions and formats throughout the eighteenth century.[31] The doctrines they had made notorious also made conspicuous appearances in highly publicized trials of heretical mystics held in Dijon and Toulon, as well as in the works of apologists such as the Jesuit Jean-Pierre Caussade.[32]

More notably still, the culture of dispossession that first emerged as an identifiable position during the Quietist Affair went on to set the parameters for Enlightenment-era polemics over the self in other arenas. In particular, orthodox Catholic theologians and moderate *philosophes* alike recognized similarities between the radical spirituality preached by Fénelon and Guyon and the radical philosophy attributed to Baruch Spinoza and his materialist followers in France. In the article on God that appeared in *Questions sur l'Encyclopédie* (1770–2), Voltaire claimed to be puzzled when it came to Spinoza's idea of a purely disinterested, intellectual love of divinity as elaborated in the *Ethics*.[33] "Is it the virtuous and tender Fénelon, or is it Spinoza who wrote these thoughts?," he demanded to know (*Questions*, 366). "How could two men so opposed, with such different notions of God, come together in the idea of God for himself?" (366). The very notion struck the *philosophe* as dangerous, if not absurd. To his mind, human morality was underwritten by the promises of a "remunerating and vengeful God" to dispense rewards to the virtuous and heap punishment on the reprobate (376). Moreover, as he explained in regard to *Le Système de la nature* – a materialist manifesto from 1770 written by Paul Henri Thiry, the baron d'Holbach – denying the existence of a willful, self-conscious deity cast doubt on his own faculties as a self-owning subject. "I have sensations and thoughts," Voltaire countered, so it was unthinkable to him that "an intelligent cause could not have given me intelligence" (375).

Not unlike Voltaire, Christian apologists quickly turned from their triumph over the Quietist menace to confront attacks on the integrity of the human person stemming from radical philosophical circles. For instance, the renowned theologian Nicolas-Sylvestre Bergier attacked d'Holbach for reducing the self to passivity and indifference, when both scripture and reason made plain that the soul directs the material body "by its will and its action" alone.[34] Furthermore, religion promises those who exercise these faculties "peace" in this life, and "immortal felicity" in the next (*Examen* I, 367). Bergier even surmised that d'Holbach's various fallacies rested on a specious understanding of nature, which conjured to his eyes "a being more *mystical,* more unknown, and more inconceivable than a spiritual God" (*Examen* II, 232).

What did Voltaire and Bergier – two of the most knowledgeable, influential thinkers of the period – mean by their remarks likening mysticism and materialism? On the surface, the two movements appear antithetical: one affirmed the existence of an all-encompassing divinity, the other excluded the possibility of God's existence. Although Fénelon died before d'Holbach was even born, had he lived long enough, the archbishop would doubtlessly have regarded his work with horrified contempt. Yet to their critics, radical spiritualists and radical materialists spoke in the same damnable terms. Both challenged theological and philosophical pronouncements on divine transcendence and human autonomy, whether in their Christian or deistic guises. Both sought to devalue spiritual and existential goods. For veterans of the eighteenth-century culture wars over the self, the lines of division shone through clearly. One could insist that the human person maintains a possessive relationship to its ideas and actions, and thus stands accountable for them as a moral agent who acts in and on the world. Alternatively, one could take the opposing view, and assert that individuals remain ultimately beholden to a determining power beyond their comprehension or control.

In this way, Enlightenment-era cultures of personhood operated as rival arsenals that furnished theologians and philosophers with logics and lexicons to be deployed in defense of their respective views. The weapons used in one battle could be refitted for use in another. To be sure, when Voltaire alluded to the similarities between Fénelon and Spinoza, he did not intend to reduce the ideas of an archbishop to those of an exile from the Jewish community in Amsterdam, whom he characterized as an inveterate atheist.[35] Rather, he related them in light of the parallel stances they had taken vis-à-vis the nature of God and the human person, which positioned them in his mind on the same side of the conflicts between partisans of self-ownership and dispossession.

In the case of Fénelon's purported doppelganger Spinoza, the crucial affinity hinged on the status of free will as a property of the thinking subject, whether human or divine. The Christian apologist Laurent François described Spinoza's supreme being as a figure with a more than passing resemblance to the debased Quietist: he "hates himself, he pleads mercy for himself and is refused it, he persecutes himself, he kills himself, he eats himself, he slanders himself, he condemns himself to the scaffold."[36] While Spinoza left his personal religious beliefs in doubt, he provided ample fodder for such criticism in the *Ethics* (1677), where he roundly rejected the idea a transcendent, intelligent, redemptive creator.[37] In its place, he substituted a monist conception of the divine as coexistent with the universe and immanently at work within it. Within such a framework, divine causes by definition lack intent or agency. It becomes reasonable to conclude that "God does not produce any effect by freedom of will," but is instead constrained by his own nature (*Ethics* 106).

Spinoza dismissed human pretensions to free will on similar grounds. As he stated in the *Ethics*, "when we say that the human mind perceives this or that idea, we are saying nothing but that God (. . .) has this or that idea" (123). In other words, one should relate to one's thoughts not as possessions unique to oneself, but rather as reverberations of God thinking through the mind. Likewise, the quest for knowledge of God through the study of nature should remain a wholly disinterested enterprise, since "he who loves God cannot strive that God should love him in return" (*Ethics*, 253). From this perspective, the most fundamental truths stem from an awareness of the determined character of one's existence, and the happiest fate is "to be and to remain chained by the bonds of (God's) love."[38] It is a love, moreover, that relates not to the individual human person, but instead forms "part of the infinite love with which God loves himself" (*Ethics*, 260). This sentiment, which Spinoza hailed as the "intellectual love of God," must by necessity be radically self-referential – not to the human subject, but to divine substance in its infinity of forms as "God, *or* Nature" (*Deus sive Natura*) (*Ethics*, 259, 198). The self who attains it, then, persists merely as an effect of this totalizing force, rather than as a distinct, self-owning individual.

As Voltaire duly noted, Fénelon and Spinoza shared a common commitment to the pure love of God – or "God for himself," as the *philosophe* would have it (*Questions*, 366). Yet their respective positions at once converged and diverged at a still more fundamental level. For both, the need for disinterestedness stemmed at least partly from a recognition of the divine's immediate proximity to the self, and of the undeniable power it exerted on all persons and things. On this view, humans were far from poised, as Descartes famously put it in *Discours de la méthode*, to become "masters and possessors of nature."[39] If anything, the opposite was the case. Fénelon and Spinoza each attempted to imagine, in distinct and significant ways, a resacralization of the material world, understood as a new means of orienting its relationship to the sacred. The physical universe no longer represented for them a profane realm apart from that of a hidden God, an inert field ceded to and awaiting the attention of a willful subject. Divinity infused the natural realm. Its looming presence encompassed, and even effaced, the real existence of all other particular beings, up to and including the individual self.

While Fénelon and Spinoza both affirmed God's immanent presence in the world, they differed significantly in their definitions of who or what God is, and why and how he acts. Indeed, Fénelon even composed what scholars agree was a refutation of the *Ethics* – though he demurred from citing its author by name.[40] The work, entitled *Démonstration de l'existence de Dieu* (1713), clarified the point at which he found Spinoza's arguments insupportable. His religious convictions, however heterodox they appeared to critics, would not allow him to affirm the infinity of a mere "assemblage of parts" (i.e. of extended substance, or matter), since doing so would obviate the need for a perfectly singular, unified, and divine creator.[41] The indeterminate status of *Deus sive* Natura, he believed, left scarcely any place for God as a sovereign being with absolute freedom of will and movement. Thus, the archbishop would only meet Spinoza half-way. He might have countenanced the self's dissolution, or even the absorption of the created universe into God within the framework of his mystic monism. He could not bring himself, however, to take the definitive step of reducing the divine to mere matter.

Materialism and the Goddess of Nature

Fénelon's stumbling block would become a cornerstone of the radical philosophy that arose in Enlightenment-era France. Its architects, to whom Diderot referred as "modern Spinozists," adhered to a staunchly materialist interpretation of their predecessor that did away with all references to the divine.[42] Among the most notorious works disseminating this view – and, according to Robert Darnton, one of the best selling – was baron d'Holbach's anonymously published *Système de la nature* (1770).[43]

The author was an avowed atheist who ridiculed the obscurantism of references to God in works such as the *Ethics*.[44] Nevertheless, he remained firmly committed to the monist, determinist vision popularized by the earlier treatise, which provided the basis for what he styled "fatalism" – a statement of atheistic principles that, paradoxically, featured its own liturgy, and even its own deity.

D'Holbach's stated aim in *Système de la nature* was to dispel the "phantoms" employed by agents of "religious and political tyranny" to justify the enslavement of their subjects' hearts and minds (I, Preface). Yet the way to liberation passed through constraints of a different order. An avid amateur scientist who contributed articles on chemistry, mineralogy, and related topics to the *Encyclopédie*, his studies had taught him that nature, taken as a whole, consists of nothing "but an immense chain of causes and effects that ceaselessly follow from one to the other" (I, 55). In sharp contrast to theologians who defended the soul as a spiritual subject, d'Holbach maintained that individual beings could never be said to possess "independent energy" or the wherewithal for "detached action" (I, 55). Their role, properly understood and simply stated, is to carry out "a necessary task in the general work" (I, 58). For centuries, priests and kings heaped false praise on the supposed grandeur of the human person. If we could only disabuse ourselves of our own significance, d'Holbach implied, and dispossess the self of the false titles that have been falsely attributed to it, then at last we might see ourselves for what we are and where we stand in the totality of matter. In the end, it sufficed to look at the world with eyes wide open to perceive that "man is in each instant of his life a passive instrument in the hands of necessity" (I, 81).

It followed that all creatures are bound by the same set of universal laws. D'Holbach rejected out of hand the theological premise that men and women are fallen beings who required otherworldly redemption. "Self-gravitation," he countered, compels them to act in accord with their own interests for the sake of preserving and improving their physical existence (*Système* I, 54). Yet this drive is in turn circumscribed by reason, which he argued directs us "toward objects of true interest for ourselves and for others" (I, 231). Social relations, then, should reflect the determined organization of things in nature.

D'Holbach made these claims in support of his overarching doctrine of "fatalism," which he believed would make it possible to found morality on an "unshakeable base" (*Système* I, 241, 258). He described fatalists who reconciled themselves to the "system of necessity" as subsisting in a state of "contented apathy" – the just reward for cultivating "a reasoned resignation to the decrees of destiny" (I, 260). As if in imitation of Pascal's famous wager, d'Holbach then inquired of the potential skeptics among his readers whether they could still believe that, given the immense influence of nature, they might be "the only being who could resist its power?" (I, 274). Confident in the assurance that their pretensions would come to nothing, he gave guidance on how best to proceed. "Let us submit ourselves then to necessity," he implored, "let us resign ourselves to nature" (I, 273).

Like Spinoza, then, d'Holbach had no use for a transcendent God or for a human soul purportedly made in his image. He set out to expose the falsehood in the claim that the universe remained "under the empire of an intelligent cause whose model was and always will be man" (*Système* I, 72). Religion perpetuated the misguided notion that humans stand apart from nature on account of their supposed likeness to divinity, and that the design of the universe favors their particular benefit. God did not create humanity; on the contrary, the human mind invented God to justify its illegitimate claims to sovereignty over the terrestrial sphere. Rather than imagine nature on the basis of a flawed conception of the self, d'Holbach insisted that human beings reconsider their existence as nature had determined it. To do so would require a concerted campaign of dispossession – one that toppled God from his throne before casting down humanity from its privileged place above all other creatures.

After spending two volumes and over 800 pages presenting his indictment against the gods of revealed religion, it is more than a little ironic that d'Holbach ultimately chose to swaddle his fatalist doctrines in quasi-religious imagery. The treatise's final pages are devoted to a long soliloquy delivered by nature to her devotees. "Descend within your self (*ton intérieur*)," she declares, before imploring them to "enjoy, and have others enjoy, the use of the goods that I have placed in common for all the children who have come equally from my womb. (. . .) It is only in making them happy that you will be happy yourself" (*Système* II, 443). Thus spoke nature, who along with reason formed a pantheon of solicitous "deities" determined to lead humankind into a new age, with a new sense of self (II, 453).

Two aspects of d'Holbach's encomium stand out in light of the arguments I have put forward regarding the eighteenth-century culture of dispossessive personhood and its role in the resacralization of nature. First, it is significant that the goddess who graces his treatise enjoins her charges to possess, but to possess in common, thereby allowing for a rehabilitation of self-ownership on collective rather than individualist grounds. Moreover, their sense of justice follows from the central tenet of philosophical fatalism: that all humans, equally and without exception, owe their thoughts, wills, and actions to the workings of nature. Once this abiding truth found universal recognition, d'Holbach asserted, the world as he and his contemporaries knew it would be forever transformed. His determinism, then, could be regarded as doubly dispossessive. It described, on the one hand, a presumably immutable condition – the human person's intrinsic dependency on nature – that demolished theological claims concerning the soul's personal identity and agency. Yet, as d'Holbach made clear, humans could lose sight of the true source of their existence. Thus, on the other hand, his system also required an act of self-surrender in the present to establish the code of nature as the basis of the social order.

Second, the rhetorical figure of the goddess signals d'Holbach's paradoxical yet undeniable effort to imagine nature as an entity with many of the powers attributed to the divine, but with none of its status. His own lapses aside, he repeatedly eschewed anthropomorphism: "When I say that nature produces an effect, I do not at all claim to personalize it. (. . .) We cannot call nature intelligent in the manner of some of the beings it encompasses" (*Système* I, 12). This qualification proved essential to d'Holbach in his attempts to arrive at the proper relationship between the human person and nature – and, by implication, the proper dynamic between transcendence and immanence. To a considerable extent, he shared the monist framework elaborated in different ways by both Fénelon and Spinoza. He approached nature as an immanent and dispossessive force that subsumed the attributes and prerogatives once thought to belong to the individual human person. In so doing, he effectively resacralized it as an atheist deity, one endowed with all the power of Fénelon's mystic God or Spinoza's *Deus sive Natura*. At the same time, he insisted that nature did not perform the same role as the divine creator of orthodox theology. Here, he embarked on the path outlined in the *Ethics* that Fénelon refused to take. More specifically, a relationship that the archbishop, as a professing Christian, regarded as an exchange between two distinct and spiritual, albeit unequal, persons (God and the soul), d'Holbach described as one between material things. In his system, nature and the self were rendered immanent to each other, bound together in the same complex, totalizing whole. "Oh Nature! Sovereign of all beings!" he proclaimed at the conclusion of his work, "and her adorable daughters, virtue, reason, truth! Be forever our only divinities (. . .) concentrate your power in order to conquer our hearts" (*Système*, II, 453).

Coda: The Enlightenment and the Sacred

It seems counter-intuitive that an atheistic materialist like d'Holbach would engage in intellectual activities analogous to those pursued by Spinoza, an alleged pantheist, or Fénelon, a confirmed Christian mystic. In certain circles, it may even be regarded as heresy. Yet, eighteenth-century critics thought otherwise. Consider again, for instance, Voltaire's dismissal of all three authors' views on God in *Questions sur l'Encyclopédie,* or Bergier's references to the "mystical" deity of the *Système de la nature.* Simply put, it was impossible to avoid theological questions during the period when these texts were written.[45] Even the most vehement nonbelievers thought long and hard about God. It is time that scholars of the Enlightenment start doing the same.

To this end, the argument presented here offers a contribution to a burgeoning literature on the religious dimensions of intellectual and cultural life in eighteenth-century France. Following some of the most innovative work in the field, my brief study takes as its point of departure the difficulties produced by the *deus absconditus.* For eighteenth-century defenders of self-ownership, the human person – along with the society and nation it made possible – derived its independence from an all-powerful but distant God who required created beings to exercise their mental and physical faculties on their own, for their own purposes. Enlightened *abbés* and moderate *philosophes* championed the cause of an active, autonomous, self-possessed subject modeled on a supreme being and destined to preside over the world. In so doing, they effectively secularized the self, thereby establishing the basis for modern individualism, but with religious referents very much in mind.

Yet, this narrative reveals only part of the story. Heretical mystics and radical materialists opposed the partisans of self-ownership at every turn, and they sought to minimize the distance separating the otherworldly and temporal domains. Moreover, they shared a common means for doing so – a wide-ranging culture of dispossession that challenged the human person's status as a willful, acquisitive agent. Their writings demanded that the human person renounce its unjust claims of ownership over its ideas and actions, and that it place itself and its powers under the direction of God and/or nature.

This dynamic, which I have termed "resacralization" as a way of differentiating it from phenomena predicated on divine transcendence, was neither more nor less "modern" than secularization. Both movements had profoundly religious origins, while also opening the way for a post-theological view of the world. The same rhetoric that Fénelon employed to describe spiritual abandon informed d'Holbach's hopes for the triumph of reason over the dictates of a false god. Despite their acute differences, the atheist no more than the archbishop could dispense with the view that either God or nature held a totalizing sway over humankind. D'Holbach's deification of nature, however uncharacteristic, belies a devotion to the sacred in perhaps its most fundamental sense: as an entity worthy of sacrifice, of a radical act of self-dispossession. It also connotes, in a manner anticipating Durkheim, the ultimate grounding of one's identity not only as a member of society, but as a living being *tout court*.[46] As such, his ideals can be seen to follow a rather different trajectory from those conventionally associated with secularization – toward collectivism rather than individualism, interdependence rather than autonomy, immanence rather than transcendence.

We must cautiously depart, therefore, from Weber's famous dictum. During the eighteenth century, the world was not only becoming disenchanted, but becoming enchanted anew – or, more precisely, resacralized. D'Holbach sought not to subjugate nature, but to reveal its immanent, determining power. To do so required him to cast off the false pretensions of a nascent individualism in favor of a highly charged awareness of the connections between all beings. In describing this state of affairs, moreover, he had recourse to a language that resonated strongly with rhetoric associated in the eighteenth century with unorthodox strands of mystic devotion. His project, and the vision of resacralized nature it sought to implement, frame a compelling perspective from which to reconsider not only the history of the Enlightenment, but also its legacy.

Notes

[1] See, for instance, *Dictionnaire de l'Académie française, 4th* edition, 2 vols. (Paris: Brunet, 1762), s.v. "Sécularisation"; *Encyclopédie, ou Dictionnaire raisonné des sciences, des arts et des métiers, par une société de gens de lettres,* 17 vols. (Paris: Chez Briasson; Neufchâtel: Chez Samuel Faulche et Compagnie, 1751–65), s.v. "Sécularisation"; and Claude-Joseph de Ferrière, *Dictionnaire de droit et de pratique,* 2 vols. (Paris: V. Brunet, 1769), s.v. "Séculariser."

[2] *Encyclopédie,* s.v. "Séculier." Cf. *Dictionnaire de l'Académie,* 4th ed., s.v. "Séculier."

[3] On the divine nature of monarchical power in seventeenth- and eighteenth-century France, see Jacques Bénigne Bossuet, *Politique tirée des propres paroles de l'Écriture sainte* (1709), edited by Jacques Le Brun (Geneva: Librairie Droz, 1967), 64–71. For a more general discussion, see Marc Bloch, *The Royal Touch: Sacred Monarchy and Scrofula in England and France,* translated by J. E. Anderson (London: Routledge and Kegan Paul, 1973) and Ernest Kantorowicz, *The*

King's Two Bodies: A Study in Medieval Political Theology (Princeton, NJ: Princeton University Press, 1966). On government interventions in the administration of Church property, see John McManners, *French Ecclesiastical Society under the Ancien Régime: A Study of Angers in the Eighteenth Century* (Manchester: Manchester University Press, 1960), 118–22.

4   On the changes in the religious status of the French monarchy, see Dale Van Kley, *The Religious Origins of the French Revolution: From Calvin to the Civil Constitution of the Clergy, 1560–1791* (New Haven, CT: Yale University Press, 1996) and Jeffrey W. Merrick, *The Desacralization of the French Monarchy in the Eighteenth Century* (Baton Rouge, LA: Louisiana State University Press, 1990).

5   Max Weber, "Science as a Vocation," in *From Max Weber: Essays in Sociology*, edited and translated by H. H. Gerth and C. Wright Mills (New York, 1946), 129–56; quote on 155.

6   Peter Gay, *The Rise of Modern Paganism*, vol. I of *The Enlightenment: An Interpretation*, 2 vols. (New York: Knopf, 1966–9) and Paul Hazard, *La Crise de la conscience européenne, 1680–1715* (Paris: Boivin, 1942). See also Michel Vovelle, *Piété baroque et déchristianisation en Provence au XVIIIe siècle: Les Attitudes devant la mort d'après les clauses de testaments* (Paris: Seuil, 1978).

7   Jonathan Israel, *The Radical Enlightenment: Philosophy and the Making of Modernity* (Oxford: Oxford University Press, 2001), quote on 7.

8   In addition to the works cited here, see, for example, Alyssa Sepinwall, *The Abbé Grégoire and the French Revolution: The Making of Modern Universalism* (Berkeley, CA: University of California Press, 2005); Jonathan Sheehan, *The Enlightenment Bible: Translation, Scholarship, Culture* (Princeton, NJ: Princeton University Press, 2005); and Jeffrey D. Burson, *The Rise and Fall of the Theological Enlightenment: Jean-Martin de Prades and Ideological Polarization in Eighteenth-Century France*, foreword by Dale Van Kley (Notre Dame, IN: University of Notre Dame Press, 2010).

9   Van Kley, *Religious Origins of the French Revolution*, 75–134, 249–368.

10 David A. Bell, *The Cult of the Nation in France: Inventing Nationalism, 1680–1800* (Cambridge, MS: Harvard University Press, 2001), 6–17, 22–48; quote on 7. Bell's thesis draws on arguments made in Marcel Gauchet, *Le Désenchantement du monde: Une Histoire politique de la religion* (Paris: Gallimard, 1985), esp. 47–130. On shifting perceptions of the relationship between human society and the heavenly city, see also Keith Michael Baker, "Enlightenment and the Institution of Society: Notes for a Conceptual History," in *Main Trends in Cultural History: Ten Essays*, edited by Willem Melching and Wyger Velema (Amsterdam and Atlanta, GA: Rodopi, 1994), 95–120.

11 Cf. *Encyclopédie*, s.v. "Propriété."

12 Mona Ozouf, *La Fête révolutionnaire* (Paris: Gallimard, 1976), 317–40; quote on 317.

13 I have previously discussed resacralization in Charly Coleman, "Resacralizing the World: The Fate of Secularization in Enlightenment Historiography," *Journal of Modern History* 82 (2010): 368–95.

14 *Catéchisme du Concile de Trente* (Bouère: Éditions Dominique Martin Morin, 1984), 7–12, 130–49; quote on 131. See also *Le Sainte Concile de Trente oecuménique et général, célébré sous Paul III. Jules III. et Pie IV. souverains pontifes*, translated

by Martial Chanut, 3rd ed. (Paris: Sébastien Mabre-Cramoisy, 1686), 37, 48, 71, 146.

[15] Henri Bremond, *L'Invasion mystique*, vol. II of *Histoire littéraire du sentiment religieux en France*, 12 vols. (Paris: Bloud et Gay, 1915–36).

[16] Jeanne-Marie Guyon, *Le Moyen court et très facile de faire oraison* (1685), in '*Le Moyen court*' *et autres écrits spirituels*, edited by Marie-Louise Gondal (Grenoble: Éditions Jérôme Millon, 1995), 118.

[17] Guyon, *Lettres chrétiennes et spirituelles sur divers sujets qui regardent la vie intérieure*, 5 vols. (London: n.p., 1767), IV, 318.

[18] On Saint-Cyr and its mission, see also Carolyn C. Lougee, *Le Paradis des Femmes: Women, Salons, and Social Stratification in Seventeenth-Century France* (Princeton, NJ: Princeton University Press, 1976), 188–201.

[19] For an account of Guyon's early relationship with Fénelon, see the letters collected in Guyon, *Correspondence*, 3 vols., edited by Dominique Tronc (Paris: Honoré Champion, 2003–5), especially vol. I, *Directions spirituelles*.

[20] Bossuet, *Instruction sur les estats d'oraison, où sont exposées les erreurs des faux mystiques de nos jours: Avec les actes de leur condamnation* (hereafter *Instructions*) (Paris: Chez Jean Anisson, 1697), 10.

[21] Archives nationales, L 22, no. 5, pp. 1–2, *Lettre du pur-amour*.

[22] Georges-Marie Butel-Dumont, *Théorie du luxe; ou Traité dans lesquel on entreprend d'établir que le Luxe est un ressort non-seulement utile, mais même indispensablement nécessaire à la prosperité des Etats*, 2 vols. (n.p., 1771). On Dumont's employment of sensationalism in support of luxury, see Michael Kwass, "Ordering the World of Goods: Consumer Revolution and the Classification of Objects in Eighteenth-Century France," *Representations* 82: 1 (2003), 87–116.

[23] François de Salignac de La Mothe Fénelon, *Explication des maximes des saints sur la vie intérieure*, in *Oeuvres*, edited by Jacques Le Brun, 2 vols. (Paris: Gallimard, 1983), I, 1017, 1011; emphasis added.

[24] Fénelon, *Oeuvres spirituelles de Messire François de Salignac de la Mothe-Fénelon* (hereafter *OS*), 2 vols. (Anvers: Henri de la Meule, 1718), I, 11.

[25] Fénelon, *Traité de l'existence et des attributs de Dieu* (hereafter *Traité*), in *Oeuvres complètes*, edited by Jean-Edme-Auguste Gosselin, 10 vols. (Paris, 1848–52; reprint, Geneva: Slatkine, 1971), I, 1–88. On the dates of composition of Fénelon's *Traité*, see Denise Leduc-Fayette, "Fénelon et infini véritable," in Jean-Marie Lardic, *L'Infini entre science et religion au XVIIe siècle* (Paris: J. Vrin, 1999), 97.

[26] Louis-Antoine de Noailles, *Instruction pastorale de M. l'Archevêque de Paris, sur la perfection chrétienne et sur la vie intérieure, contre les illusions des faux mystiques* and Fénelon, *Troisième lettre à M. l'Archevêque de Paris, sur son Instruction pastorale*, in Fénelon, *Oeuvres complètes*, II, 458 and 495–7. On Noailles's criticisms, see also Alain Niderst, "Le Quiétisme de Télémaque?," in *Fénelon mystique et politique (1699–1999)*, edited by F.-X. Cuche and J. Le Brun (Paris: Honoré Champion, 2004), 208–14.

[27] Bossuet, *De la Connaissance de Dieu et de soi-même* (hereafter *Connaissance*), edited by Émile Charles, new ed. (Paris: Librairie classique d'Eugène Belin, 1875).

[28] Bossuet, *Relation sur le quiétisme* (Paris: J. Anisson, 1698), 144.

[29] *Condamnation et prohibition faite par nostre tres-Saint Pere le Pape Innocent XII. du livre imprimé à Paris l'an MDCXCVII. qui a pour titre:* 'Explication des *maximes des saints*

  sur la vie intérieure, &c.,' in *Relation des actes et délibérations concernant la Constitution en forme de bref de N. S. le Pape Innocent XII* (Paris: Chez François Muguet, 1700), 24–36.

30 On the archbishop's political aspirations, see Fénelon, *Plans de gouvernement,* in *Oeuvres complètes,* 7: 182–94, as well as Gilbert Gidel, *La Politique de Fénelon* (Paris, 1906; reprint, Geneva: Slatkine, 1971) and Patrick Riley, "Fénelon's 'Republican' Monarchism in *Telemachus,*" in *Monarchisms in the Age of Enlightenment: Liberty, Patriotism, and the Common Good,* edited by Hans Blom, John Christian Laursen, and Luisa Simonutti (Toronto: University of Toronto Press, 2007), 78–100. It is worth pointing out that *Les Aventures de Télémaque* (1699), the allegory Fénelon originally composed for the Duke of Burgundy, went on to become one of the best-selling titles of the eighteenth century. See Riley, "Fénelon's 'Republican' Monarchism," 81.

31 See Albert Cherel, *Fénelon au XVIIIe siècle en France (1715–1820): Son Prestige – Son Influence* (Paris, 1917; reprint, Geneva: Slatkine, 1970). For a list of Fénelon's posthumous eighteenth-century publications, see Cherel, *Fénelon au XVIIIe siècle,* "Supplément, Tableaux Bibliographiques," 1–33.

32 Jean-Pierre de Caussade, *Instructions spirituelles, en forme de dialogues sur les divers états d'oraison* (Perpigan: Jean-Baptiste Reynier, 1741). On the Quietist trials, see also Mita Choudhury, "'Carnal Quietism': Embodying Anti-Jesuit Polemics in the Catherine Cadière Affair, 1731," *Eighteenth-Century Studies* 39:2 (2006), 173–86; Choudhury, "A Betrayal of Trust: The Jesuits and Quietism in Eighteenth-Century France," *Common Knowledge* 15:2 (2009), 164–80; and Jason Kuznicki, "Sorcery and Publicity: The Cadière-Girard Scandal of 1730–1731," *French History* 21:3 (2007), 289–312.

33 François-Marie Arouet, Voltaire, *Questions sur l'Encyclopédie* (hereafter *Questions*), s.v. "Dieu, Dieux," in *Oeuvres complètes de Voltaire,* edited by Louis Moland, new edition, 52 vols. (Paris: Garnier, 1877–85), XVIII, 366–9.

34 Nicolas-Sylvestre Bergier, *Examen du matérialisme* (hereafter *Examen*), 2 vols. (Paris: Humblot, 1771), I, 144.

35 See Voltaire, *Questions sur l'Encyclopédie,* s.v. "Athéisme," in *Oeuvres complètes de Voltaire,* XVII, 474.

36 Laurent François, *Preuves de la religion de Jésus-Christ, contre les spinosistes et les deistes,* 3 vols. (Paris: La Veuve Estienne & Fils, 1751), I, 276–80; quote on 278.

37 Benedict de Spinoza, *Ethics,* in *A Spinoza Reader,* edited and translated by Edwin Curley (Princeton, NJ: Princeton University Press, 1994), especially 85–114.

38 This quote is taken from Spinoza's supplement to the *Ethics,* published as *Dieu, l'homme et la béatitude,* translated and introduction by Paul Janet (Paris: G. Balière, 1878), 124.

39 René Descartes, *Discours de la méthode,* introduction and notes by Etienne Gilson (Paris: J. Vrin, 1989), 128.

40 On Fénelon's relationship to Spinoza, see Paul Vernière, *Spinoza et la pensée française avant la Révolution* (Paris, 1954; reprint, Geneva: Slatkine, 1979), 271–2, 275–8.

41 Fénelon, *Démonstration de l'existence de Dieu,* in *Oeuvres,* II, 623–31; quote on 626.

42 *Encyclopédie*, 15: 474, s.v. "Spinosiste." On the rise of French materialism and its relationship to Spinoza, see Vernière, *Spinoza et la pensée française*, 374–5, 413, 528–9 and Israel, *Radical Enlightenment*, 684–713.

43 Robert Darnton, *The Forbidden Best-Sellers of Pre-Revolutionary France* (New York: W.W. Norton, 1996), 25–8, 48–9, 63–6.

44 Paul Henri Thiry, baron d'Holbach, *Système de la nature, ou Des Loix du monde physique & du monde moral* (hereafter *Système*), new ed., 2 vols. (London: n.p., 1771), II, 188–93. On d'Holbach's engagement with Spinoza, see also Vernière, *Spinoza et la pensée française*, 630–42.

45 D'Holbach's writings on theological and doctrinal issues include *Le Christianisme dévoilé* (1756), *La Contagion: la Bible devant La critique rationaliste* (1768), *Examen des prophéties qui servent de fondement à la religion chrétienne* (1768), *Théologie portative* (1768), *Histoire critique de Jésus-Christ* (1770), and *Tableau des saints* (1770).

46 I draw here on the definitions of the sacred formulated in Gauchet, *Désenchantement du monde*, 10–25 and Georges Bataille, *Théorie de la religion*, edited by Thadée Klossowski (Paris: Gallimard, 1973), 58–84, as well as Émile Durkheim, *Les Formes élémentaires de la vie religieuse* (Paris: Presses Universitaires de France, 1960), 49–66.

Chapter 6

Permutations of the Theological–Political Analogy: Political Voluntarism, "Transfer," and Secularization

Stephanie Frank[1]

During the Revolutionary summer of 1789, the Abbé Sieyès made arguments on the floor of the National Assembly for the sovereignty of that body. Nearly exactly a century earlier, in the context of the major theological polemic of the seventeenth century, Nicolas Malebranche had offered the same constellation of arguments regarding the sovereignty of the Church. Both arguments justify their respective institutions with respect to a so-called *volonté générale* (of God in the one case and of France in the other); both arguments include the same differently oriented and somewhat contradictory constructions of the relation between the *volonté générale* and the representative body; both arguments use institutional constraints to preclude opposition.

Particularly in the context of the theological derivation of the notion of the *volonté générale* itself, the reiteration of the logic of Malebranche's argument in Sieyès is striking.[2] And I have made a case elsewhere for the derivation of Sieyès' argument from Malebranche's – for a claim that posits some sort of narrative of causation between the theological original and its "secularized" image.[3] This suggestion relates to Carl Schmitt's claim that all the modern concepts of the theory of the state were "secularized" versions of theological concepts.[4] Schmitt's claim hinges on the etymological sense of "secularizatio," which originally named a transfer of land from ecclesiastical to secular control. In the Malebranche-Sieyès case, it would appear that the structures of the arguments are the same; the argumentative logic has simply been transferred from religion to politics.

Perhaps still more striking than the identity of the arguments, though, is the acute divergence of the two arguments beyond the level of rhetoric. Malebranche was interested in the ways God's actions necessarily reflected the sort of being that he was: God's *volonté générale* was constrained by his justice, goodness, etc. In fact, he eventually articulated a political theory that – while maintaining its roots in certain questions about the nature of God's salvific plan – held universal standards derived from God's nature to be binding on human exercises of sovereignty. However, when Malebranche's original argument was redeployed in a political context a century later, it gave rise to a position quite opposed: in Sieyès, France's *volonté générale* is constrained by nothing other than itself. (For purposes of this essay, I call this latter position "voluntarist.")

That is, while it may be the case that the form of the two arguments is identical, the arguments have very different purchases. This suggests that, even if "transfer" comprises one element of the phenomenon, it does not exhaust it. Indeed, Schmitt's problematic has always hinted at uncharted depths. Owing to his phrasing of the original claim, the transfer problematic has been associated with the broader array of changes generally (if vaguely and unsatisfyingly) categorized under the heading of "secularization." Nevertheless, I do not think there has been a serious attempt to imagine how Schmitt's "secularization theory" – pertinent to transfer in the "history of ideas," – or something like it – might align with more general accounts of secularization.

Toward answering the narrow question of the divergent politics of the two arguments and making a start on the broader question of intellectual–historical "transfer" and "secularization," I want to compare the arguments of Malebranche and Sieyès and the way each of them regard the relation of politics and theology. First, I will sketch briefly the arguments' structural homology. Then I will consider more closely the political ramifications of Malebranche's argument, as he spells them out, and his changing sense of what we might call the political–theological analogy. Finally, I show the way Sieyès' argument undoes the trajectory of the evolution of Malebranche's argument. Ultimately, Sieyès and Malebranche offer us different models of the relation of politics and theology, legible in their uses of political–theological analogy. I suggest that this difference explains their divergence on the question of voluntarism and begins to suggest how Schmitt's "transfer" problematic could fit into a more general account of secularization.

Malebranche's and Sieyès' Homological Arguments for the Legitimacy of Representation

Sieyès' argument of September 7, 1789, is addressed to the question of the *sanction royale*. In keeping with the French tradition of regarding the king as a bastion of protection against the encroachments of the aristocracy, the chief arguments for the royal veto were broadly democratic in nature.[5] On "suspensive" conceptions of the royal veto, the king would put his own proposal alongside that of the National Assembly so that the people could decide between the two at the next elections; on "absolute" conceptions, the king would simply dissolve the National Assembly and call for new elections. However, even if both versions of the royal veto tended more toward democracy than despotism, neither – as Sieyès of course realized – was consonant with the sovereignty of the National Assembly. Sieyès' argument, then, is chiefly directed at asserting that France's government was representative and not democratic.

Sieyès' first foray seems to be in keeping with treatments of Sieyès' thought that emphasize its relationship with political economy.[6] Thus, for instance, Sieyès explains:

> It is for the common utility that [citizens] name for themselves representatives much more capable than they to know the *general interest* and to interpret in this regard their proper will. . . . The very great majority of our fellow citizens has neither enough instruction nor enough leisure to want to occupy themselves directly with the laws that must govern France; they have decided therefore to name representatives. . . .[7]

Considering the realities of limited time and poor education, Sieyès argues, France's general will can best be discerned by representatives. This argument generally dovetails with Sieyès' political writings, which emphasize the centrality of the division of labor to modern society and suggest that representation is just one species of the same.

However, this motif is juxtaposed, in the same speech, with quite a different argument, which suggests that more than practical considerations are at stake:

> The national will has come to be considered as if it could be something other than the will of the representatives of the nation, as if the nation could speak in any other way than through its representatives. Here, false principles become extremely dangerous. . . .[8]

Sieyès here makes a very strong claim: not only is the national will most prudently accessed through the National Assembly, it can only be accessed through the National Assembly. In fact, Sieyès' contention goes still further, beyond questions of access: the national will can only *be* the will of the members of the National Assembly.

This claim is peculiar both for its strength and for its combination with the more prudential argument. However, it is less peculiar when viewed in the context of the broader discourse of the *volonté générale*. As Patrick Riley has brilliantly shown, this discourse was originally theological. Its root lay in the seventeenth-century Jansenist–orthodox controversy over the question of the interpretation of 1 Timothy 2:3–4, "God wills all men be saved," and in particular, the polemic between the orthodox theologian Nicolas Malebranche and the Jansenist Antoine Arnauld.[9] The problem was how, considering the plain sense of the Scripture, one could account for the fact that so many people were so clearly (to the minds of the participants in the debate) not saved. Arnauld ventured that, before the Fall, God would truly have saved all men, but after the Fall, he only had a "general will" for human salvation, which meant that "all men" were saved only in the sense that God saved representatives from all classes of humanity (i.e. salvation did not discriminate by wealth, race, sex, etc.).

Nicolas Malebranche appropriated the term *volonté générale* but gave it quite a different import. For Malebranche, *volonté* implies not just an idle wish for an end (as Arnauld contended) but also the establishment of a means to that end. *Générale* characterizes this means. That is to say, the principles by which salvific grace is distributed are elegantly simple laws befitting the unfathomable wisdom of God. Since the finer points of the orthodox–Jansenist controversy all referred back ultimately to the question of the Church's authority, it is unsurprising that Malebranche's considerations of both "means" and their "generality" find their resting places in the institution of the Church. The Church was, by Malebranche's orthodox lights, both the means God had prepared for realizing human salvation and an elegantly simple way to distribute grace.

The ecclesiology that Malebranche developed from the central idea of the *volonté générale* anticipates in its structure Sieyès' peculiar combination of arguments. I will consider here his *Entretiens sur la Métaphysique et sur la Religion* (1688). In this text, we see the conventional argument that the masses cannot "discern truth from error," such that God, in all his providence, provided the Church for them. Thus this dialogue:

ARISTES. I understand you to say, Theodore, that the way of inquiry might correspond to God's will to save the savants: but God wants to save the poor, the simple, the ignorant, those who do not know how to read, as well as gentlemen critics. . . . It corresponds perfectly to God's will that all men could come to knowledge of the truth. But where will we find this infallible authority, this certain way that we can follow without fear of error?[10]

Theodore chimes in that the infallible authority is to be found in Holy Scripture, but "it is by the authority of the Church that we know this. Saint Augustine was right to say that without the Church he would not have believed in the Gospel."[11]

We saw Sieyès combine a prudential argument regarding the National Assembly's discernment of France's *volonté générale* for the masses with an alternatively oriented argument to the effect that the will of the National Assembly just *was* the *volonté générale* of France. Similarly, Malebranche combines his own prudential argument (the Church is the means to render accessible to the masses God's *volonté générale* for salvation) with an alternatively oriented argument to the effect that the Church just *is* God's *volonté générale* for salvation. Malebranche had earlier come under pressure from his critics on the issue of miracles – surely, they asked pointedly, he was not suggesting that God did not intervene in particular historical moments? In the *Entretiens*, then, Malebranche scaled back his use of the term of *volonté générale* and replaced it with *dessein*. The rhetoric of *desseins* suggests that the means/end distinction is, so far as divine providence is concerned, a false one, that the means are "built in" to the design itself. Thus:

> THEODORE. Remember that God can act only according to His nature, in a way that bears the character of His attributes; that thus He does not form plans independently of the means of executing them but that He chooses together the work and the ways [to accomplish it] which express the perfections which He is glorified to possess better than any other work by any other means.[12]

For Malebranche of the *Entretiens*, the Incarnation and the Church are the "chief among the designs of God" (*le principal des desseins de Dieu*), foreseen as integral parts of the cosmic drama of redemption: "Certainly, before the fall of the first man, God already had the design to sanctify his Church by Jesus Christ."[13]

In the *Entretiens*, then, it is not just that the Church exemplifies God's general willing. Since there is no distinction between ends and means, on Malebranche's understanding of divine power, it is not too much to say that the Church *is* God's *volonté générale*. We might then frame Malebranche's ecclesiology as Sieyès framed his theory of representation: given that God has a *volonté générale* for human salvation, it is ridiculous to imagine that it could be anything other than the Church. That is, Malebranche combines a prudential argument (regarding the accessibility of the relevant *volonté générale* to the masses via the relevant institution) with what we might call a metaphysical argument that identifies the *volonté générale* with the institution. For Malebranche, "the Church of the living God," is – as Theodore says, quoting and glossing the Vulgate – simultaneously "the pillar and firm support of the truth" and "the pillar and ground of the truth."[14] And so, the argumentative logics of Malebranche's ecclesiology and Sieyès' theory of representation are strikingly homologous.

If the position Sieyès took in the National Assembly's debates about representation appears to be indebted to Malebranche's ecclesiological argument, so too does the strategy that he used to foreclose debate. On July 8, 1789, the National Assembly was debating the *mandat impératif*, which would have bound the National Assembly's representatives to vote according to the expressed wishes of their constituents. For Sieyès the fundamental theoretical issue anticipated that of the *sanction royale* debate: were the people the ultimate arbiters of the national will? Or was, instead, the Assembly? After extensive debate, Sieyès took the floor to "remind" his listeners, "My opinion has been and is still, about the matter, that relative to the Assembly there are no grounds to deliberate. The principles about which my opinion is founded have already been consecrated through the order of 17 June."[15] There were "no grounds to deliberate" about the *mandat impératif*, for Sieyès, just because the matter had already been resolved against it when the National Assembly constituted itself as the sovereign authority. By virtue of being members of the National Assembly, the argument ran implicitly, the representatives had already come out against the *mandat impératif*.

Malebranche similarly deploys institutional considerations to preclude debate. To see how, we will have to understand the way in which Malebranche pursued the question of the authority of the Church through a restaging of the Eucharistic controversies. In the *Entretiens*, Malebranche recodes the *volonté générale-volonté particulière* polemic as an iteration of the Protestant–Catholic debates about the hubris of those who would maintain their own individual inspirations against the weight of the institution of the Church. For Sieyès, the National Assembly's sovereignty had to be secured against the vision whereby the people directly accessed France's *volonté générale*. Similarly, in Malebranche's assimilation of the Jansenist position to the Protestant position, the legitimacy of the Church had to be buttressed against the claim of individuals to directly access God's *volonté générale*.

I want to look at just one aspect of Malebranche's strategy of revisiting the Reformation here: a thought-experiment that revolves (at least in theory) around the question of the nature of Eucharistic representation.[16] To settle the intractable Protestant–Catholic dispute (Is the wafer Christ's body? Or merely a symbol of Christ's body?), Malebranche imagines convening a representative body.

> Let us take an example. We are at a loss to know whether it is the Body of Jesus Christ or the symbol of His body that is in the Eucharist. . . . What do we do to clarify what is contested? We convene the most general assemblies that we can . . . The Bishops know whether, in the Church in which they preside, it is or is not believed that the Body of Jesus Christ is in the Eucharist. We ask them then what they think of this. They declare it to be an article of their faith that the bread is changed into the Body of Jesus Christ. They pronounce anathema on those who maintain the contrary. The Bishops of the other Churches, who were not able to be at the assembly, approve affirmatively the decision; or, if they are not in touch with those at the Council, *they remain silent and give sufficient testimony by their silence that they are of the same opinion* . . . That being so, I maintain that . . . we should have to renounce common sense to prefer the opinion of Calvin or of Zwingli to that of all these witnesses who attest a fact that it is *not possible for them not to know*[17] (Emphasis mine)

Malebranche's thought experiment is structured around the assumption that if Christ is not actually in the wafer, then the Holy Spirit must not be guiding the Church. The Church, faced with a challenge, invites its bishops to assemble to articulate the *volonté générale*, but this effort is wasted. After all, if Christ is not in the wafer, neither is he in the Church and therefore neither is he with those in the Church's representative council. However, how could those in the convened assembly of the Church cast a vote implying that the Church had been deserted by God? The question is moot. As in Sieyès' famous foreclosure of debate on the matter of the *mandat impératif,* everyone at Malebranche's theoretical convention can be assumed to agree by the constraints of the institution itself.

The Analogies before the Homology: Theology and
Politics in Malebranche's *volonté générale*

As it turns out, Sieyès' argument was not the only one to evince an analogical structure. Even the earliest arguments surrounding the *volonté générale* invoked a theological–political analogy. In his early work, Malebranche, on at least one occasion, used politics as a kind of analogy to aid in conceptualizing divine sovereignty. In the *Meditations Chretiennes et Métaphysiques* (1683), Malebranche deployed a political–theological analogy as part of his case against *volontés particulières*. The position espousing *volontés particulières* implied that God willed specifically the various evils of the world. Malebranche instead used a political analogy to point up the difference between actions of commission and omission:

> When you hear it said that God permits some natural disorders . . . [it is in] the same fashion that a Prince lets his ministers act, and permits the disorders that he is not able to prevent. It is God who does all, the good and the evils. . . but God *does* the good and *permits* the evils, in the sense that he wills positively and directly the good, and he does not so will the evil.[18]

Arnauld proposed a different political–theological analogy, more in keeping with his own theodicy:

> There is no contradiction whatever [in the fact] that God wills by a *volonté absolue et particulière* the contrary of what he wills *en général*, just as a good king wills by an antecedent will that all his subjects live contentedly, though by a consequent will he executes those who disturb public tranquility by murders and violence.[19]

Arnauld likens God's salvific will before [*antécédent*] and after [*conséquent*] the Fall to a king's will before and after one of his subjects commits a crime.

Initially, then, Malebranche and Arnauld – though they differ on the particulars – inhabit the same framework governing the relation of the political to the theological. The problem motivating their political–theological analogies is basically epistemological: they use their understandings of comparatively fathomable political sovereignty to cast light on the more difficult question of God's sovereignty. Importantly, this form of the political–theological analogy, advanced by both Malebranche and Arnauld, presumes the very assumption that Malebranche claimed he did not share with Arnauld: that God is recognizably like humans. Here, Malebranche's eagerness to imagine the nature of God's willing apparently trumped his insistence on the essential discontinuity between the human and the divine – which was, of course, the major argument shoring up the *volonté générale* position.

It is hard to imagine that Malebranche was not aware of this problem, and indeed, a year later in their polemic, Malebranche engages a point that Arnauld made through political analogies by sidestepping the analogy through which he made it. Arnauld argued (as Malebranche quoted at length) that Malebranche must believe that God, constrained as he is to will only generally, intervenes in history only through angels; but this (contended Arnauld) was as absurd as imagining that a king had one of his ministers make and execute all plans on his behalf without even consulting him. Arnauld's analogy reaches its climax with a pointed question: "To whom would the subjects of [this] king . . . address themselves in order to obtain succor for the evils that menaced them?"[20] Arnauld's point, of course, is that titles notwithstanding, this system elevates the minister above the king, and thus that Malebranche's system elevates the angels above God. In the *Réponse*, Malebranche addresses Arnauld's argument only by suggesting that it is a straw man: "everything said by M. Arnauld . . . is such strange nonsense and gross fraud . . . that people of good sense do not need me to see that he combats only the products of his own imagination."[21] Malebranche goes on to diagnose Arnauld as having misunderstood the sense of "general laws"; he does not have a word to say about the theological–political analogy.

Malebranche likely skirted the problem of the theological–political analogy here because he had taken up a new framework for thinking the relation between theology and politics. In his *éclaircissements* to the *Traité de la Nature et de la Grâce*, appended in 1684, Malebranche developed the idea that the relations between God's many perfections constituted an order of justice, which was binding on God rather as Malebranche had originally conceived God's nature to be.[22] The final paragraph summarizes this new contention in this way:

> A general cause ought not act by particular willings. The conduct of God ought to bear the character of his attributes, if the immutable and necessary order of justice obligates him to change it. For order, to God, is an inviolable law: he loves it invincibly, and he always prefers it to arbitrary laws through which he could execute his designs.[23]

And so Malebranche subsumes the generality of God's will in the broader matter of this "immutable and necessary order of justice."

The continuity between the original *volonté générale* argument and this argument about the "order of justice" is witnessed by the fact that this final *éclaircissement* responds to the foremost critique of the original formulation of the *volonté générale*; the quoted passage is part of an argument that Old Testament miracles "do not at all show that God often acts by *volontés particulières*." Once again, we have the notion that God is averse to particular willings; this time, though, the aversion is attributed to the "immutable and necessary order of justice." That the shift of terminology is continuous with Malebranche's position is suggested by the persistence of the rhetoric of *volonté générale* and *particulière* in treatments of the problems of theodicy and providence for the rest of Malebranche's life.[24]

What, exactly, did this recontextualization of the *volonté générale* argument secure for Malebranche? It provided a better footing vis-à-vis the major critique of his opponents, but even beyond the polemic, there was an important shift in his position.[25] God had been bound to act in accordance with his nature even in the earlier articulation of Malebranche's position. Yet Malebranche's restatement entailed the new idea that God's nature (in particular, the relation between his perfections) was equally binding on human action. If the universe was governed by the principles of the relations obtaining between God's perfections, these principles held true for humans as for God.[26]

> In supposing that humans should be reasonable, certainly one can argue that they know something of that which God thinks and of the manner in which God thinks it. Because, in contemplating the substance of the Word . . . I am able to discover, at least dimly, the relations of perfection which exist between these same ideas; and these relations are the immutable order that God consults when he acts: the order which also ought to regulate the esteem and love of all intelligent beings.
>
> From this it is evident, that there exists true and false, just and unjust, and this in regard to all intelligent beings: what is true, with regard to man, is also so with regard to God. Because all souls that contemplate the same intelligible substance necessarily discover there . . . the same practical truths, the same laws, the same order, when they see the relations of perfection between intelligible beings who contain the same substance of the Word, which is the immediate object of all our knowledge.[27]

The generality of God's willings was just one entailment of the order of justice by which all willings ought to be evaluated. Therefore, it is incumbent upon humans to "follow a law that God loves invincibly":

> Since truth and order are the relations of grandeur and of perfection—the real, eternal, necessary relations that the substance of the divine word

contains—he who sees these relations, sees what God sees: he who regulates his love by these relations, follows a law that God loves invincibly.[28]

Of course, humans, feeble as they are, generally fall short of this call.

It seems clear, from the prevalence of political motifs in Malebranche's later work, that Malebranche was particularly concerned with not human conduct but human *sovereignty*. In fact, it seems difficult to avoid the conclusion that at least part of Malebranche's motivation, in recontextualizing the *volonté générale*, lay in rethinking human politics. For Malebranche's new articulation of his theodicy carried in its train the transformation of the relation between politics and theology. Politics and theology resembled each other analogically, but only incidentally – only insofar as they exemplified the same immutable "order of justice" derived from the nature of God. God necessarily carried out the order of justice – he couldn't help but act in accordance with his own nature, after all – but humans had to be enjoined to do so, and often fell short. Here, unlike in his first deployment of the political–theological analogy, Malebranche underscored the discontinuity between humans and God.

More importantly, though, Malebranche's new political–theological analogy had leverage for political critique. The first articulation of the political–theological analogy had taken as given a certain structure of human sovereignty in order to think divine sovereignty, thus naturalizing that understanding of human sovereignty and insulating it from critique. However, on the new understanding, the political–theological analogy provided a standard from which to critique human sovereignty. Thus, Malebranche writes in the *Traité de Morale*:

> No less than the pope, the prince holds only his authority over other men by God alone, and the one and the other ought to use it as God himself, by relation to the immutable order, universal reason, the inviolable law of all intelligences and of God himself.[29]

In the *éclarcissements* to the *Traité*, Malebranche wields his new apparatus vis-à vis human politics, while simultaneously discrediting his polemical opponents. He strongly criticizes human leaders who fail to abide by the order of justice, even as he uses the specter of their despotism to tar his theological enemies.

> I do not say that God chooses and abandons [his plans] simply because he wills it, because I fear making God seem like a man, who conducts himself

by caprice and lacks regard for his work. It will not suffice to understand that God is powerful, and that he does what he wants with his creatures. . . . It is necessary to render him worthy of love and adoration at least as much as to render him formidable. . . . [T]he principle of the predestination of the Saints . . . is not a blind, bizarre, imperious will, of the sort that is often noted among the great powers [*les Grands]* of the Earth.

. . . [M]en make God such as they would like to be themselves; and since they prefer power to wisdom, God will always be just enough and wise enough for them, so long as he is powerful and sovereign. People love independence: to them it is a species of slavery to submit to reason . . . they fear making [God] powerless by making him wise.

These people will never understand that the Word of God is sovereign and universal reason; that this reason is coeternal and consubstantial with God himself; that he loves it necessarily, invincibly, inviolably; and that although he is obligated to follow it, he remains independent. Thus all that God wills is just, wise, and constant, because God is only able to act according to his lights, because he is only able to love according to his order, because he is not able to misunderstand his wisdom and deny himself . . .[30]

Here, those who would disagree with Malebranche on the matter of the nature of God's willing are implicitly likened to despots and discredited thusly. Like unjust sovereigns, Arnauld and his ilk "prefer power to wisdom" and are willing to sacrifice wisdom and every other value to secure the fantasy of the completely unconstrained will.

The political entailments of Malebranche's theodicy are still more clearly manifest in his last work, *Réflexions sur la Prémotion Physique* (1715), which was a response to the critique directed at Malebranche by Laurent Boursier's *De l'action de Dieu sur les créatures*. Along the lines we have just seen Malebranche anticipate, Boursier held what I will call the voluntarist position, i.e., that God's will is completely sovereign and unconstrained. For Boursier, to suggest (as Malebranche did) that God was confined by anything like reason, goodness, or justice – let alone *necessarily* so confined – was to render him "impotent."[31] Malebranche responded to this charge by explaining that the "constraints" on God were actually just the contours of his own nature.

God is the essential justice . . . because the eternal, immutable, original law can only consist in the immutable and necessary relations that exist between the attributes and perfections of a necessary and immutable nature. God is thus able neither to deny nor to neglect it; for he loves invincibly what he is essentially. . . . God depends only on himself, because the eternal law is consubstantial with him.[32]

For Malebranche to say that God is "confined" by his nature is actually to misspeak – God is simply acting in accord with his nature and his love for all of his attributes and perfections, which are also the foundation of all knowledge.

Malebranche contended that the real denigration of God's power was to detach it from his goodness and justice – for that was to assimilate him to a certain unfortunate sort of earthly prince.

> If God were only omnipotent, without wisdom, justice, goodness, and if his attributes did not have any order or relation among them, . . . if he was similar to princes who glory more in their power than in their nature, then his sovereign domain, or his independence, would give him the right to all. . . . Hobbes, Locke and several others would have discovered the true foundation of morality: authority and power giving, without reason, the right to do anything one wants, when one has nothing to fear.[33]

Malebranche considers it self-evident that Hobbes (not to mention Locke, bizarrely included here) has in fact not discovered the true foundation of morality: thus, it must not be the case that God is like these deficient earthly princes. Note that the very sort of reasoning that Malebranche had once himself undertaken – that from the (known) character of human sovereignty to the unknown character of divine sovereignty – is now the basis for Malebranche's *reductio ad absurdum*.

Malebranche's politics here is not deployed to discredit his adversaries in theological controversy; for him, politics appears to have become an end in itself. And yet, even though the originally theological polemic is no longer legible, Malebranche's argument still evinces its roots in the question of salvation. Thus Malebranche argues,

> The choice of the elect is not the effect of a will of God that is absolute and bizarre, or a will that has no reason other than the will itself, such as certain people are pleased to attribute to God; [these people] apparently prefer force, the law of brutes, that which has given the Lion empire over

the animals, to reason. Preferring power to wisdom and to justice, they make God as they would like to be themselves.[34]

And indeed, we could multiply instances where Malebranche returns to God's intention to save all men.[35] So although it is no longer the motivating issue, Malebranche is still concerned with the question with which his polemic with Arnauld began. However, by assimilating this question to the broader question of the order of justice implied by God's perfections, Malebranche used his theodicy to wield his political critique. If it was the case that God's perfections constituted an order of justice, not only God but also human sovereigns should be constrained by it. His new position reflected also a new configuration of human and divine sovereignty, now indirectly analogical, insofar as both reflected the same independent "order of justice."

The Problem of Voluntarism: Intellectual History and the Political–Theological Analogy

As we have seen, Sieyès' political argument partakes of a structure homologous to that of Malebranche's ecclesiological argument. Nevertheless – the parallels in the geometry of the arguments notwithstanding – the quality of the legitimacy claims is different in the two cases. For while Malebranche's Church is legitimate because it instantiates God's *volonté générale*, which (in turn) derives from the universal order of justice, Sieyès' National Assembly is legitimate just because it instantiates France's *volonté générale*.

Because Sieyès makes no recourse to independent moral standards, his argument takes on the quality of the position I have identified as voluntarist. Consider again Sieyès' perversely strong claim:

> The national will has come to be considered as if it could be something other than the will of the representatives of the nation, as if the nation could speak in any other way than through its representatives. Here, false principles become extremely dangerous . . .[36]

Sieyès is here incensed by the notion that the national will could be anything other than the will of National Assembly's representatives. This is no mere rhetorical flourish: slightly later in the speech, after insisting that France could only ever have a representative government, Sieyès explains the folly of the *appel au peuple* by explaining that, in the relevant situation, the people quite simply lack *volontés particulières*:

> Thus the citizens who name representatives, renounce and should renounce making the law themselves immediately. *They do not have a particular will to impose.* Every influence, every power belongs to them about the person of their *mandataire*; but that is all. If they dictate willings, it would no longer be a representative state: it would be democratic.[37]

Malebranche's Church is legitimate because it partakes of what we might call capital-J Justice; Sieyès' Assembly is just, it seems, because there is nothing else to which questions of justice could refer.

What exactly should we make of the reversal on what we might call the voluntarist question? It would be possible to read it as a consequence of the "bracketing" of God: God's absence from Sieyès' argument means also the absence of the relations between his perfections, which is to say, the perfections which acted as a kind of constraint on God's sovereignty in Malebranche's ultimate argument. If we bracket God and the order constraining God out of the original argument, all that is left is the *volonté générale* and the institution exemplifying it. Thus (the argument would run) it is not possible in the Sieyèsian context to make recourse to something like a "necessary and immutable order of justice" as constraining the *volonté générale*. The *volonté générale* is the only possible rationale for itself.

Such a hypothesis is elegant but not, I think, ultimately persuasive. Can it be the case that the geometry of Malebranche's argument was this magnetic for Sieyès? That Malebranche–Sieyès analogy is exclusively a rhetorical "form" that has become historically sedimented, even at the cost of what would seem to be critical "content" (to wit, the question of the ethical valence of politics)? Moreover, of course, the hypothesis would in the end just gesture to a more fundamental (and more intractable) question of why, exactly, God came to be bracketed in Sieyès' argument.

In fact, we might ask whether God has in fact been bracketed at all. Historians sometimes talk (in perhaps less than rigorous terms) about the "deification" of the "nation" in Revolutionary political thought. The Malebranche–Sieyès homology gives traction to this claim, if a claim it is. It is certainly the case that the nation (and in particular, the national will) occupies the place that God (and God's will) had held in the original theological argument. And if we think of "God" rather narrowly, as naming a certain sort of legitimizing work, then the claim will hold: it is true that (at least on one construction) France's *volonté générale* does the same work, in Sieyès' argument, that God's *volonté générale* does for Malebranche's. Incidentally – though I suspect it employs a rather more reductionist understanding of "sacrality" than such historians would prefer – this might lend an intelligible, nonmystifying construction to the formulation of the "transfer of sacrality" that cultural historians have advanced for thinking about the nature of the investment in certain categories of Revolutionary politics.[38]

At any rate, it does not seem as though God's "bracketing" –if it obtains at all– can explain the change in the argument. Alternatively, it might be tempting to suggest that the critical moment in the production of the voluntarist quality of Sieyès' argument predates Sieyès. Perhaps the heart of the question lies in the adoption of France's *volonté générale*; as soon as France was conceived to have its own *volonté générale*, we might think, Sieyès' argument necessarily ran (analogically) parallel to Malebranche's early position.

Actually, though, the historical trajectory of the *volonté générale* claim gives the lie to this possibility. While the specificity of France's general will – it is after all the general will of *France* – would seem to pull against the universalist timbre of Malebranche's argument, the framework of Malebranche's late position could have made space for France's *volonté générale* alongside God's *volonté générale*. After all, Malebranche did position the wills of earthly princes in just this way – as governed, like divine sovereignty, by the "immutable order of justice" that derived from God's nature. It is worth noting, though, that in this case there could have been no Schmittian "transfer": the "political" image of the "theological" original would have just turned out to be a restatement of Malebranche's late position. Since the position already espoused a politics alongside a theology, Malebranche's late position could not "secularized."

Schmitt's famous claim about the secularization of concepts in the modern theory of the state is in his *Political Theology*. In spite of the incoherence of the category of "political theology" in current theoretical discourse, I will adopt it here (à la Schmitt) to describe cases such as that of Sieyès' argument. By the lights of the late Malebranche, on the other hand, the question of the ways in which sovereignty ought to be wielded ultimately finds its answer in the very nature of God; we might then use "theological politics" (rather rudimentarily) for a politics that explicitly derives its normative force from propositions pertinent to God.

The difference between "political theology" and "theological politics" could be a shorthand for that between Malebranche and Sieyès, but my interest is not in classification. Rather, I would like to map this difference onto the forms of political–theological analogy that undergird

Malebranche's and Sieyès' arguments. In particular, what interests me is the way that Sieyès' "voluntarist" argument seems to correlate with the reversal of the trajectory of the evolution of Malebranche's position.

We can (at least tentatively) read this reversal in Sieyès' work. Sieyès' position in the *sanction royale* debate on September 7 seems clearly voluntarist. However, the position he had taken just months earlier, in *Qu'est-ce que le tiers état?*, was deeply ambiguous.

> The nation exists prior to everything; it is the origin of everything. Its will is always legal. It is the law itself. Prior to the nation and above the nation there is only natural law. . . . [T]he sequence of positive laws all emanat[e] solely from the nation's will. . . . A nation is formed solely by *natural* law. Government, on the other hand, is solely a product of positive law. A nation is all that it can be simply by virtue of being what it is.[39]

We see here Sieyès divided on the ultimate source of the just and good. On the one hand, there is a very explicit assertion to the effect that the nation is the uncaused cause, "the origin of everything," "the law itself." If we translate between theological and political idioms, this recalls, in its fashion, the position of Malebranche's critics: there could be no cause of and thus no explanation for God's *volonté* outside of the will itself – certainly no universal "order of justice."

At the same time, though – even as he asserts that the nation exists "prior to everything" – Sieyès seems to inhabit a position analogous to Malebranche's: "prior to the nation and above the nation there is only natural law." "Natural law" figures elsewhere in Sieyès' political writings as a kind of law above the law, "the mother-law from which all the others should follow."[40] That is to say, while on the one hand Sieyès wants to figure the nation as uncaused cause, on the other, he seems to suggest that the nation *is* in fact beholden to something ("natural law") occupying the position of Malebranche's universal order of justice. In addition, in the earliest of his political writings – a few months prior to *Qu'est-ce que le tiers état?* – Sieyès takes this position more explicitly:

> Thus since the national will is the product of every individual will, the legislative power belongs to the nation, necessarily and in all its fullness. The only thing that can be set above it is natural law that, far from contradicting it, serves rather to enlighten and guide it towards the great end of the social union.[41]

The focus here is not on the positive law that the nation establishes but rather on the "natural law" that exists prior to (even as it is enlightening of) the nation.

From these data points – admittedly limited and comprising a rapid succession – we might construct a narrative of Sieyès' shift between two positions on the voluntarism question. In Sieyès' earliest political writing, he espouses a position analogous to Malebranche's; "natural law" pre-exists and informs the *volonté générale,* though of course the question is about the *volonté générale* of the nation rather than of God. Slightly later, in *Qu'est-ce que le tiers état?* we see the *malebranchiste* position alongside a new (and contradictory) position, asserting the primacy of France's *volonté générale* and figuring it as the uncaused cause of its own order of justice; that is, we can see alongside each other the voluntarist position and the position holding to a "law before the law." Finally, on the floor of the National Assembly several months later, considerations of "natural law" have fallen out entirely – Sieyès seems to suggest that there are no standards independent of the *volonté générale* (nor in fact of the National Assembly) by which it might be judged.

The fact that the trajectory of Sieyès' argument reverses that of Malebranche's suggests that this trajectory is significant. Moreover, indeed, we might read their divergence on the voluntarism question as a corollary of their different conceptions of the political–theological analogy – which is to say, their different conceptions of the relation between politics and theology. Malebranche's argument considered divine and human sovereignty together as independent articulations of the same set of norms derived from the divine nature. The domain of politics was a subset of the theological domain, whence (as the hierarchy would imply) all normative force ultimately derived. Sieyès' argument, functioning as it did by a Schmittian "transfer," relied on the construction of politics and theology as distinct and nonoverlapping domains. In the structure implicit in Sieyès, of politics and theology as independent and nonhierarchical domains, it is not clear whence norms with any sort of ultimacy would derive.

It is perhaps fair to suggest that – despite their engagement in parallel polemics about institutional authority – this shift also colored the nature of the enterprise of legitimation. Malebranche conceptualized divine power as bound up necessarily with the good and the just – this is just what (on his analysis) separates his position from that of his opponents. That is to say, in what I have called "theological politics," legitimacy is underwritten by the goodness guarantee of God's nature. For Sieyès, by contrast, there were no corresponding specifications of nature for France's *volonté générale*. In fact Sieyès has precious little to say about the *volonté générale* in his speeches; it would seem to be an empty category – even a placeholder. However, this is in fact integral to his (voluntarist) sense of what sovereignty is: sovereignty is just what makes no recourse to anything outside itself. Accordingly, the case for legitimacy becomes a case for the genuineness of the sovereignty of France's *volonté générale*, which is to say not its goodness but its unconstrainedness.

In concluding, we might step beyond Sieyès and Malebranche to gesture briefly toward the potential implications of broader questions of intellectual history and secularization. If my analysis of the Malebranche–Sieyès case is correct, the phenomenon that Schmitt described in *Political Theology* would seem to be correlated with a contraction of the purview of theology. That is to say "political theology" in Schmitt's sense seems to be bound up with something like functional differentiation – roughly, the transformation of "religion" to become one sphere among many, in late modernity. This might suggest the beginnings of an approach to the question of the sense in which Schmitt's "secularization theory" (about the history of ideas, or something like it) relates to the broader phenomenon generally described as "secularization."

Notes

[1] I have profited from criticism and conversations at many stages of the development of the broader project of which this forms of a piece; I am especially thankful to William Sewell, Michael Sonenscher, John McCormick, and Sam James. And I would like to particularly acknowledge Bruce Lincoln, who suggested to me, in the first version of this project, that the differences between Malebranche and Sieyès were as worthy of pursuit as the similarities, and Sanja Perovic, whose editorial acumen has sharpened the argument of this piece of the project.

[2] Patrick Riley, *The General Will Before Rousseau: The Transformation of the Divine into the Civic* (Princeton, NJ: Princeton University Press, 1988).

[3] See Stephanie Frank, "The General Will Beyond Rousseau: Sieyès' Theological Arguments for the Sovereignty of the National Assembly." *History of European Ideas* 37 (2011): 337–43.

[4] Carl Schmitt, *Political Theology*, translated by George Schwab (Chicago: University of Chicago Press, 1985).

[5] A good overview of the debates on the royal veto, with helpful contextual information, can be found in R. R. Palmer, *The Age of the Democratic Revolution* (Princeton, NJ: Princeton University Press, 1969), 490ff. The relevant transcripts are in *Archives parlementaires* 8: 588ff.

6 See, for instance, three excellent treatments (to which I am in many ways indebted): Keith Michael Baker, "Redefining Representation" in *Inventing the French Revolution* (Cambridge: Cambridge University Press, 1990); Michael Sonenscher, "Introduction" in *Sieyès: Political Writings* (Hackett: Indianapolis, 2003); William Sewell, *A Rhetoric of Bourgeois Revolution: The Abbé Sieyès and What is the Third Estate?* (Durham, NC: Duke University Press, 1994).

7 *Archives parlementaires* de 1787 à 1860 (Paris, 1875), 8: 594.

8 *Archives parlementaires* 8: 593.

9 Riley, *General Will Before Rousseau.*

10 Nicolas Malebranche, *Entretiens sur la Métaphysique et sur la Religion* (Rotterdam: Reinier Leers, 1688), 541.

11 *Entretiens,* 542.

12 *Entretiens,* 533.

13 *Entretiens,* 443–4.

14 *Entretiens,* 547.

15 *Archives parlementaires* 8: 207.

16 For more on the intersections of questions of representation and questions of sovereignty in Malebranche's treatment of the Eucharist, see Stephanie Frank, "Re-imagining the Public Sphere: Malebranche, Schmitt's Hamlet, and the Lost Theatre of Sovereignty." *Telos* 153 (2010), 70–93.

17 *Entretiens,* 550.

18 Nicolas Malebranche, *Méditations Chrétiennes et Métaphysiques* (Lyon: Leonard Plaignard, 1707), 139–40.

19 Quoted in Riley, *General Will,* 48.

20 Quoted in Malebranche, *Réponse,* 226.

21 Malebranche, *Réponse,* 227.

22 Riley argues that Malebranche's late emphasis on the "order of justice" may have developed from the influence of his friend and correspondent Leibniz. Riley, "Malebranche and Cartesianized Augustianism," in *A Treatise of Legal Philosophy and General Jurisprudence,* edited by E. Pattaro, D. Canale, P. Grossi, H. Hofmann, and P. Riley (Amsterdam: Springer, 2009), 463–90.

23 Malebranche, *Traité,* 336.

24 See, for instance, the seventeenth *éclaircissement* in the last edition of the *Recherche* published in Malebranche's lifetime (1712).

25 The critique arose vis-à-vis the issue of miracles. Whatever reasons there were to think of God as willing particularly various events in human history, such concerns faded into the background of Malebranche's broader framing. For clearly it was more immediately appealing to imagine that the universe was governed by an eternal and changeless order that derived from God's very nature than that God was constantly and capriciously changing the very fabric of the universe for no reason other than the willing itself.

26 It is also the case, for Malebranche, that in the Word of God (and the divine intelligence) are contained the eternal and necessary truths of mathematics. For a fuller treatment, and a comparison of Malebranche and Leibniz on this point, see Patrick Riley, "Malebranche and Cartesianized Augustinianism."

27 Malebranche, *Traité de Morale* (Rotterdam: Reinier Leers, 1684), 5.

28 Malebranche, *Traité de Morale,* 9.

[29] Malebranche, *Traité de Morale*, 122.

[30] Malebranche, *Traité de Morale*, 306.

[31] Laurent Boursier, *De l'action de Dieu sur les créatures* (Paris: Babuty, 1713), 70.

[32] Malebranche, *Réflexions sur la Prémotion Physique* (Paris: Michel David, 1715), 179.

[33] Malebranche, *Réflexions*, 186–7.

[34] Malebranche, *Réflexions*, 177–8.

[35] See, for instance, Malebranche, *Réflexions*, 231, 318.

[36] *Archives parlementaires* 8: 593.

[37] *Archives parlementaires* 8: 594 (emphases mine).

[38] See, most notably, Mona Ozouf, *Festivals and the French Revolution*, translated by Alan Sheridan (Cambridge: Harvard University Press, 1988); Roger Chartier, *The Cultural Origins of the French Revolution*, translated by Lydia Cochrane (Durham, NC: Duke University Press, 1991).

[39] Sieyès, *Écrits Politiques*, edited by Roberto Zapperi (Paris: Éditions des archives contemporaines, 1985), 160–1. The translation I have supplied here is Michael Sonenscher's, from his edition *Sieyès: Political Writings* (Indianapolis: Hackett, 2003), 136–7.

[40] Malebranche's concern for the "universal order of justice" can similarly be parsed as a "natural law" concern (see Riley, "Malebranche and Cartesianized Augustinianism"). Sieyès, "Essai sur les privilèges," in *Écrits Politiques*, 91.

[41] Émmanuel-Joseph Sieyès, "Views of the Executive Means Available to the Representatives of France in 1789" in *Sieyès: Political Writings*, edited by and translated by Michael Sonenscher (Indianapolis: Hackett, 2003).

Chapter 7

The French Revolution as World Religion

Sanja Perovic

It is common to affirm revolution as a secular religion of modernity. As recently as 2006, in a posthumously published book, the historian Martin Malia described the various revolutions of world history as ascribing to the same religion or cult of the way that history works. He is certainly not the first to claim that although the French Revolution was "militantly antireligious," it reproduced "millenarian expectations of a new world-historical epoch," ushered in by a "violently creative historical process."[1] In this regard, he belongs to a host of scholars who, ever since the collapse of the Marxist paradigm in studies of the revolutionary period, have been reconsidering the impact of religious categories on the so-called secular events of modern history.[2] But what does it mean to yoke together history and religion in such a way when the former belongs to the terrestrial time of human actors and their actions and the latter to a transcendent time in which human agency plays, at best, an oblique role? Is this characterization of the French Revolution as a secular version of Christianity simply a case of reasoning by analogy, a way of redescribing the revolution in religious terms without adding explanatory power to our understanding of the event? Or can it tell us something more about the structure and experience of revolutionary time?

It is indisputable that the French Revolution opposed the past by adopting a secular perspective on historical time. Human time and its agents became the material through which a break with the political and religious structures of the past was accomplished. This historical break was symbolized by a series of measures aimed at destroying the Church that reinforced the Revolution's self-image as a wholly secular event. However, as historian Dale Van Kley has argued, just because the revolutionaries had invented dechristianization does not mean that the Revolution had no Christian origins.[3] The difficulty, as he points out, is in making sense of a

Revolution that claimed to be without origins of any kind, to be "absolutely *sui generis*," in a way that makes it impossible to accept at face value any claim made by the revolutionaries about their own relation to the past (2). This self-image makes it particularly difficult to distinguish between what Hans Blumenberg has called descriptive claims about the "secularization thesis," namely claims about the empirical decline of religious influence, and argumentative claims, such as the one put forward by Martin Malia, in which a specific aspect of Western European culture is explained by reference to the Christian world that preceded it.[4]

Yet, it is precisely with the Revolution's claim to have ruptured with the past that the analogy with Christianity becomes most compelling. Just as Christianity is a religion based on the event of Christ's birth, death, and resurrection that forever changed the meaning of history, so too did the Revolution understand itself as a rupture in time that forever changed the meaning of history. Moreover, just as Christianity is a religion of both history and the calendar, so too did the French Revolution understand itself as belonging to a new time that was historical as well as calendrical. Although Christianity may have been the first religion to be rooted in a concrete event dividing time into a *before* and *after*, it only became a universal religion once it mapped the story of Christ's birth, death, and resurrection onto the cosmic time of the calendar, thereby transforming this claim of rupture into a new experience of time and its duration. Similarly, the French Revolution also claimed to start time anew in the form of a new calendar that simultaneously vindicated secular time and affirmed the Revolution's structural affinity with Christianity. This new calendar replaced the Christian chronology with a secular timeline starting from Year I, the Christian saints with natural images, and the seven-day Judeo-Christian week with a new ten-day decimal week called the *décade*.

Taking this analogy between the Christian and French Republican calendars as its starting point, this chapter seeks to demarcate and circumscribe the extent to which the French Revolution can and cannot be considered a "secular religion of modernity." As even this brief comparison makes clear, the revolutionary calendar shared an intentional structure with Christianity that went far beyond an emotional response to social upheaval. In both cases, the aim was to transform an event that is limited to participants and followers into a "binding" orientation for all peoples and all times. Moreover, in both cases, the cyclical repetitions of a natural calendar time were used to elevate this historical event into an "objective" and "universal" truth. And yet, it is the Christian calendar – and not its revolutionary rival – that has become the de facto universal calendar used around the world today. The Republican calendar, in contrast, failed to impose itself as the modern time-schema. Despite its claim to have replaced a "hierarchical," "religious" past with a "secular" representation of time, it proved even less compatible with a "modern" understanding of history than the Christian calendar it tried to replace. Significantly, it failed at precisely the points in which its analogy with the Christian calendar became the most acutely apparent: in its attempt to translate a phenomenological experience of living in a "new time" into an objectively valued truth and to elevate the French Revolution into a "universal" structure of history valid for all peoples.

Without wishing to minimize the historical factors that might have led to the calendar's failure, this article argues that one important source of its failure relates directly to its attempt to correlate the linear time of "secular" historical events with the natural, cyclical time of the calendar year. As Reinhart Koselleck has observed, the calendar's failure derives from a fundamental contradiction, namely the attempt to combine a secular understanding of history, predicated on an open and unknown future that is always "new," into the everyday lived experience of time, which depends on repeatable patterns derived from nature.[5] This raises the question as to why the revolutionaries felt compelled to embark on this enterprise. It also suggests a deeply ambivalent view taken by the revolutionaries regarding human agency, which was imagined as both historical and yet also somehow as natural. This essay builds upon Koselleck's observation in order to consider how the Revolution's intentional understanding of history – itself derived from religion – contributed so profoundly to structuring its own expectations of history even as it failed to sustain them. It suggests that if such a thing as a "secular" religion of revolution can be said to exist, it emerged here, in the Revolution's failure to reoccupy a temporal paradigm no longer adequate to its own experience of history.

Secular Time as Structure

The problem of assessing the Republican calendar's contribution to the "secularization" of time is two-fold. The first concerns the calendar's difficulty in translating what Mona Ozouf has neatly characterized as the difference between *temps voulu* and *temps vécu*.[6] The feeling of flying high and living in a new time was very much the experience for revolutionary participants when viewed phenomenologically – that is, from the inside and internal to their own experience. This feeling was captured in the establishment of a new timeline beginning in Year I whose aim, as Walter Benjamin famously put it, was to "make the continuum of history explode."[7] This rupture with tradition – and the implied orientation toward the future – is frequently taken as evidence for the "modernity" of revolutionary time. However, this interpretation overlooks the fact that Year I signaled not just a new timeline but also a new calendar, which, by definition, involves the natural, cyclical time of repetition. That is to say, the new calendar was also intended as a secular institution, which would parallel the emotional and (as I will show) political logic of religious time by grounding the Revolution's new experience of history onto referents derived from nature.

The second problem arises from our own relation to the Gregorian calendar that the revolutionaries tried to displace, which tends to act as a screen obscuring the differences between a revolutionary and "modern" experience of time. As Hannah Arendt has remarked, the secular version of the Gregorian calendar that is in near-worldwide use today constitutes the "actual content of our concept of history."[8] It does so in two ways, both of which differ considerably from the revolutionary understanding of secular time. First, the BC/AD timeline, slowly implemented over the course of the seventeenth and eighteenth centuries, enables us to go both backwards in time toward an infinite past and forwards into an infinite future. Second, the calendar's neutral grid of numbered dates allows us to cut up and divide historical time at will. The former, as Arendt has noted, was essential to overcoming the Judeo-Christian conception of history as a rectilinear process with an origin and end. The latter is essential to our "revisionist" understanding of history. Once dates are associated with a homogenous, linear, empty time that can be partitioned in any number of ways (rather than, say, important symbolic events), we can go back and privilege different dates as historically important ones.[9] Thus, although Christ's birth still persists as a marker dividing time, it has been neutralized by a timeline that is infinitely dividable in both directions.

Neither of these assumptions apply to the revolutionary understanding of "making history," which remained very much indebted to an extensive eighteenth-century understanding of universal history as consisting of both "origins" and "ends." One important assumption that the eighteenth century shared with the Christian model was the belief that there was, if not quite a center to history, at least a unity, whether this was expressed in the form of universal histories that emphasized moral progress and mankind's increasing freedom (Voltaire, Condorcet), secular versions of Biblical narratives (Condorcet, again, or Condillac), or cyclical accounts of history (Vico). Even for those thinkers who rejected the unique examples of Christ's life and resurrection, secular history was mainly envisioned as a storehouse of examples, as "lessons" that repeat and therefore hold equally true for the future as for the past. If it took so long to establish a universal timeline, it was in part because secular history still followed an exemplary model in which the action or deed was self-illuminating and did not need to be synchronized alongside other events on a historical timeline in order to be meaningful.

Nowhere was this exemplary model more apparent than in the self-representation of French kings, who frequently represented themselves as the center of both secular and sacred history. The preferred symbol for this center or unity was the sun: the king ruled over his kingdom like the sun ruled over the world. His great deeds illuminated not just the earthly realm but also united earthly and heavenly power in the very image of divine enlightenment. Recourse to the sun image was of course a very ancient one, as Rolf Reichardt has shown.[10] Before the Bourbon dynasty took it up, the image of a "sun-king" had been used first by the Pharaohs in Egypt, and then by a series of Roman Emperors. In addition to this secular heritage, the solar myth of divine kingship also reflected a long tradition of Christian and Catholic imaginary in which the battle of light over the forces of dark featured prominently.

However, if this monarchical version of the solar myth perpetuated the idea that history had a unity – in which Christ's birth, death, and resurrection were mirrored in the king's heavenly body, which also promised religious deliverance – it also came under increasing attack over the course of the seventeenth and eighteenth centuries. In his rich survey of the visual iconography of solar images, Reichardt has demonstrated how opposition to absolutism, especially on the part of French Protestants after the revocation of the Edict of Nantes, frequently took the form of a reversal of values in which the heavenly sun of the divine-king was pitted against the natural sun of the "light of reason." While scholars have frequently noted the transference of this Christian imagery to the Enlightenment, especially in theories of natural law and Republicanism, less attention has been paid to the specific role of calendar time in secularizing the solar myth. Yet, it is the calendar that best represents a time dictated by a natural sun and a natural "light of reason" that is freely available to all.

It therefore comes as little surprise that calendars became privileged source documents in the secular versions of universal history that became especially popular in the more radical circles of the late eighteenth century. The discovery of the new world and with it other calendars, including those (like the Chinese calendar) which had chronologies longer than biblical history would allow, prompted the realization that there was no one single narrative or framework for universal history.[11] This led to a reconsideration of how natural symbols associated with calendar time (the length of the year, month, and day) became invested with political and religious authority. Protestant thinkers such as Court de Gébelin popularized the notion that the astronomical calendar was a central artifact subtending all the world religions, thereby offering a "universal" frame in which a rational interpretation of religion could emerge.[12] Court de Gébelin shared this erudite fascination with calendar time with other *érudits* who gathered at the *Loge de Neuf Soeurs*, many of whom, like Bailly the future mayor of revolutionary Paris, would have influential roles during the French Revolution.[13] What these thinkers had in common was the desire to impose a synchronic or structural framework on history that relativized religious mythology, including that of Christianity, by showing how it could be compared and even converted into other similar "allegories" of natural time.[14] They thus simultaneously dislodged the idea of one civilizational origin – in this case a Christian one – even as they sought a stable, more "originary" account of origins in the postulate of a natural, solar calendar that was the foundation of all state religions.

As many of these same thinkers would go on to occupy important social and political positions in postrevolutionary France, their understanding of the relation between calendar time and state formation was enormously influential in subsequent formulations of Republican *laïcité*. Both Constantin-François Volney and Gilbert Romme, the future designer of the official Republican calendar, traced the origins of state religion to ancient Egypt, where the true length of the solar year was first accurately calculated. Unlike lunar calendars that required the intercalation of an extra month now and then to keep the year in line with the seasons, the solar calendar enabled accurate prediction of the seasons and therefore control over the cycles of harvest. Volney and other like-minded thinkers traced the emergence of large-scale agriculture and a centralized state organization to ancient Egypt where the priests chose to keep the true length of the solar year a secret, thus enabling them an effective cognitive monopoly over the telling of time.[15]

If the Egyptian priests relied on a lunar calendar for civil use in order to maintain control over the people, the situation had been no better in ancient Rome where the calendar also suffered the same sort of abuse. Until the imposition of a solar calendar under Julius Caesar (itself imported from Egypt), the *pontifices*, the body of priests, who decided when the extra 27-day month was added, also controlled when assemblies were met, wars were fought, taxes paid, and officers elected.[16] The intent of Caesar's reform was precisely to establish a universal time independent of priests and kings. I will return later on to the importance of the Julian calendar for the revolutionary imagination. For now, it suffices to note that religious calendars were considered prime evidence of a more general cognitive monopoly by religion over the works of nature. As Condorcet bluntly put it:

> It has always been the case that a class of individuals has arrogantly affected exclusive rights, separating themselves from other humans the better to enslave them. Seizing hold of medicine and astronomy, this class has used all possible means to subjugate the human mind, not allowing anyone to see through its hypocrisy and to break the chains.[17]

D'Holbach was even more explicit, tracing the wars of religion themselves to this conflict between secular and sacred orders: "In all political orders in which Christianity has been established, two rival powers are continually at war, usually resulting in the destruction of the state."[18] For d'Holbach, the religious monopoly on education in particular was a surefire way of ensuring that "the priesthood was and will always be the rival of the crown" (xvii).

Because secular time was largely conceived as something that had been misappropriated by the political and theocratic orders, it did not reflect the assumptions about calendar time that we are familiar with today. First, although the solar calendar consisted of "transparent," "homogenous" time, it was not, like our calendars today, "empty" of significance. For the Church, the solar year made it possible to align the liturgical calendar directly with the natural changes of the seasons, thereby investing natural time with religious significance. For its detractors, in contrast, a solar calendar meant freedom from such religious overdeterminations. The solar calendar was transparent insofar as it was a perpetual calendar that could run independently of the calculations of astronomer–priests. It was associated with "self-governance" or the ability to tell time without the interference of a political or religious authority. Thus, when Charles-François Dupuis argued that "the passion and resurrection of Christ celebrated at Easter belongs to the mysteries of an ancient solar religion or cult of universal nature," he was postulating the existence of an original "natural" measure of time subtending all religions.[19] Second, the postulate of an original natural religion implied a structure of historical development common to all peoples. Social roles were still imagined as inhering in natural concepts, and there was little room for an understanding of history as an independent process. A "secular" critique of the (perceived) political and religious control over time thus went hand in hand with a "cosmological" understanding of nature, which defined – as well as confined – the process of history. Third, and consequently, this oppositional, secularizing vision of historical intentionally was resolutely backwards-looking and had little room for a vision of a "future" that did not resemble the past. "Stripping," "peeling back," "returning to" the astronomical layer that subtends all calendars – these were the dominant verbs used to describe the process of secularization. This suggests that, prior to the Revolution, the idea of a radical rupture and break with the past was first articulated using a notion of calendar time that emphasized stasis over dynamism, origins over ends, and natural concepts over historical ones.

It is significant in this regard that this emphasis on natural time as a homogeneous continuum did not preclude a growing fascination with the concept of an axial age to which the development of all the major world religions could be traced. Although this term, from twentieth-century philosopher Karl Jaspers, did not form part of the revolutionary lexicon, it nonetheless expresses the widely shared belief that the discovery of writing and astronomy were linked not just to the origins of feudalism but also to the birth of a political theology that had remained current up to the Revolution. In other words, the ability to control calendar time was not just crucial to the emergence of a centralized religion; it also subtended a system of values or norms that determined the subsequent development of human history.

Before the Revolution, then, and before any allegedly "messianic" experience of rupture, French thinkers and writers were already engaged in a sustained reflection on the nature and political function of secular time. In this regard, the revolutionary attack on the Christian calendar is to be understood as an extension of – rather than a break from – the enlightenment project of restoring the original source of time in the astronomical layer of the Julian calendar that preceded it, the first calendar to institute a universal, civic time in the Mediterranean world.

State Religion or Religious State?

However, there is a further reason why the revolutionaries believed that the birth of a new secular politics required a new calendar time. This is because the history of the Gregorian calendar, from its Roman Imperial origins to its Roman Catholic incarnation, was a history of secularization in reverse, encapsulating the increasingly tighter union of religious and political power that the revolutionaries were seeking to undo. As the classicist Denis Feeney has remarked, the original Julian calendar represented a "watershed" in the organization of time, eventually extended to the modern world, because it was the first to associate the calendar "exclusively with measuring time."[20] This same universalizing structure was used by the Emperor Constantine who, in his bid to institute Christianity as the state religion of the Roman Empire, grafted religious symbolism onto the Julian calendar, renaming the days of the week, fixing Easter, attributing saints to the days and establishing Sunday as the official day of rest. Christianizing the Julian calendar not only enabled Constantine to exercise state control over religion; it also allowed him to ground the first Christian state as a temporal as well as geographical unity.

If Constantine had been the first to align Christianity with a state calendar, he also subordinated religion to politics, prompting Voltaire to identify him as the origin of every single great revolution that had since then marked the Western world: "Constantine . . . changed both religion and the empire, authoring not just this great revolution but all others subsequently witnessed in the Western world."[21] Even Voltaire, who otherwise detested Constantine, had to concede that his most lasting contribution was to grant freedom of conscience and religious worship to all the religions in the Empire and to establish a definitive separation of sacred and secular powers: "Of all the emperors he was without doubt the most absolute. He entirely separated the robe from the sword. (. . .) Constantine's overall aim was to become master of everything, over the Church as well as the State."[22] As Voltaire makes clear, secularization in this case did not imply a loss of absolute power but rather its ascendancy. A similar association of monarchical with religious power was later appropriated by the Bourbon monarchy when it sought to make good on its claim that it alone could transcend the religious antagonisms between Protestants and Catholics, because it, like the sun, was "above" them both.[23] In both cases, the key image remains that of a union of earthly and heavenly powers in a solar, astronomical, universal, and perpetual time.

When the Roman Catholic Church established itself as heir to the Roman Empire, it used this calendar to extend religion into all aspects of political life even as it marked the emergence of a new political order by altering key aspects of this calendar. The secular, political timeline, which for Constantine still followed the regnal years of the Roman emperors, was replaced by a new chronology that counted years from the birth of Christ. Martin Malia is one historian who has attempted to trace the revolutionary impulse, as it culminated and went beyond the French Revolution of 1789, back to the Year 1000, when this new chronology was first established.[24] Although this Christian chronology was far from universally observed and in fact took several centuries to be established,[25] for Malia it marks a turning point in the historical self-awareness of a distinctively Western European Christianity. Unlike the Roman Empire, for which religion was still subordinated to the state, Western Christianity sought to fuse Church and state in a new kind of religious society. As Malia notes, this political change was accompanied by changes in the everyday structure of calendar time. Pagan holidays were Christianized and the liturgical calendar was aligned with the agricultural year. Later, the invention of automated Church bells extended Benedict's monastic timetable, which had combined the Christian calendar with the divisions of the Roman army day, to all of society.[26] For Malia, this fusion of political and religious symbolism meant that any social unrest would henceforth be directed not just against political authority but also against the Church as the "all-embracing unit of European society."[27]

Whatever one may think of an approach that seeks to explain revolution with reference to the social role of Catholic Christianity, there is no denying that this medieval Christian calendar loomed large in the imagination of the French revolutionaries. In France, unique among European nations, Gallicanism had ensured that papal primacy was limited by the temporal power of the monarch whose divine will was inviolable. From the perspective of the king's temporal authority, this meant a considerable separation of Church and state. From the perspective of monarchical power, however, the two were closely related, because the king's authority was divinely ordained; it stemmed from a fusion of earthly and divine authority. Indeed, far from undergoing a gradual process of secularization, the effort to anchor royal authority in the divine became ever more vehement throughout the seventeenth century. This implies two things. Firstly, that for the greater part of the seventeenth and eighteenth centuries, the separation of Church and State alone was not enough to yield an overall "secularization" of either time or authority. Second, given that the sacred and secular swords were both represented by the king, attacking the one meant attacking the other. There was no way to simply criticize the Church without also invoking the "civil" authority of the state.

This political arrangement explains in part why in France the Revolution came to stand for an absolute rupture with the past and why its privileged expression became a new secular calendar, beginning with a new timeline in Year I. Indeed, one of the problems of overarching "secularization" narratives is that they frequently assume a uniform transnational process that overlooks the fact that the secular itself always implies a certain relation to authority and the limits of temporal power. Nowhere is this more evident than when we compare the French decision to change calendar time with other challenges to the Gregorian calendar that had taken place in Europe. As is well known, Pope Gregory XIII reformed the Julian calendar, which was 11 minutes too long for the solar year in 1582. Protestant countries initially rejected Gregory's reform as an unacceptable intrusion of papal power on civil time.[28] Some, like England, even considered a radically reformed and rationalized calendar even though Gregory's reform itself was widely understood to be "scientific."[29] In France, however, the calendar represented the union of civil and liturgical time right up until the Revolution. Indeed, the idea of radically altering the calendar became urgent only with the trial and execution of the king. Only then was the calendar explicitly linked to the recently instituted metric system and the demand for "universal" measures derived from nature and science.

Secularization as Revolutionary Event

The French Revolution may have sought to represent itself as the outcome of a much longer process of secularization, but it was also, essentially, a political event like no other in world history. Both these understandings of secularization – as scientific process and as political event – came together in the decision to institute a new Republican calendar. The French Republic marked the moment when a theoretical separation between religion and politics became the foundational act of a new political state; so too the Republican calendar marked the moment when the gradual and implicit replacement of religion by science became explicit and real. Thanks to the new calendar, the political event of secularization could be traced to a specific time and place: September 22, 1792. This way, the day of the autumn equinox corresponded to the day in which the new Republic was officially proclaimed. As Gilbert Romme famously put it, the moment when day and night occurred in equal measure was the moment when the French people threw off their past to become free and equal citizens.

Nevertheless, was the French Revolution one event or several? By the time the new calendar was instituted, the Revolution had already declared several new beginnings and endings. July 14, 1789, had been immediately hailed in the popular press as Year I of Liberty. The *Fête de la Féderation*, celebrated a year later, was similarly hailed as the true moment of regeneration.

Three years later, the deposition of the king, on August 10, 1792, was held up as the Revolution's "true" beginning, and was immediately baptized in the popular press as Year I of Equality. Indeed, it was partly to unify all these various beginnings into one timeline that the committee for calendar reform had first been assembled.

For the historian of secular time, the institution of the Republican calendar raises interesting questions. How did a revolutionary horizon of expectation, in which rupture was first imagined as a secularization of religious time, come to be mapped onto the historical experience of events as they unfolded in linear sequence? Moreover, what does this tell us about the emergence of our own modern understanding of history as a linear narrative of events? There are no easy answers, but one thing is clear: the linear chronology that was to mark the Revolution's new beginning had little in common with the secular timeline that we are familiar with today. On the contrary, one of the first acts of the new Republican calendar was to use linear time to establish an exemplary understanding of revolutionary events as stations on the road to freedom, that is, as events that organized the timeline of history (rather than the other way around).

This is nowhere more apparent than in Romme's original proposal for the Republican calendar, which insisted on mapping the linear timeline of revolutionary rupture onto the cyclical time of the calendar year. Although this calendar was not adopted in the end, it is crucial for understanding both the religious structure of revolutionary intentionality and the "horizon of expectation" (Christological in nature) that eventually came to be suppressed in the name of an entirely natural, cyclical conception of time. Romme's calendar directly imitated the Christian liturgical calendar, which mapped the historical narrative of Christ's birth, death, and resurrection onto the months of the year associated with Christmas, Lent, and Easter. In Romme's proposed version, the narrative of Revolution began on the spring equinox, in the month now called *régéneration* (corresponding to March 21–April 19 on the old calendar). Although the calendar year started in the fall, its narrative began and ended in springtime. Just like the Christian liturgical calendar, it began with "advent," a preparation of a Revolution that was yet to come. Moreover, like in the Christian calendar, in which the first months of the year are dedicated to Christ's earthly teachings, the first three months of Romme's calendar were named after specific historical events. The month renamed *réunion* (April 20–May 19) celebrated the opening of the *Etats généraux*, followed by the month commemorating the *jeu de paume* (May 20–June 18) and culminating in the month named *La Bastille* (June 19–July 18). However, then Romme's historical narrative jumped ahead by three years. If the first three months were dedicated to the events of 1789, the following three months were dedicated to the events of the summer of 1792, which led to the deposition of the king and the establishment of a new Republic and a new calendar beginning in Year I. For the remaining months, all that was left was for history to follow its logical progression to its end. Accordingly, the last three months of the year were named after abstract political concepts: *l'unité* (October 22–November 20), *la fraternité* (November 21–December 20), *la liberté* (December 21–January 19), *la Justice* (January 20–February 18), and *égalité* (February 19–March 20).

Thus, if Romme used the calendar to superimpose a linear understanding of history onto revolutionary events, he also borrowed a Christological image that allowed him to transfer an expectation of closure to the future. To take but one glaring example, the month of *La Justice*, corresponding to the trial and execution of the king, was here presented as leading ineluctably and necessarily to the establishment of *égalité*, the final month of the year, before returning full circle to *régénération*, the first month of the following year. By condensing the three to four years of revolutionary tumult into a 12-month frame, the calendar not only produced the impression that the Revolution unfolded as a single event, but also sought to ensure that this event would be re-experienced every year like an eternally repeating truth. However, as Mona Ozouf has pointed out, between the time the committee on calendar reform was assembled and the time the proposal was delivered, it was not just the king who had been executed. The Constitution had been suspended, the revolutionary government proclaimed on October 10, 1793, the revolutionary tribunal created, and the Girondins purged. All these events cast doubt on the government's claim to have terminated the Revolution.[30]

This incompatibility and even contradiction between a secular "religion of history" and the historical experience of events as they unfolded in chronological succession was evident from the outset. This explains in part why Fabre d'Eglantine's proposal, in which references to history were dropped altogether in favor of a calendar representing a strictly natural time, became the winning one. It is to Fabre d'Englantine that we owe the famous revolutionary months named after the seasons and days of the week named after various fruits, vegetables, and farming utensils. New time was no longer to be associated, as in Romme's suggestion, with an awareness of revolutionary history but rather the cyclical repetitions of an entirely natural time drawn more from the pages of Linnaeus and Buffon. It should be clear by now that the French Revolution chose to commemorate itself using a conception of time that, although resolutely secular and scientific, had very little in common with our modern time-schema. It was not just that Romme's calendar presupposed a horizon of expectation drawn from religion; Fabre d'Eglantine's final version of the calendar too relied on a solar myth of a natural time to establish a linear, irreversible understanding of rupture.

If the founding of a Republic or any new form of government is a founding event by definition, then the paradox of the Republican calendar is that it tried to derive a historical intention from this event that would determine the future as well as the past. In fact, it is precisely around the issue of historical intentionality – the desire to give history a vector – that the analogy between the Revolution and Christianity breaks down. This is because, contrary to its religious counterpart, the revolutionary calendar was consubstantial with the historical events it sought to date and classify. Here was a calendar that attempted to stabilize the meaning of events which still existed as a field of possibilities and not yet as the only future for the Revolution. In this sense, the French Republican calendar anticipated a Marxist understanding of history in which the end of history is the outcome not just of a process, but also of political action that in turn determines the understanding of both "beginnings" as well as "ends." Thus, if the new chronology affirmed the irreversibility and political necessity of rupture, it did so by rejecting a secular understanding of history as something that gains meaning only by going forward in time.

More crucially, it is only by maintaining the union of cyclical and linear time in the form of a new calendar that the revolutionaries hoped to project the Revolution itself as a new "axial age." Like Condorcet before him, who identified ancient Greece as a period of epoch-making transformation, Jaspers defines the axial period as originating between 800 and 200 BC, during a period when several world religions emerged more or less simultaneously without knowledge of one another. What these religions shared was a belief in a transcendent God and a literate clergy able to codify this belief in a set of universally applicable dogmas that gave rise to an axis of world history common to all people.[31] It is important to note, however, that what Jaspers called the "axial age" did not appear with the emergence of a belief in transcendent authority, but only much later. It is only when this belief was externalized in, among other things, a calendar reflecting the power of the clerical hierarchy that this transcendent authority became part of the lived experience of time.

This concept of an axial age offers insight into some of the problems the revolutionaries faced in seeking to model the Revolution as a universally applicable history of humanity, analogous to those of the great world religions. Where the Roman Church had used the calendar to retroactively express the historical consciousness of an axial age, the revolutionaries attempted to communicate a similar world-historical rupture in their own time. The problem was twofold. Not only were the revolutionaries attempting to achieve the same sense of rupture in an immanent time of history but their very claim to be returning to a purely astronomical time of nature also posed another problem, that of time's uniformity. Natural time is certainly always "present." However, precisely because it is continuous, it cannot reflect a history of human making, which presupposes discontinuity. At the same time, *some* appeal to a universal, homogenous time was necessary if the French Revolution was to transform itself from a contingent event to a universal social order. The problem of trying to extrapolate a world-historical pattern out of an immanent and natural understanding of time is evident in Romme's conceit that the fall equinox represented the "sacred" union of natural and historical time: "And so the sun passed from one hemisphere to the other the same day that the people, triumphing from the oppression of kings, passed from a monarchical government to a republican one."[32] Instead of reflecting a transcendent time (the way in which, in Genesis, God creates the world by giving light, or a king enlightens his nation), this new epoch demarcated itself from the past simply thanks to a natural light, an original distinction between night and day.

Nevertheless, when applied to recent historical events, this appeal to a natural time revealed deep fissures between the Enlightenment's understanding of an original solar time that subtended all religions and revolutionary experience. As Koselleck has observed, the calendar's insistence on natural metaphors contradicted its claim to usher in a new historical epoch.[33] On the one hand, the calendar's cyclical time reflected a natural sun that illuminates half the world while the other remained in darkness; on the other hand, the Revolution's claim to start a new universal time valid for the entire globe was predicated on an eternal, ever-shining sun. This solar metaphor presupposed, in other words, an absolute standpoint on human history, that those who control time occupy, as it were, the position of the sun even though this sun itself is only experienced *in time on earth* in the form of a calendar. From the vantage point of the sun, history assumes an absolute, unchanging rather than relative meaning; from the perspective on earth, this same absolute standpoint is experienced as the reduction of all time to its measure. In neither case does it represent a new understanding of *history* as an ongoing, open-ended process with no discernable conclusion.

This is significant, because it shows how a revolutionary culture that tried to undo the feudal structures of the *ancien régime* ended up reproducing a very similar cosmological understanding of historical agency. In asserting that priests and kings had seized control of, and diverted, a solar myth already in place, the revolutionaries also restricted themselves to a belief that history could be made in only one of two ways: either by returning to this solar myth and adapting social structures to it, as the revolutionary calendar claimed to do, or by violating it completely, as they claimed the Christian calendar had done. Moreover, by privileging cyclical time and by representing the Convention as if it occupied an absolute standpoint on the Revolution itself, the calendar's premise of a new time contributed to radicalizing the demands to reconcile social and natural time. If, after 1792, the political aims of the Revolution also became social ones, it is partly because this utopian promise of perfect synchrony between natural and social time was still left open so long as the revolutionary administration continued to privilege the Republican calendar as the correct model for revolutionary history.

Conclusion

The comparison between these two calendars shows that the question of whether the French Revolution can be considered a secular version of Christianity cannot be answered by any straightforward linear narrative of secularization. This is especially the case if we accept the premise that what was new about the French Revolution was not just its perspective on history, but also the fact that it represented this new time in the form of a new calendar. Renewed attention to the revolutionary calendar offers the possibility to assess the deeper links between natural and historical time common to both religion and revolution in a way that avoids a binary logic of either their mutual exclusion or wholesale substitution. After all, if the Republican calendar expressed the retrospective legitimation of the French Revolution by stripping the Christian calendar of its religious connotations, it also denied the very thing that made secular history go forward, namely the accumulation of historical meaning. Indeed, what the comparison of these two calendars shows is that a "synchronic" point of origin can only be established "diachronically," after the fact. One cannot be the mediator of one's own historical moment. A history of the present will never look like the history of the past. This is nowhere more apparent than in the Republican calendar itself, which continued to be propped up by every single revolutionary administration for almost 13 years even as each used the calendar to project its own interpretation of revolutionary history.

This paper began by suggesting that although the French Revolution failed to reoccupy the temporal paradigm established by religion, it nonetheless borrowed from religious history its belief that history has an intention or vector. It did so, however, not simply by analogy – substituting one calendar for another – but also by applying to the future an understanding of history that can only be established retrospectively. In this sense, the French Revolution can be considered both more and less than a world religion. Like Christianity, the French Revolution sought to establish a universalizable pattern of history applicable to all times and all peoples. In addition, like Christianity, it ultimately failed in this endeavor. However, to say that the French Revolution resembles a religion insofar as it only holds true for its believers is to downgrade the extent to which it in fact succeeded in becoming a yardstick or norm, if not for all human history, then at least for our understanding of modernity. The French Revolution may have failed to project itself as a closed system of beginnings and ends, but it nevertheless succeeded to a considerable extent, and fairly quickly, in altering the periodization of the period before 1789, which became the *ancien régime*. As the Republican calendar so clearly demonstrates, history was made modern by passing through the crucible of religion. In this sense, the French Revolution can rightfully be called a "religion" of modernity. Through its failure to become a universalizable event, it succeeded in establishing a new horizon of expectation. Along this horizon, in the absence of a closed system and in the absence of transcendence, the Revolution can only ever be repeated again and again.

Notes

[1] Martin Malia, *History's Locomotives: Revolutions and the Making of the Modern World* (New Haven: Yale University Press, 2006), 6.

[2] Notable titles include Dale K. Van Kley, *The Religious Origins of the French Revolution* (New Haven: Yale University Press, 1996), Susan Desan, *Reclaiming the Sacred: Lay Religion and Popular Politics in Revolutionary France* (Ithaca: Cornell University Press, 1990), Thomas Kselman, *Death and Afterlife in Modern France* (Princeton: Princeton University Press, 1993), Marcel Gauchet, *The Disenchantment of the World: A Political History of Religion*, translated by Oscar Burge (Princeton: Princeton University Press, 1993), as well as the many works by Michel Vovelle.

[3] Dale K. Van Kley, 2.

[4] Hans Blumenberg, *The Legitimacy of the Modern Age*, translated by Robert Wallace (Cambridge, Mass: MIT Press, 1987), 10 and 65. Malia argues that radical social

change originated in feudal Europe because the unity of political and religious beliefs meant that religious dissent entailed political dissent. See Malia's Introduction, Chapter One, and 187–92.

[5] Koselleck, "Remarks on the Revolutionary Calendar and Neue Zeit" in *The Practice of Conceptual History: Timing History, Spacing Concepts*, translated by Todd Samuel Pressner and Others (Stanford: Stanford University Press, 2002).

[6] Mona Ozouf, *La fête révolutionnaire, 1789–1799* (Paris: Editions Gallimard, 1976).

[7] Walter Benjamin, *Illuminations*, edited by Hannah Arendt, translated by Harry Zohn (New York: Schocken Books, 1977), 261.

[8] Hannah Arendt, "The Concept of History: Ancient and Modern" in *Between Past and Present* (London: Penguin, 1977), 75.

[9] For the salient aspects of the modern time schema and its relation to historical revisionism, see Lynn Hunt, *Measuring Time, Making History* (Budapest: Central European University Press, 2008), 24–30.

[10] See Rolf Reichart, "Light Against Darkness: The Visual Representations of a Central Enlightenment Concept" in *Representations* 61: Winter (1998): 95–148.

[11] Reinhart Koselleck, "Time and History" in *The Practice of Conceptual History*, 106.

[12] Antoine Court de Gébelin, *Histoire du monde primitive, analysé et comparé avec le monde modern* (Paris: 1773–83), Vol. IV.

[13] Founded by Jérôme Lalande, this loge is notable for having produced many of the future members of the *Institut de Paris*, who were enormously influential in setting up France "Republican" educational institutes.

[14] See, for example, the debate between Bailly and Rabaut de Saint Etienne in *Lettres à M. Bailly sur l'histoire primitive de la Grèce* (Paris: 1787), 11–14.

[15] Constantin-François Volney, *Les ruines, ou méditation sur les révolutions des empires*, tome 1 (Paris: Firmin Didot, 1826 [1791]), 166–87.

[16] Leofranc Holford-Strevens, *The History of Time: A Very Short Introduction* (Oxford: Oxford University Press, 2005), 28–30.

[17] Marie Jean Antoine Nicolas de Caritat, marquis de Condorcet, *Esquisse d'un tableau historique des progrès de l'esprit humain* (Paris:1795), 36.

[18] Paul Henri Thiry, baron d'Holbach, *Le Christianisme dévoilé ou Examen des principes et des effets de la religion chrétienne* (London: 1767), 188.

[19] Charles-François Dupuis, *Abrégé de l'origine de tous les cultes* (Paris: 1797), 336.

[20] Denis Feeney, *Caesar's Calendar: Ancient time and the Beginnings of History* (Berkeley, CA: University of California Press, 2007), 193–6.

[21] Voltaire, "De Constantine" in *Oeuvres de 1753–1757 II, Mélanges de 1756, Les Oeuvres completes de Voltaire* (Oxford: The Voltaire Foundation, 2010), 179.

[22] Voltaire, 186–7.

[23] For an earlier elaboration of this trope in the context of the religious wars, see Denis Crouzet, *La nuit de la Saint-Barthélemy; un rêve perdu de la Renaissance* (Paris: Fayard, 1994), 213–24.

[24] Malia, 19.

[25] See Robert Favreau "La datation dans les inscriptions médiévales françaises" in *Construire le temps: normes et usages chronologiques du moyen âge à l'époque contemporaine* (Paris and Geneva: Champion and Droz, 2000).

[26] See David S. Landes, *A Revolution in Time: Clocks and the Making of the Modern World* (Cambridge, MA: Harvard University Press, 1983).

[27] Malia, 19.

[28] The Protestant states of Germany, Netherlands, and the Protestant cantons of Switzerland did not accept Gregorian reform until 1701, England and its dominions until 1752, and Sweden until 1753. Interestingly, when the Quakers adopted the Gregorian calendar along with the rest of England, they replaced the months named after the pagan gods with numbers.

[29] For a comprehensive survey of these attempts, see Robert Poole, "Calendar Reform in Eighteenth-Century England" *Past and Present*, no. 149 (November 1995): 95–139, especially, 106–9.

[30] Ozouf, "Republican calendar," 540.

[31] Karl Jaspers, *Origin and Goal of History*, translated by Michael Bullock (London: Routledge and Kegan Paul, 1953), 1–29.

[32] Gilbert Romme, "Rapport sur l'ère de la République fait à la Convention nationale dans la séance du 20 septembre de l'an II de la République." *Archives parlementaires* 77: 499–506.

[33] Koselleck, "Remarks on the Revolutionary Calendar and Neue Zeit," 51.

Chapter 8

The Secularization of Execution: Heresy, Sacrifice, and the Inquisition from Montesquieu to Maistre

Francesco Manzini

One could easily construct a history of the French Enlightenment's attitude to execution that begins with the various demands for its secularization (e.g. in the writings of Montesquieu and Voltaire), moves on to Cesare Beccaria's call for its abolition (via André Morellet's translation), and ends with its democratization as demonstrated by the invention of the Guillotine, that emblem of the new secular laws of the modern state.[1] The Guillotine radically symbolized the citizen's equality before the law – an equality that went hand in hand with the various rights, passive and active, proclaimed by the *Déclaration des droits de l'homme et du citoyen* (1789). Yet, paradoxically, the Guillotine would very soon come to be associated not with the freedoms of opinion, conscience, expression, and assembly enshrined, *inter alia*, in the *Déclaration*, but rather with the repressive excesses of the Terrorists, determined as they were to extirpate political heresies. Furthermore, the workings of the Guillotine came, again very soon, to be associated with the figure of sacrifice, whether by the Counter-Revolutionaries who tended to exalt the redemptive calvaries of the royal family (Louis XVI, Marie-Antoinette, Madame Élisabeth) or by the Revolutionaries themselves, who sought to present the shedding of politically tainted blood as a ritualized act of national purification.

This chapter will investigate the persistence of the religious categories of heresy and sacrifice during and after the French Revolution. It will do so by examining the polemical debates that surrounded a number of eighteenth-century executions, whether real or imagined. In particular, it will look at those executions that most clearly belonged to the religious past, namely the *auto-da-fés* instigated by the Spanish and Portuguese Inquisitions.[2] These were the executions foregrounded by Montesquieu, Voltaire, and

Morellet, before the Revolution, as they wrote arguing for the secularization of capital punishment. These same executions were then revisited, after the Revolution, by the reactionary Savoyard theosopher Joseph de Maistre, as he sought instead to blame the very drive toward secularization for the political violence of the Terror and, in particular, its incontinent use of the Guillotine. It will be shown how Maistre's concerns in this regard feed into, and at times prefigure, an ongoing debate within critical theory centered around interlinked conceptions of sovereignty and sacrifice.

Maistre used his various works to attack what he considered to be the most pernicious ideas to have emerged from the Enlightenment.[3] By his own logic, he need hardly have bothered, for he liked to argue that Providence had only allowed these ideas to flourish in order that they might better bring themselves into discredit, just as the Revolutionaries had only been permitted to seize temporal power (and implement these ideas) in order that they might turn this power against themselves, for, as Maistre puts it in the third dialogue of *Les Soirées de Saint-Pétersbourg* (1821), "every wicked man is a HEAUTONTIMOROUMENOS," that is to say "AN EXECUTIONER OF HIM-SELF."[4] Founded on human error, the ideas of the Enlightenment immolated themselves by mutating into the fallacies of an ever more deranged Revolution. More generally, no idea founded on human error, whether barbaric or Enlightened, can stand as far as Maistre is concerned, for his conservative world view rests in large part on the conviction that the great mass of humanity bases its judgments not on cold reason but on a common-sense intuition informed by ancient lore and a divinely implanted store of innate ideas.[5] It is in this sense that the uneducated possess better judgment than the learned, for the masses turn out to be incapable of the sustained Promethean effort required to keep (bad) faith with the pitiful inductions of human reason. Popular beliefs and superstitions are everywhere more reliable than the elucubrations of self-appointed philosophers. God, the light of the world, illuminates; reason merely enlightens. Secularization, viewed from this optic, represents a determined rejection of divine truth in favor of human error. By extrapolation, the secularization of execution consists in an attempt to turn redemptive sacrifice into the senseless act of killing.

With the posthumous publication of *Les Soirées de Saint-Pétersbourg* (1821), Maistre became infamous for his claim that the executioner functions as "the cornerstone of society" (*StPD*, 207), "the horror and the bond of human association" (20). A superficial reading of this claim might suggest that Maistre was simply advocating public execution as a means of maintaining order, everywhere preferable to liberty. Stendhal, for example, cynically reduces Maistre's argument in this way in the articles that he prepared for the English press in the second half of the 1820s.[6] Certainly, Maistre is himself capable of advancing this argument, for example, when he claims that the Spanish Inquisition, by clamping down on heterodoxy and heresy, ensured political and social stability, thereby preventing the horrors of a Spanish war of religion, or that a French Inquisition would have prevented the Revolution.[7] However, Maistre also means something more by his claim, for, according to his *Éclaircissement sur les sacrifices*, appended to *Les Soirées*, the executioner carries out sacrificial acts that serve to bind the community before God. These sacrificial acts are intended not just as earthly punishments but also as so many acts of redemption, analogous to Jesus Christ's great act of redemption on the cross. This is the central truth that the Enlightenment and then the Revolution had sought to evacuate from the workings of the law – the truth that Maistre hoped would come to reanimate the laws of the Restoration and towards which the ministers of Charles X were groping as they stumbled their way toward the 1830 Revolution.[8]

In the *Éclaircissement*, Maistre insists that the figure of execution should not be detached from its religious underpinnings. In the process, he goes out of his way to counter one of Voltaire's many polemical attacks on the Spanish Inquisition, namely his claim that the executions it instigated were a hundred times more abominable than the human sacrifices of antiquity (*StPD*, 373).[9] Maistre objects to two aspects of Voltaire's assertion: first, that he should consider the Inquisition, "a legitimate tribunal in virtue of a previously solemnly promulgated law," to be "a *hundred times more abominable* than the horrible crime of a mother and a father putting their child on the flaming arms of Moloch! What atrocious madness! What negligence of all reason, justice, and modesty!" (374); second, that he should misunderstand human sacrifice as no more than the "tardy result of animal sacrifices" (373). For "*always* and *everywhere* where the true God was not known and adored, men were sacrificed" (373).

From Maistre's perspective, human sacrifice represents a pagan groping toward the great truth of redemption by blood as finally revealed by the self-sacrifice (as opposed to self-execution) of Jesus on the cross. For "paganism could not be mistaken about an idea as universal and fundamental as that of sacrifices" (380). Thus, the properly Christian theory of sacrifice – its rectified archetype – rests on the mechanism of reversibility that allows for the voluntary substitution of the merits of the innocent for the sins of the guilty. However, the innocent and the guilty are bound together not just by the operation of reversibility, but also by age-old notions of the sacred. As a consequence, the ancients had come to confuse voluntary self-sacrifice with the figures of execution and (forced) human sacrifice, this last described by Maistre as a "horrible superstition" (364):

> It is very likely that the first human victims were criminals condemned by the laws, for every nation believed what the Druids believed, according to Caesar: *that the punishment of criminals was something very pleasing to the Divinity.* The ancients believed that every capital crime committed in the state *bound* the nation, and that the criminal was *sacred* and bound to the gods until, by the shedding of his blood, he was *un-bound,* both himself and the nation.
>
> We see here why the word *sacred* (SACER) was taken in the Latin language in both a good and a bad sense, why this same word in the Greek language (*HOSIOS*) meant both what is holy and what is profane; why the word *anathema* means at the same time what is offered to God as a gift, and what is delivered to his vengeance; and finally, why in Greek as in Latin it is said that a man or a thing has been *desacralized* (expiated) to express the idea that someone has been cleansed of a stain they contracted. This word *desacralize* (*asposioun, expiare*) seems contrary to the analogy; the uninstructed ear would require *resacralization* or *re-santification,* but it is only an error of appearance, and the expression is very accurate. To *sacralize,* in the language of antiquity, means that which is *delivered to the Divinity,* no matter what the reason, and that which is found *bound,* so that punishment *desacralizes, expiates,* or *unbinds,* just like religious *ab-solution.* (365)

Thus, execution, the ultimate temporal punishment, functions also as a religious expiation that serves to redeem the nation. The criminal is made sacred by his impending execution, hence the phrase "SACER ESTO (*that he be sacred*)!" (365) used by the Romans to pronounce the death penalty, for execution serves as a dedication to God. It is in this sense that, according to *Les Soirées,* "the scaffold is an *altar*" (290).

The Inquisition functions as an exemplary tribunal in this respect, illustrating the complex interplay between temporal and spiritual authority that alone can prevent the figure of execution from being corrupted "by the force that corrupts everything" (364). Far from representing an embarrassing and barbaric religious past, the Spanish Inquisition – abolished in 1808, restored in 1814, suppressed in 1820, and only definitively abolished in 1834[10] – offers a modern model of best judicial practice.

Maistre had outlined his position with regard to the Inquisition in the *Lettres sur l'inquisition espagnole* (1815, first published posthumously in 1822), then, as now, a relatively neglected work. It had been written to challenge not only the various sensational claims made by Voltaire with regard to the Inquisition's barbaric methods and crazed bloodlust – claims illustrated by Morellet's equally sensational *Abrégé du Manuel des Inquisiteurs* (1762) – but also to argue against Montesquieu's dangerous insistence, in *De l'esprit des lois* (1748), that temporal and divine law should be kept entirely separate. In the *Lettres*, Maistre pursues his familiar tactic, attacking his opponents by seeking to overturn what appeared to be the strongest of their arguments. For although Voltaire and Morellet may eventually have felt themselves in sympathy with Beccaria and his radical call for the abolition of the death penalty in *Dei delitti e delle pene* (1765), they tended to advance weaker versions of this argument, suggesting that capital punishment be limited, rather than abolished. For, surely everyone could agree that executions for crimes of conscience must be done away with, particularly those inspired by the blind fanaticism exhibited by the Inquisition or the judicial murderers of Jean Calas? The religious and legal worlds must be kept separate, as Montesquieu had argued; divine and civil punishments must not be confused with one another. Maistre turns this argument on its head: the use of the death penalty is sanctioned precisely by its religious purposes, for otherwise executions would be no more than human punishments meted out by the powerful on the powerless, with no greater legitimacy than the judicial murders of the Terror.

In *De l'esprit des lois*, Montesquieu unambiguously argues in favor of the secularization of justice: "penal laws must be avoided in the matter of religion. They impress fear, it is true, but as religion also has its penal laws which inspire fear, the one is canceled out by the other. Between these two different fears, souls become atrocious."[11] Thus, "one should not enact by divine laws that which should be enacted by human laws, or regulate by human laws that which should be regulated by divine laws" (495). He embellishes his argument with various denunciations of the Inquisition and its arrogation of lay judicial powers, most notably in his "*Very humble remonstrance to the inquisitors of Spain and Portugal*" (490–2) nominally composed by "an eighteen-year-old Jewess, burned in Lisbon at the last auto-da-fé" (490). Montesquieu's "Jewess" pathetically claims her right to freedom of conscience. Maistre, in the *Lettres*, notes that her crime, had she existed, would not have consisted in her adherence to her religion but in her willfully false conversion to Christianity; he therefore dismisses Montesquieu's remonstrance as "a pitiful calumny" (*LSI*, 26).

Montesquieu clearly considers the fate that befalls his "Jewess" to constitute an indefensible extreme case, just as Voltaire, in *Candide* (1759), was to offer his account of a Lisbon *auto-da-fé* as a kind of *reductio ad absurdum* of public execution (admittedly one of many in this particular *conte philosophique*). Voltaire's account, however, is most emphatically not written from the viewpoint of a persecuted Jewish (or rather *converso*) minority: Cunégonde is required, problematically, to share her favors between a Grand Inquisitor and Don Issacar, a Jew. Candide saves her from the clutches of both these predatory men by killing (murdering?) them. There is of course an enormous difference between the way in which these two crimes are viewed by Portuguese society, as demonstrated by the differing fates that befall the two corpses: the Grand Inquisitor is buried in a beautiful church, the Jew is thrown on to the rubbish heap. However, the *auto-da-fé*, in Voltaire's fictional account, loses its properly religious dimension. It is no longer motivated by sincere religious fanaticism. Instead, the Inquisition is presented as an essentially hypocritical institution that seeks to dress up its will-to-power in robes of Catholic piety and superstition.[12]

Any sense Voltaire might have had that he had maligned the Inquisition in *Candide* was dispelled by Morellet's explosive exposé of Inquisitorial practices, the *Abrégé du manuel des inquisiteurs*, a redacted translation of Nicholas Eymerich's *Directorium inquisitorium* (1376). Morellet used his *Abrégé* as a kind of calling card to allow him greater entry in *philosophe* circles. He sent the book to d'Alembert with a view to it being forwarded to Voltaire. Traces of the latter's reactions survive in his correspondence. To Damilaville, he writes on February 4, 1762: "je lis toujours avec édification le manuel de l'inquisition, et je suis très fâché que Candide n'ait tué qu'un inquisiteur."[13] (I am still reading the manual of the inquisition with edification, and I am very sorry that Candide was responsible for killing only one inquisitor.) To d'Alembert, he writes on February 10: "Les hommes ne méritent pas de vivre puisqu'il y a encore du bois et du feu et qu'on ne s'en sert pas pour brûler ces monstres dans leurs infâmes repaires. Mon cher frère, embrassez en mon nom le digne frère qui a fait cet excellent ouvrage. Puisse-t-il être traduit en portugais et en castillan" (19). (Men do not deserve to live, given that they still possess wood and fire and yet do not use these to burn those monsters in their vile lairs. Dear brother, embrace for me the worthy brother who wrote this excellent work. May it be translated into Portuguese and into Castilian.) It is worth noting in passing that Voltaire, however facetiously, is here calling for the ritual execution of Inquisitors or an Enlightenment version of the *auto-da-fé*.

Voltaire's imagined history of execution – as adumbrated in the *Lettres philosophiques*, a text that was itself executed when it was burned by the

Parisian public executioner in 1734 – turns out to be strikingly similar to Maistre's account:

> From earliest times the fate of the Gauls, the Germans, [and] the inhab-
> itants of the British Isles were to be governed by their druids and the
> chieftains of their villages. (. . .) These druids claimed to be mediators
> between men and their gods: they made laws; they excommunicated;
> they condemned to death.[14]

Voltaire and Maistre could only speculate as to the religious origins of capital punishment and the religious meanings that might or might not have
attached themselves to this practice in ancient times. Voltaire clearly views
such meanings as essentially hypocritical and fraudulent; Maistre, when he
in turn refers nebulously to druids, appears not so much to be commenting on the antiquity and persistence of a religious category (sacrifice) as
asserting its absolute necessity, for it alone could make sense both of the
Terror, figured as a slaughter of the innocent, and of the continued use of
the death penalty in Restoration France.

The expiatory function of the death penalty became a staple of Counter-
Revolutionary propaganda, because it helped to valorize the aristocratic
victims of the Terror. Without it, the Terror would have no meaning and
one would already be in the fully modern world of senseless mechanical
slaughter, the world not of the holocaust but of the Shoah analyzed by Jean-
Luc Nancy.[15] To paraphrase Voltaire, if the death penalty had not formerly
performed a sacrificial function, then such a function and its origins would
need to be invented. Otherwise, the salutary repression that Maistre hoped
would characterize the administration of justice under the Revolution –
the repression required to stave off further revolutions – would start to
look very like the Revolutionary and Napoleonic repressions that it had
replaced: a point already all too eloquently made by Louis XVIII's re-em-
ployment of Joseph Fouché as his first Minister of Police.

Viewed from this optic, Jacques Derrida's pessimism regarding the possibility of moving beyond Christian sacrifice, as outlined in such works as
Donner la mort (1992) and *Le Toucher, Jean-Luc Nancy* (2000), might be taken
more as evidence of an inability on the part of Western thinkers, starting
with Maistre, to move beyond the French Revolution and the worrying implications of its political violence. Nancy and Giorgio Agamben have sought to
investigate these implications – and in the process to imagine beyond sacrifice – in their respective theorizations of "the 'Unsacrificeable'" and the
"homo sacer." Agamben, in particular, develops his position by looking at

the same legal history as Maistre. For Agamben, the "homo sacer," according to the laws of Ancient Rome, is he who can be killed but not sacrificed.[16] His focus is therefore on a different form of desacralization to that identified by Maistre, whose position is instead closely echoed by René Girard in his repeated investigations of the (Christian) scapegoat. Whatever these often radical differences, the speculations of Derrida, Nancy, Agamben, and Girard, like those of Maistre before them, insist both on a continuity in, and a transfiguration or sublimation of, "early" sacrificial thinking. However, this insistence, in the final analysis, takes the form of assertion: a myth of the past is simply fabricated to stand in counterpoint to a myth of the present.[17] Nancy appears well aware of this myth of the past, arguing that "there is precisely nothing we can say about 'early sacrifice' except that all representations of it are constructed on the basis of transfigured sacrifice" (*AFT*, 55), that is to say Christian and neo-Christian sacrifice.

Foucault, in his famous opening chapter to *Surveiller et punir* (1975) relating the botched execution of the supposed attempted regicide Damiens, shows his readers that in 1757 the executioners of France had little practical experience in hanging, drawing, and quartering their patients. Implicit to the subsequent development of his argument is the idea that the French were starting to forget quite why a man should be hung, drawn, and quartered. Maistre covers similar ground in *Les Soirées*, describing at some length a fictional executioner breaking a condemned criminal on the wheel. Maistre goes on to stress the unintelligible, hermetic aspect of the executioner's conduct:

> Remove this incomprehensible agent from the world, and in a moment order gives way to chaos, thrones fall, and society disappears. God, who is the author of sovereignty, is therefore also the author of punishment. He has suspended our earth on these two poles; *For the pillars of the earth are the Lord's, and he has set the world upon them.* (*StPD*, 20)

Maistre is here identifying the executioner as an agent who mediates, somewhat obscurely, between sovereignty and punishment, that is to say between the sovereign and the *homo sacer* who, according to Agamben, together constitute a sovereign exception beyond the extremes of civil society.[18] Similarly, the figure of the Inquisitor serves to mediate between a doctrinally infallible pope – described at some length by Maistre in *Du pape* (1819) – and the heretics who reject the finality of his decisions, thereby threatening religious and social order. In this sense, Maistre presents the pope as a sovereign, standing above and outside the main body of the

Church.[19] In the *Lettres*, however, Maistre takes great pains to stress that whereas the figure of the Grand Inquisitor derives his spiritual authority from the pope, he derives his temporal authority – his authority to execute – from the sovereign monarch.

Maistre views both the sovereign monarch and the sacred criminal as essential to the proper, legitimate, divinely ordained functioning of society. Otherwise, there is the chaos and senseless bloodletting of the Terror or, extrapolating into the future, the senseless destruction of the Shoah (as opposed to the Holocaust) analyzed by Nancy. This, presumably, is the obscure reason why the remains of Damiens had to be burnt: he needed to become a holocaust, a religious sacrifice – that which, etymologically, must entirely be consumed by flames – if he was to be given over to God. All this was not, however, sufficiently clear, or sufficiently accepted, at the time of his execution.

The Damiens affair generated a great deal of polemic, for it brought to a head the various conflicts between the French monarchy and the Paris Parlement, as well as between the Jesuits and the Jansenists, and was followed in quick succession first by the (in some ways analogous) Malagrida affair and then by the Calas affair, this last prompting a redoubling of Voltaire's efforts against "*l'infâme*" (the constellated forces of religious intolerance and oppression).[20] One of the ironies of the Damiens affair – hardly lost on the *philosophes* – is that it involved the religiously ritual execution of an apparent religious fanatic, for the unemployed manservant Damiens had maintained, in the course of his various interrogations, that he had attacked Louis XV for religious motives. A martyr was being martyred, contributing to the general sense of official embarrassment that attended his botched execution. This same irony was contained in the Malagrida affair that did so much to reignite the Enlightenment debates surrounding the Spanish and Portuguese Inquisitions originally sparked by Montesquieu.

The Jesuit priest, Gabriel Malagrida, was executed in Lisbon for heresy in 1761. His political crime – for which he had been condemned to death but not executed in 1758–9 – took the form of an alleged participation in the murky Tavora plot to assassinate the King of Portugal; his religious crime took the form of heresy in its most florid forms, as demonstrated by his unhealthy fixation on the uterus of St Anne. He did not help his cause by refusing to apologize for, or desist from, onanistically polluting himself when in solitary confinement.[21]

Malagrida's eventual execution for the crime of heresy in 1761 appeared topical to French audiences, coming so shortly after the Damiens affair. In particular, it allowed both the Jansenists and the *philosophes* to attack the

Jesuits (and then the *philosophes* to attack the Jansenists for the hypocrisy of their attacks on the Jesuits). Hence the flurry of polemical materials with which Malagrida's execution was greeted. More importantly, the case was useful to the *philosophes* because it appeared to unmask *l'infâme*, revealing all its hypocrisy and bad faith.[22] For Malagrida's condemnation and execution appeared to rest on a convoluted legal fiction: the real crime for which he was executed was the political crime of (allegedly) conspiring to assassinate the king and, more generally, of being a prominent Jesuit at a time when the Jesuits were being expelled from Portugal. The religious crime (heresy) was therefore no more than a pretext, ironically required to get around the pope's reluctance to see a Jesuit priest executed on a secular charge, but helpful also as a means of getting around the problems posed by Malagrida's evident insanity (Damiens had of course posed the same problem to the French authorities.).[23]

Yet, the *philosophes*, in their response to the Malagrida affair, made no mention of a second legal fiction that attended not only Malagrida's execution but also all other executions instigated by the Spanish and Portuguese Inquisitions: technically speaking, Malagrida was sentenced to death not by the Inquisition but by a royal court. Maistre makes much of the fact that no tribunal of the Spanish (and by extension Portuguese) Inquisition ever passed sentence of death, although, given that the royal court automatically passed this sentence on all those returned to it by the Inquisition, his arguments would no doubt have appeared hair-splitting to a Voltaire or a Morellet. Maistre, however, is not just trying to get the Inquisition off on a technicality (although he is also trying to do this); he is also insisting on the proper separation of powers between church and state. The state, in this case a monarchy, has passed laws, including laws that seek to regulate religious crime (heresy, blasphemy, sacrilege, etc.). The state then enforces these laws, delegating some of its responsibilities and powers to a royal institution (the Inquisition or Holy Office) partly staffed by members of the religious orders.

> Whatever in this tribunal is rigourous, and frightful – but, above all, the punishment of death, – all this is purely the concern of the civil government: – it is its affair; and it alone is accountable for it. Whereas, all the clemency, which is so remarkable in this tribunal, is the act and influence of the Church, which interferes in punishments, only in order, either to suppress, or to mitigate, them. (*LSI*, 11)

In particular, the religious functionaries of the Inquisition endeavor to find grounds for excusing the guilty by accepting their repentance. Only when these efforts have failed do they turn the accused back over to the royal authorities, absenting themselves from the passing of sentence, because it is the "eternal axiom" of the Catholic faith that *"The Church Abhors Blood!"* (8). The Inquisition therefore illustrates, in exemplary fashion, the process whereby the Church endeavors to bind society – the flock – together, bringing as many strays as possible back into the fold. When it fails, it passes the unrepentant and any recidivists back to a temporal authority that would otherwise already have imposed punishment. It is the Inquisition that dedicates the condemned to God; the organs of the state that perform the incomprehensible role of the executioner, mediating between the sovereign and the criminal, both standing outside society (the flock).

Maistre goes on to point out the extreme leniency of the Inquisition in the eighteenth century. In this respect, he is rather borne out by the historical record. Jean-Pierre Guicciardi, in his introduction to Morellet's *Abrégé*, points out the *"curieux problème de cécité politique et historique"* (*AMI*, 45) (curious problem of political and historical blindness) posed by the French Enlightenment's denunciations of the Spanish and Portuguese Inquisitions and their largely imaginary crimes. He goes on to suggest that this blindness might be deliberate: the fight against *l'infâme* had proved too arduous for the *philosophes* to consider fighting fair.[24] Yet, there might be another reason for this blindness: a desire on the part of the *philosophes* to posit repressive violence as an exclusive feature of the religious past, about to be swept away by the brave new modern world of their devising. Thus, it was important for them to assert the opposite of what Maistre would go on to claim: that clemency belonged to the emergent modern state, and severity to the remnants of neo-druidical theocracy.

Execution, too, belonged to *l'infâme*; once rationalized and brought into the modern age, presumably it would wither away as Montesquieu had implied when he predicted that liberty would bring with it ever gentler punishments (*SL*, 83). Maistre uses almost exactly the same argument with regard to repression: the success of the Inquisition is reflected not only in the avoidance of religious wars and social or political revolution, but also in a progressive softening of sentences. Thus, Maistre cites the following punishment handed out by the Inquisition, as related by Joseph Townsend, an Anglican minister (and therefore self-evidently hostile to the Holy Office), traveling through Spain between 1786 and 1787:

> "A beggar," he tells us, "named Ignazio Rodriguez, was condemned by the tribunal of the Inquisition for having distributed certain love potions of a very indecent nature, and of having, in the administration of the

infamous remedy, pronounced certain words of necromancy. It was, moreover, proved, that he had administered the disgusting dose to all ranks of persons. Rodriguez had two accomplices in his crimes, who were equally condemned, as he was, – their names, Juliana Lopez, and Angelo Barrios. One of these imploring the Judges to spare her life – they told her "*that it was not the practice of the Holy Office to condemn any one to death*." Rodriguez was condemned to be led through the streets of Madrid mounted on an ass; and to be whipped. They, likewise, imposed upon him certain practices of religion; and to be banished from the Capital, for five years. The reading of the sentence was frequently interrupted by peals of laughter, in which the beggar himself joined."

"Accordingly, the criminal was led through the streets; but not whipped. On the way, and during the procession, the people offered him wine and biscuits," (cruel creatures) "to refresh him." (*LSI*, 43)

Maistre goes on to point out that "if we only consider the words of the traveler, we find, that the *ingredients*, employed by Rodriguez, were such as would, in any other country, have condemned him to the pillory, to the galleys, or even to the gallows" (44). In other words, the softening of sentences is the product not of liberty and democracy, as in Montesquieu, but of successful (religious) repression. The old theocracies can afford to be lenient where the modern state feels compelled to assert itself through violence.

Maistre is clear that executions must perform, and be understood to perform, a sacrificial function. Otherwise, punishment has no meaning, sovereignty is abrogated, and order gives way to chaos. This "truth" came to be lost in the eighteenth century of the French Enlightenment and Revolution. Maistre "finds" it largely by asserting it as eternal and innate. More recently, many critical theorists have agreed with him on the perennial quality of Western sacrificial thinking, citing the extreme difficulty with which the modern world has tried to move beyond Christian sacrifice (Derrida) or worrying about the possible shapes that this beyond of sacrifice might take (Nancy and Agamben).[25] Sacrifice as a religious category has persisted as a means of accounting for the ever more efficient modern use of execution and other forms of violence. The French Revolution briefly oversaw a massive increase in executions, at times on a new, industrial scale. Its insistence on execution as a form of national purification designed to bind the nation more tightly together testifies to the persistence of a sacrificial logic. This persistence impressed itself on Morellet when, in his mid-sixties, he found himself confronted with the political violence of the Revolution and even forced to negotiate with the Terrorists when they began to suspect him of new crimes of thought (secular political heresy). In his *Mémoires,* Morellet bears witness to the "massacres" of the Terror; he goes on to describe an anti-Revolutionary satire that he composed, but wisely did not publish, "dans un moment de fureur contre les destructeurs de l'homme" (in a moment of fury against the destroyers of humanity).[26] This satire is plainly modeled on Swift's *A Modest Proposal* (1729), as indeed Morellet's first published work, his *Petit écrit sur une matière intéressante* (1756), had been. Entitled *Le Préjugé vaincu, ou Nouveau moyen de subsistance pour la nation, proposé au comité de salut public en messidor de l'an II de la République (juillet 1794),* this new work proposed that the recent food shortages be remedied by citizens being required, at least once a week, to eat the flesh of the victims of the Terror, "sous peine d'être emprisonnés, déportés, égorgés comme suspects" (433) (under pain of being imprisoned, deported, or having their throats cut as suspects). Morellet further proposed that "dans toute fête patriotique, il y ait un plat de ce genre, qui serait la vraie *communion* des patriotes, *l'eucharistie* des Jacobins" (433–4) (as part of every patriotic festival, there be a dish of this type, that would be the true patriotic *communion,* the *eucharist* of the Jacobins). Morellet's contemptuous use of italics serves to underline his scorn for this return to barbarism figured as a return to the religious past. Sacrifice had returned, as of course had the methods of the Inquisition: once again, it was possible for men and women to be imprisoned and deported, and even for their throats to be slit, on simple suspicion, without even the semblance of due, that is to say modern, secular legal process. Morellet makes this point at length in the *Mémoires* (426–7). He also makes it in the course of recently published extracts from his "Matériaux pour servir à l'histoire de la Révolution." In a trenchant discussion of the Revolutionary "loi des suspects et arrestations qui l'ont suivie" (law on suspects and the arrests that followed it), Morellet compares this new measure to the formal procedures of the Inquisition that he had been the first to expose to public scrutiny:

> Selon une maxime de l'inquisition extraite fidelement des canonistes qui ont enseigné cette horrible jurisprudence, l'inquisiteur peut citer à son tribunal et soumettre à l'obligation de se purger de soupcon d'heresie tout homme que le bruit public accuse d'avoir dit ou fait quelque chose contre la foi [,] et pour avoir contre lui une preuve complète il suffira que deux temoins disent qu'ils ont entendu dire à tels et tels que l'accusé est heretique quand ces deux temoins n'auroient pas entendu tenir ce propos aux mêmes personnes. Et si on leur demande ce que c'est que la *reputation d'heretique* il n'est pas necessaire qu'ils en donnent une definition exacte. Il suffit qu'ils disent que c'est ce qu'on dit communément. Telle est

la doctrine de l'auteur ancien *du directoire des inquisiteurs* dont j'ai donné abregé, intitulé le *Manuel des inquisiteurs* et on voit que de ces deux juris-prudences ce n'est pas celle de l'inquisition qui est la plus monstrueuse.[27]

(According to a maxim of the inquisition taken faithfully from the can-onists who taught this horrible jurisprudence, the inquisitor may cite before this tribunal and require to clear himself of the suspicion of her-esy any man that public rumor accuses of having done or said something contrary to the faith. In order to have against him a complete proof, it will be sufficient for two witnesses to declare that they heard from such and such persons that the accused is a heretic so long as these two wit-nesses did not hear these things from the same persons. And if they are asked what a *reputation for heresy* might mean, it is not necessary that they provide an exact definition. It is enough that they declare it to be that which it is commonly said to be. Such is the doctrine of the author of the *directory of the inquisitors* of which I have given an abridged version, enti-tled the *Manual of the Inquisitors* and one can see that, of these two juris-prudences, it is not that of the inquisition that is the most monstrous.)

The secular state, it turned out, was even more intent on extirpating heresy than the eighteenth-century Inquisitions that the Enlightenment had imagined as its dark, barbarian Other.[28] The figures of sacrifice and heresy had persisted in ways that appeared incomprehensible to Morellet: "ce phénomène moral n'est pas encore expliqué, si même il est explicable" (*M*, 427) (this moral phenomenon has yet to be explained, if indeed it can be explained). It would be left to Maistre to start providing an explanation and so lay the foundations for Schmitt's new discipline of political theol-ogy – since taken up by Agamben and others – through his interlinked analyses of heresy, infallibility, sacrifice, and sovereignty.

Notes

1 See Daniel Arasse, *La Guillotine et l'imaginaire de la Terreur* (Paris: Flammarion, 1987) for an influential account of the Guillotine's place in the Revolutionary consciousness.

2 In her recent book on the mythical figure of the Grand Inquisitor that even-tually emerged in the nineteenth century, Caroline Julliot observes that the Inquisition constituted the archetype of barbarism, religious oppression, and obscurantism against which the *philosophes* of the Enlightenment sought to do battle. Caroline Julliot, *Le Grand Inquisiteur, naissance d'une figure mythique au XIXe siècle* (Paris: Champion, 2010), 33 (hereafter *GI*).

[3] See *Joseph de Maistre and the Legacy of Enlightenment*, edited by Carolina Armenteros and Richard A. Lebrun (Oxford: SVEC, 2011), for an alternative account of Maistre as the heir as well as the foe of the *philosophes*.

[4] Joseph de Maistre, *St Petersburg Dialogues or Conversations on the Temporal Government of Providence*, translated and edited by Richard A. Lebrun (Montreal and Kingston: McGill-Queen's University Press, 1993), 91–2 (hereafter *StPD*).

[5] Maistre uses both his *Examen de la philosophie de Bacon* (1814–16, published posthumously in 1836) and *Les Soirées de Saint-Pétersbourg* to reassert the theory of innate ideas ridiculed by Voltaire in the *Lettres philosophiques* (1734).

[6] See Stendhal, *Chroniques pour l'Angleterre*, translated by Renée Dénier, edited by Keith G. McWatters, 7 vols (Grenoble: ELLUG, 1993), V, 100–1.

[7] Joseph de Maistre, *Letters on the Spanish Inquisition*, translated by John Fletcher (London: Keating, Dolman and Jones, 1838), 31, 56–7 and 75 (hereafter *LSI*).

[8] The most notable example of this process took the form of the paper introduction of the law against sacrilege of 1825, with its seemingly absurd reapplication of the death penalty for certain crimes of profanation and blasphemy.

[9] Maistre provides his own unimprovable endnote by way of bibliographical reference: "See note xii to his decrepit tragedy, *Minos (Les Lois de Minos)*" (373).

[10] Francisco Bethencourt, *The Inquisition: A Global History, 1478–1834*, translated by Jean Birrell (Cambridge: Cambridge University Press, 2009), 416.

[11] Charles de Secondat, baron de Montesquieu, *The Spirit of Laws*, translated and edited by Anne M. Cohler, Basia C. Miller and Harold S. Stone (Cambridge: Cambridge University Press, 1989), 489.

[12] Voltaire, *Candide and Other Stories*, translated and edited by Roger Pearson (Oxford: Oxford University Press, 1990), 19–22. See also *GI*, 31–7 on the Enlightenment's polemical representations of the figure of the Grand Inquisitor as, in essence, a (comical) hypocrite.

[13] André Morellet, *Abrégé du Manuel des Inquisiteurs*, edited by Jean-Pierre Guicciardi (Grenoble: Jérôme Millon, 2000), 19 (hereafter *AMI*).

[14] Voltaire, *Philosophical Letters*, translated by Prudence L. Steiner, edited by John Leigh (Indianapolis: Hackett, 2007), 27.

[15] Jean-Luc Nancy, *A Finite Thinking*, edited by Simon Sparks (Stanford: Stanford University Press, 2003), 69 (hereafter *AFT*).

[16] Giorgio Agamben, *Homo Sacer: Sovereign Power and Bare Life*, translated by Daniel Heller-Roazen (Stanford: Stanford University Press, 1998), 81–5 (hereafter *HS*).

[17] See Hent de Vries, *Religion and Violence: Philosophical Perspectives from Kant to Derrida* (Baltimore: Johns Hopkins University Press, 2002), 200–10 for an excellent and extended discussion of these issues (the main lines of which I have followed here).

[18] See Carl Schmitt, *Political Theology: Four Chapters on the Concept of Sovereignty*, translated by George Schwab, edited by Tracy B. Strong (Chicago: University of Chicago Press, 2005), 5–15 (hereafter *PT*) and *HS*, 15–29, for discussions of the paradox of the sovereign exception, whereby the sovereign "stands outside the normally valid legal system," but "nevertheless, belongs to it" (*PT*, 7). Agamben develops this analysis to show how the sovereign and the "*homo sacer*" together function as "the two poles of the sovereign exception" (*HS*, 110).

19 Schmitt offers an illuminating discussion of Maistre's linked conceptions of infallibility and sovereignty (*PT*, 55). More generally, Schmitt links the notion of sovereignty to the power to make a final decision: "sovereign is he who decides on the exception." (5).

20 See Dale K. Van Kley, *The Damiens Affair and the Unraveling of the* Ancien Régime *1750–1770* (Princeton: Princeton University Press, 1984) for a classic account of the political ramifications of the Damiens affair. *L'Attentat de Damiens: discours sur l'événement au xviiie siècle*, edited by Pierre Rétat (Lyon: Presses Universitaires de Lyon, 1998), offers a useful overview and analysis of contemporary reactions to Damiens's attack and contains an interesting account of his execution as a form of sacrifice (241–66).

21 Anon., *Relation de l'Autho-da-Fé de Lisbonne* (Paris [?]: n., 1761), 6–7.

22 Voltaire, for example, provides an irreverent account of the Malagrida affair in his *Précis du Siècle de Louis XV* (1768). See Voltaire, *Œuvres historiques*, edited by René Pomeau (Paris: Gallimard, 1957), 1532–4 (hereafter *OH*).

23 Voltaire notes that Malagrida was put on trial for being a prophet and executed for being mad. His participation in what Voltaire presents as a very real political crime – even as a form of parricide – is silenced by the Inquisition. Voltaire goes on to observe, sarcastically, that Malagrida's political crime had been committed against a mere representative of the secular world, whereas his madness constituted a crime against God (*OH*, 1534).

24 See also *GI*, 33, for a brief discussion of this point.

25 More generally, these theorists have, to varying degrees, followed Schmitt, who suggests that "all significant concepts of the modern theory of the state are secularized theological concepts not only because of their historical development – in which they were transferred from theology to the theory of the state, whereby, for example, the omnipotent God became the omnipotent lawgiver – but also because of their systematic structure" (*PT*, 36). See also *GI*, 179–80, on the ways in which the nineteenth-century figure of the Grand Inquisitor, *pace* Maistre, constitutes a sovereign exception in this sense and, more generally, 153–217 on the Grand Inquisitor as a theologico-political figure.

26 André Morellet, *Mémoires de l'abbé Morellet de l'Académie française*, edited by Jean-Pierre Guicciardi (Paris: Mercure de France, 2000), 433 (hereafter *M*).

27 *André Morellet (1727–1819) in the Republic of Letters and the French Revolution*, edited by Dorothy Medlin and Jeffrey W. Merrick (New York: Peter Lang, 1995), 128.

28 This idea became a staple of Counter-Revolutionary attacks on the Terror. See *GI*, 151, for a development of this point, as well as 81–152 more generally on the figure of the Grand Inquisitor as a mirror-image of the Terror.

Chapter 9

Religion and the French Revolution –
or The Politics of Incarnation

Craig Carson

Well before the academy's recent "religious turn" exhumed concepts such as political theology and secularization, Claude Lefort, in his essays *On the Permanence of the Theologico-Political?* and *Revolution as New Religion*, had begun reassessing the continuing, if often obscured, imbrications of politics and theology.[1] In a pre-9/11 world, where secularism and democracy had become virtually uncontested truths, Lefort casts a critical eye on the origins of these mythologies, especially as they concern the separation of Church and State or, in the French context, *laïcité*. In this light, Lefort's interpretations of the French Revolution and the work of Jules Michelet in particular play a decisive role. Throughout his now infamous *History of the French Revolution*, Michelet insists that the Revolution, simultaneously the emergence and collapse of modern democracy, fails due to its inability to address religious concerns in a sufficiently nuanced fashion. Michelet's *History* belies the mythology of the French Revolution as a fundamentally secular event, if not the event of our secular political modernity, more generally. Lefort continues where Michelet leaves off: modern democratic institutions, like the French Revolution of Michelet's *History*, will continually fail until they can address the interdependence of religion and politics, or the "permanence of the theologico-political." It is Michelet, therefore, who anticipates much of the so-called post-secular reappraisal of the role of religion within contemporary politics. If the *History* continues to speak to us today, it is less as an atavistic curiosity in an age of scientific historiography (as in the work of Roland Barthes or Georges Bataille) or as a mythology of the people (as in Bettina Lerner's *Michelet, Mythologue*), and more as a theory of the political–theological dimensions of our modern democracy.[2] To this end, Lefort's rallying cry is that, "rather than imputing [Michelet's] conviction immediately to [his] romantic imagination, one would undoubtedly be better advised to ask oneself what was seeking to be said through these words *new religion.*"[3] It is precisely this task, the inquiry into Michelet's identification of the Revolution with a "new religion," beyond Lefort's inaugural gestures, that is the driving force behind this chapter.

In this context, what is most interesting and timely about Michelet's work is not simply the paradoxes of revolutionary historiography that, as Marie-Hélène Huet describes in her book, *Mourning Glory: The Will of the French Revolution*, must "reclaim the very past that repudiated the burden of history."[4] More than this, his work must reclaim the past in order to reassess how the repudiated *religious* elements continue to exert an inextricable force on a supposedly secular, political world. Certainly, a distinct strand of secularism runs throughout the philosophical origins of the Revolution as well as its official rhetoric even if, as Ernst Cassirer argues in his *Philosophy of the Enlightenment*, the French Enlightenment and its revolutionary inheritors were reevaluating, rather than the rejecting, religious faith. A suspicion of religion is clear, however, as when Robespierre states in speech to the Convention on February 5, 1794, that tyranny of any kind, "A king, a vainglorious Senate, a Caesar, a Cromwell must above all veil their plans in a religious shroud."[5] Michelet maintains, however, that it is the Revolutionaries' fear of addressing religion in any sustained way, beyond the antics of the Festival of the Supreme Being for instance, which destabilizes the Revolution and leads to The Terror. More illuminating still, however, is the Revolution's eighteenth-century commentators, especially its English proponents and the counterrevolutionary detractors, both of whom understand the Revolution in thoroughly theological terms. Yet, Michelet also rejects these eighteenth-century religious interpretations, whether revolutionary (such as the English Dissenters, Richard Price and Joseph Priestley, who envision the French Revolution as a positive step forward in a messianic history), or counterrevolutionary (such as Edmund Burke and Joseph de Maistre, who view the Revolution as a negative moment or even purgation contained within a Providential history). Echoing these arguments, Michelet appropriates them, bends them to his specific ends and makes them say something entirely original.

The objective of this chapter is to demonstrate that Michelet not only rejects the notion of the French Revolution as a secular event, but also develops a political theology that does not simply fall back into the banalities of the Dissenters such as Price and Priestley, or counterrevolutionaries, such as Burke and Maistre. What, in fact, does a new revolutionary religion look like when it is not, as in the case of the revolutionary upheaval of the English Civil Wars, a revolution in the name of religion? This chapter will answer this question –what is Michelet's revolutionary political–theological vision?– by focusing specifically on one aspect of Michelet's text: the engagement with Pauline theology. This engagement, I will argue, defines Michelet's unprecedented depiction of the relationship between politics and theology, one that may also shed light on contemporary political realities.

From Romanticism to Political Theology

In the deeply personal Preface to his *History*, Michelet famously describes the period of reflection afforded by the summer as a respite from teaching, when the "crowd" of students dissipates and the Parisian masses diminish. In this regained tranquility, "the pavement grows more sonorous around my Pantheon."[6] Despite the prominence of the Pantheon, which the National Assembly transformed from a Catholic church into a grand architectural mausoleum for the heroes of the Revolution, Michelet seeks elsewhere his inspiration for reigniting the flame of the Revolution. No monument can aid Michelet because, as he states, the "Revolution lives in ourselves – in our souls; it has no outward monument."[7] Yet, a monument – or, even, an anti-monument – he seeks nonetheless as he turns his footsteps and his pen toward the Champs de Mars.

> The Champs de Mars! This is the only monument that the Revolution has left. The Empire has its Column, and engrosses almost exclusively the arch of Triumph; Royalty has its Louvre, its Hospital of Invalids; the feudal Church of the twelfth century is still enthroned as Notre Dame: nay, the very Romans have their Imperial Ruins, the Thermae of the Caesars! And the Revolution has for her monument – empty space [*le vide*].

It does seem that the emptiness of the Champs de Mars fascinates the historian who, as Huet remarks, desires his project "to fill a wasteland deserted by language."[8] However, this logic of monuments meanders, first, from the obvious monument of the Pantheon to the internal realm of the human soul (which has no need for monuments), and then to the negative "empty" monument of the Champs de Mars. More than simply needing an "empty space" in which to construct a linguistic monument to rival the architectural grandeur of other powers of French history, this non-monument also effaces the one existing monument of the Revolution – the

Pantheon – and buries the embarrassing appropriation from the Catholic Church.

If, as a monument to the Revolution, the Champs de Mars functions more readily as an absolute rupture with the past and a future-oriented *tabula rasa*, the Pantheon nonetheless appears to be much more pertinent to Michelet's explicit project. The subject of both the Preface and the Introduction, if not the project as a whole, is the relation between Christianity and the Revolution. Possibly in the case of the Pantheon, this intersection appears overly determined, too easily read as an allegory of the Revolution's debt to – or, even, to use Michelet's crucial term, "fulfillment" of – Christianity. In the controversial 1847 "Introduction" to his *History*, Michelet claims that, "If the Revolution was nothing but the accomplishment (or fulfillment) of Christianity" or if it was nothing but Christianity's "age of Reason," then "the eighteenth century and the *philosophes*, the precursors and the directors [*les maîtres*] of the Revolution were wrong, and put into motion something entirely contrary to their desires" (54). In this respect, Michelet clearly distances himself from the Revolutionary messianism of the English Dissenters, for whom the French Revolution prefigured the coming Millennium. Michelet's Revolution must be something other than another chapter in the annals of thoroughly Christian history; not the "completion" of Christianity, according to Michelet, but something much more radical.

Despite the Revolution's oscillation between the secular Cult of Reason and vaguely theist Festival of the Supreme Being, Michelet's retrospective gaze sees in every event during the Revolution a univocal rejection of religious "superstition." He appears, therefore, to subscribe to Diderot's distinction between the enslavement of the "yolk of religion" and the laws of human nature where one "find[s] flowers strewn upon the pathways of life."[9] In pursuit of liberty, humanity must turn away from the idolatry of "wooden gods" toward the natural freedom, the guarantee of which is nothing other than the earth itself. Famously, Michelet's purported "romanticism" shifts from the register of the theological to the language of natural phenomena, so that in Michelet's topography the *Encyclopedia* devastates the intellectual world like the volcanic eruption of Etna or the earthquake at Lisbon, and the Revolution irrupts like a rock formation jutting out from the center of the earth. In this respect, Michelet's romanticism appears to push for a repudiation of the "supernatural" world of theology (to appropriate the words of M. H. Abrams) in favor of a romantic "naturalism," in which the theological elements have been repressed.[10] These repressed elements, however, necessarily return.

In the exuberant and partisan preface appearing in the 1979 Robert Laffont edition of Michelet's *History*, Claude Mettra writes:

> For the French nation, the Revolution is a resurrection. From the hidden depths of the soul of the people [*l'âme populaire* – common, of the people, or even working-class] rises a glorious song which both abolishes a sterilized reality and celebrates the advent of a new humanity.[11]

Nevertheless, Mettra's praise for the Revolution itself is understated in contrast with his unbridled enthusiasm for Michelet's text. Of this, he writes:

> Just as the Roman Empire formerly embraced the word of the gospel, Europe will embrace the word of the Revolution: it opens a heretofore ignored passage wherein future generations will locate their roots.[12]

On first blush, Mettra's overtly theological language, both his messianic description of the Revolution as well as identifying Michelet's history as the new Gospel, appears incongruous with the secular and decidedly anti-Christian tenor of the text being described.

If the explicitly stated purpose of Michelet's Introduction is to distinguish the Revolution from Christianity – a distinction which Michelet states "historically" and "logically" must precede any inquiry into the Revolution – its pages nonetheless do or perform something very different. The first line of the "Introduction" itself uses precisely the same overtly Christian lexicon that permeates Mettra's Preface. Here, Michelet writes, "I define the Revolution as the advent of the Law, the resurrection of Rights, and the reaction of Justice" (51). What becomes clear very early in Michelet's Introduction is that Mettra's theological language – or more precisely, his discourse of messianic expectation promising the "advent of a new humanity" – simply mirrors the theological language that, ironically, permeates Michelet's diatribe against theology itself. Already, Michelet's anti-theological stance within the Introduction is a paradigmatic gesture of what the twentieth century will come to define as political theology, generally understood following Carl Schmitt's formulation as the appropriation of religious concepts by the secular political world.[13]

The Revolution has stalled and its promise remains unrealized, not because Robespierre corrupted it, but because in the wake of Thermidor the Revolution resigned itself to allowing politics and religion to exist side by side, in a state of contradiction, even mutual hostility. Michelet's

Introduction begins with the imperative to speak about the relation between Christianity and the Revolution, a point about which everyone now passes over in silence, afraid of disrupting the tenuous balance of power, shrouding this question in a "mute empire." Before this continuation of the Revolution's discursive register can proceed, however, its relation to religion needs to be determined precisely. The life of the citizen, the potentially revolutionary subject, remains divided between political and theological existence, between the sphere of the *polis* and the sphere of the *oikos*, private and public life, like so many latter-day Antigones. In order for the Revolution to continue its historical unfolding, the relation between religion and revolution must be reconciled; this is the positive task that Michelet's work sets for itself.

Yet, even from Michelet's perspective, the writing of the *History* is more than simply the work of a revolutionary partisan; it is, in the final instance, an act of faith. Perhaps most importantly, it is not simply a history that records past events, closed off to us. Beyond Huet's insistence on the impossibility of Michelet's writing of the Revolution's end, the language of missianiasm transforms Michelet's "history" into something very different: not history, but a blueprint for a revolutionary future. Michelet's *History* is by no means an act of commemoration; on the contrary, it is the Revolution's continuation, picking up precisely where Robespierre left off, picking up just before Thermidor. In the same way that, as Lefort points out in the essay "Revolutionary Terror," Robespierre's discourse was itself the Terror, Michelet's text is the Revolution, not simply a liturgy of revolutionary history. Michelet's fidelity to the Revolutionary event looks much more like the work of an evangelist than a historian. Moreover, this fidelity requires that he speak, that he bears witness to the event, precisely, as Mettra has suggested, in the way that the Gospel functioned as the legacy of Christianity, or like Paul with respect to the Resurrection. Subtly, Michelet begins to don the rhetorical mantle of the least of the apostles, insisting that his "weakness" [*faiblesse*] is his strength, or that he writes this history "not according to the law, but according to his heart" (53).[14] However, significantly, if Michelet takes up the discourse (if not the position) of St. Paul, it is in order to repudiate the principle legacy of Paul's epistles: the doctrine of grace. "Christianity," Michelet claims, "can be reconciled with Papinan [here, a metonymy for Justice] only by withdrawing from Saint Paul – quitting its proper base, and leaning aside at the risk of losing its equilibrium and being dashed to atoms" (21). So, when Michelet writes that he defines the Revolution as "the advent of the Law, the resurrection of Rights, and the reaction of Justice," he takes up his position – on the side of the Law and Justice – against the arbitrary logic of divine grace and ultimately against the political implications of Pauline theology (51).

The Politics of Incarnation

Even if Michelet addresses the political–theological dimension of the Revolution, it not entirely true that the *"philosophes*, the precursors and the directors of the Revolution" were themselves advocating for a strict division between politics and theology. One need only reach back into the Revolution's immediate prehistory, to the work of Jean-Jacques Rousseau (who is, for Michelet, the Revolution's principle architect) to find a similar inquiry into political theology. The division between the Church and the state, which leads more problematically to an individual divided between citizen and saint, is also the central problem addressed in the final section of Rousseau's *Social Contract*, entitled "The Civil Religion." Michelet makes the rather imprecise claim that the *philosophes*, Rousseau and Voltaire in particular (Michelet's "apostles of the Revolution"), have generated an anti-Christian movement; Rousseau's discussion of religion and the state in the *Social Contract* finds itself opposed to Christianity only indirectly, or precisely because Christianity has not grasped political realities firmly enough. Despite his qualifications and caveats, Rousseau's text looks back nostalgically to a pre-Christian era – Roman as well as Judaic – in which religion and the nation were indistinguishable. Theocracy, according to Rousseau, reconciles the division between the spiritual and the material worlds. The disjunction of politics and religion first arises with the emergence of Christianity: "It was in these circumstances [i.e., theocracy] that Jesus came to establish a spiritual kingdom on earth; this kingdom, separating the theological from the political, meant that the state ceased to be a unity, and it caused the intestine divisions which have never ceased to disturb the Christian people."[15]

As a response to the division introduced by Christianity, Islam attempted to reconcile Church and state: Rousseau writes that, "Mahomet had very sound opinions, taking care to give unity to his political system, for as long as the form of his government endured under the caliphs who succeeded him the government was undivided and, to that extent, good" (179). However, even the "good" theocratic unity of Islam fell apart with the emergence of the clash between Sunni and Shiite (the "sect of Ali"). Ultimately, Rousseau's notion of a civil religion and its necessary "profession of faith" results neither from a secularization of the state nor a return to a theocratic state, of which Rousseau says admiringly that every war is a "holy war" and every dead soldier a "martyr"; it is, instead, an imperfect stopgap measure intended to reunite politics and religion. A need for religion, any religion, becomes a political necessity. Even if one does not believe in the articles of the profession of faith, he must act as if he does, otherwise he will "be banished not for impiety but as an antisocial being" (186). Demanding an even more profound unity than a simple "profession of faith," however, Michelet argues that the Revolution must struggle against Christianity, because the latter threatens to engulf the former. Many "eminent minds," Michelet argues, have gone so far as to suggest that the Revolution is simply a development of Christianity, but:

> . . . if there was but one actor, there would be no drama, no real crisis; the struggle we witness is a pure illusion, and while the world appears to stir, in reality it remains immobile. But no, such is not the case. The struggle is all too real. This is not a simulated combat between one and the same being. There are two combatants. (54)

Yet, the Revolution does not aim to end Christianity; it looks to buy it out.

The precise relation between two different actors on the stage of history, Christianity and the Revolution, needs to be spelled out in explicit terms. First, Michelet suggests the much debated concept of accomplishment or fulfillment (or, in Greek, *pleroma*) featured in the "Sermon on the Mount," proposing in effect that the Revolution would be the fulfillment of Christianity in precisely the same way that, from the perspective of Christianity, the messianic event was the fulfillment of the law, or that Christ "accomplished" or "fulfilled" Judaic Law. Michelet writes that "it is in vain that the younger, sure of its life and much more peaceful, says to the older, 'I come, not to abolish, but to accomplish . . .'" while "the older has absolutely no thoughts of being accomplished" (54). And yet the allusion lingers, even if it is "in vain" that the Revolution says to the religion of the *ancien regime* I have come as your accomplishment, Michelet provides no alternatives. To define more precisely the nature of this fulfillment, Michelet writes that "the Revolution both continues and contradicts Christianity, it is at the same time its inheritor and its adversary." Indeed, what he suggests here is that the relation between Christianity and the Revolution is precisely the fulfillment in the sense of the much debated Greek word *pleroma*, which is, not by chance, central to understanding Christianity's own perception concerning the law and grace as well as the Old and the New Testaments. It is, therefore, Michelet's ambiguous appropriation of this term, *pleroma*, on which the weight of his political theology rests.

Traditionally, since at least Martin Luther's remarks on the subject, the Sermon on the Mount has been perceived as fundamentally apolitical, functioning as the proof that Christianity could never foster a theocracy (a point, I will simply mention in passing, that history itself refutes time and again). For instance, Otto von Bismarck, Chancellor of Germany, insisted that "no State can be ruled by the Sermon on the Mount."[16] W. D. Davies, in his book *The Sermon on the Mount*, points to the central role played by the question of authority in the Sermon: Davies suggests that the most significant difference between Moses, who receives the Law on Mount Sinai, and his typological double, Jesus, who "fulfills" the Law on the mount, is that while "Moses was there as a mediator of the Law which he had received from God," Jesus "either gives a new law or a new interpretation of the Law . . . on his own authority."[17] The relation between Jesus and Moses is a dialectical one, operating in view of the foundation of the authority of the Law. God gives the Torah to the Israelites only to expropriate, complete, or fulfill it in the words of Christ, who speaks not on behalf of God, but *in his own voice*. Therefore, it is not the completion of the Law but the authority of Christ that is shocking: "The multitudes were astonished at his teachings, for he taught them as one who had authority" (Matt. VII.28). A central dimension of the Sermon, therefore, is the refounding of the law on the authority of a single individual – Jesus. Moreover, Davies suggests that the Sermon's crux – "not an iota, not a dot will pass from the law until all is accomplished/fulfilled"[18] – is in fact a refutation of the Pauline doctrine of grace that had so thoroughly devalued "works" as necessary for salvation that morality had been lost in the transaction (92). The Sermon, according to Davies, is a reconstitution of the Law over and against a Pauline notion of grace.

Like Davies, Michelet appropriates the Sermon's term "accomplishment" in order to re-establish the notion of the law and justice over against a Pauline notion of grace, which he associates with the arbitrary judgment of tyranny. However, against Davies' notion that it is the incarnation of Christ that provides a new foundation for the law, Michelet argues that "the advent of the Law, the resurrection of Rights, and the reaction of Justice" takes place precisely as the undoing of the Christian notion of the Incarnation. He must write his history, because his generation has "forgotten that the eighteenth century founded liberty on the enfranchisement of the mind, [which was until] then bound down by the flesh, bound to the material principle of the double incarnation, theological and political, kingly and sacerdotal." As such, Michelet points to the parody of the incarnation perpetuated by the monarchy that, reversing the Pauline opposition of spirit and flesh, binds the spirit of the law to the corruptible and finite human flesh of the monarch. In addition, the arbitrariness of Pauline grace makes the monarch all the more necessary: as "man has a need for justice," Michelet writes, and "as he is a captive in the precinct of a dogma depending entirely on God's arbitrary grace, he believes to secure justice in the political sphere, creating from man a *God of justice*, hoping that this visible God will guard the light of equity which the other [God] has obscured" (67). The political and theological logics, therefore, intersect in order for the former to counteract the latter: if, according to Pauline Christianity (which Michelet says determines the Catholic Church of France as well as the Protestants), the Incarnation nullifies works in favor of grace, a political incarnation appears necessary as its counterbalance.

In this light, Michelet's position vis-à-vis the Incarnation appears entirely unique in the history of the Revolution, and he develops it through the appropriation and transformation of Christianity's scaffolding. Prior to the Revolution, the unity of the French nation rested entirely, as Michelet writes, "on the notion of incarnation, either religious or political. A human god, a god in the flesh was necessary to unify the Church or the State. Human weakness ascribes its unity to a sign, a visible sign, living, a man, an individual" (75). This "material condition" for human community was, however, at odds with what Michelet called the "spiritual community," and it is precisely this community that the Revolution worked to realize.

Nevertheless, what then is the principle of unity for the new, revolutionary community underlying the structure of the burgeoning French Republic? What must take place in order to reverse the adverse effects of a political regime grounded on the Christian logic of incarnation resulting from law and justice having been supplanted by grace, the term Michelet finds most politically dubious? Certainly, one reads in these pages the clichés of Michelet's romantic return to the living community and rhythms of natural history. However, more precisely, Michelet focuses on the question of the voice: referring to the work of Rousseau (who, along with Voltaire, Michelet singles out as the intellectual precursors of the Revolution), he writes that even counterrevolutionaries who "don't listen to [Rousseau's] words, are nonetheless subjugated by the music. . . . The gods' profound harmony, thundering tempestuously on the banks from the Rhine to the

Alps, has itself felt the all-powerful incantation of the sweet melody of the simple human voice . . ." (80).

The voice of Rousseau, like the people uprising during the Revolution, comes to us, not in the immediate living presence of the incarnation of the individual human form, but in the voice that reaches us from beyond the grave, once its physical presence is no longer there. In this respect, Michelet's project is a turning to the past, not simply as an historian, but as an evangelist of the new gospel that bears witness to the advent of the law which takes place as a shift from a politics of the bodily incarnation to the disincarnated voice of the people. *The History of the French Revolution* is itself this new gospel which, mirroring the relationship of fulfillment of the two halves of the Christian Bible: recording the voice emerging during the Revolution, making the Revolution not simply a rejection of religion, and a return to nature, but an appropriation and inhabitation of the very Christian logic that Michelet hopes to counteract. Like a new, revolutionary Paul, Michelet writes the yet unfilled promise of revolutionary messianism, the entire force of which is determined as its writing and its voice cancels a fallen political order of the flesh. However, Michelet's secularism, rather than simply rejecting the discourse of Christianity, adapts its formal structures, turning them against themselves. More precisely, while the formal aspects of Christian discourse remain intact, especially the temporal or historical structures associated with a messianic expectation, Michelet's transformation of this explicitly theological discourse evacuates its content, like the palimpsest of the Pantheon and the Champs de Mars. Michelet's text is a polemic against Christianity that transposes messiansim into the discourse of Revolutionary history by making one significant alteration: the erasure of the incarnation. As such, Michelet's political–theological presentation of the secular Revolution becomes a messianism without a messiah, a messianism that promises the coming not of an individual human, but of the "advent of humanity" or of a people, which can itself never be embodied.

Notes

1 Claude Lefort, "On the Permanence of the Theologico-Political?," in *Democracy and Political Theory* (Minnesota, Minneapolis: University of Minnesota Press, 1989); "The Revolution as New Religion," in *Writing: The Political Test*, edited and translated by David Ames Curtis (Durham: Duke University Press, 2000).

2 Georges Bataille, *Literature and Evil*, translated by Alastair Hamilton (London: Marion Boyars Publishers, 2001); Roland Barthes, "Michelet, Today" and "Michelet's Modernity," in *The Rustle of Language*, translated by Richard Howard (Berkeley: University of California Press, 1989); Bettina Lerner, "Michelet, Mythologue" in *Yale French Studies*, edited by Dan Edelstein and Bettina Lerner, 111 (2007), 61–72.

3 "Revolution as New Religion," 159. While certainly the discourse of political theology appears to have been at the forefront of religion's resuscitation within academia, it was also notably shadowed by the unlikely reemergence of philosophical work on St. Paul by prominent figures such as Giorgio Agamben and Alain Badiou. Badiou's book, however, reminds us that Paul has never been marginal to the philosophical tradition: "Hegel, Auguste Comte, Nietzsche, Freud, Heidegger, and again in our own time, Jean-François Lyotard, have found it necessary to examine the figure of Paul and have done so, more or less, in terms of some extreme dispositions" (5). And yet, even against the horizon of these "extreme dispositions," Badiou's treatment of Paul appears to be unique. Indeed, the objective is the distilling from this religious figure, the religious content of which is a mere "fable," a model of secular and revolutionary universality. Badiou, *Saint Paul: The Foundations of Universalism*, translated by Ray Brassier (Stanford: Stanford University Press, 2003).

4 Marie-Hélène Huet, *Mourning Glory: The Will of the French Revolution* (Philadelphia: University of Pennsylvania Press, 1997), 101.

5 Maximilien Robespierre, "On the Principle of Political Morality" in *Robespierre: Virtue and Terror* (London: Verso, 2007), 109.

6 *History of the French Revolution*, translated by C. Cocks (London: H.G. Bohn, 1847).

7 *History of the French Revolution*.

8 Huet, *Mourning Glory: The Will of the French Revolution*, 102.

9 From Diderot's addendum to *Bougainville's Voyage* quoted by Ernst Cassirer, *Philosophy of the Enlightenment*, translated by Koelln and Pettegrove (Princeton: Princeton University Press, 1951), 135.

10 M. H. Abrams, *Natural Supernaturalism: Tradition and Revolution in Romantic Literature* (New York: W.W. Norton and Company, 1971).

11 Michelet, *Histoire de la Révolution française* (Paris: Éditions Robert Laffont, 1979), 6–7 (my translation).

12 *Histoire de la Révolution française*, 6–7 (my translation).

13 Carl Schmitt, *Political Theology: Four Chapters on the Concept of Sovereignty*, translated by George Schwab, edited by Tracy B. Strong (Chicago: University of Chicago Press, 2006).

14 So, rather than the analogy developed within the Marxist hagiographies, such as Alain Badiou's recent work on St. Paul or even Passolini's unfinished film of St. Paul's mapped onto a Nazi-occupied France, both of which equate the Christ–Paul relation with that of Marx–Lenin, here Michelet situates himself as an evangelist of the Revolutionary event. At the same time, however, Michelet attacks the Pauline inversion of the relation between law and grace, arguing in fact that Revolution is precisely the return of justice and the law over and against the Christian regime of grace.

[15] Jean-Jacques Rousseau, *The Social Contract*, translated by Maurice Cranston (London: Penguin Books, 1968) 178.

[16] Pinchas Lapide, *The Sermon on the Mount: Utopia or Program for Action* (Chicago: Orbis Books, 1986). Lapide outlines eight "misinterpretations" of the Sermon, the fourth of which is the contrast between the utopianism of the Sermon and the "sober realpolitik of the past four thousand years of world history" (5). This utopia, Lapide argues, is "something without place, not of this world, homeless on our earth and so of no consequence whatever for politics."

[17] W. D. Davies, *The Sermon on the Mount* (Cambridge: Cambridge University Press, 2000).

[18] Lapide suggests that "fulfillment" is a weak translation because, despite the fact that the gospel is written in Greek, "'fulfill', which, when used in connection to the Torah, is alien to the Semitic spirit of the language" (18). He suggests that "for Jews it is the words (1) 'keep' (Matt. 19:17), (2) 'do' (Rom. 2:12), or (3) 'establish' in the sense of (4) 'make effective'." Rather than "ending" or "finishing" the Law, the Sermon, according to Lapide, is concerned with "establishing" the Law. In that both texts are concerned with making the law effective, the comparison of their political agendas becomes substantially more obvious.

Chapter 10

Postface: The Signature that Remains

Sophie Fuggle

Over the past two decades, there has been a shift in continental philosophy toward what might be termed "post-secular" modes of thinking. While there is always something suspicious and slightly disingenuous about the use of the prefix "post," it serves here as a useful umbrella term for delineating a whole series of philosophical engagements with overtly Christian, and more specifically, New Testament motifs. It also attests to the long-overdue recognition on the part of political thinkers that religion and belief can no longer be subtracted from questions of government and state. Thus, where Michel Foucault's journalistic accounts of the 1978 Iranian Revolution were deemed an enormous *faux pas* due to his failure to appreciate the emancipatory force of religion within the collective consciousness of the Iranian people, recent work by philosophers, such as Slavoj Žižek and Alain Badiou, who proclaim themselves atheist, acknowledge the need, post-9/11, for a heightened engagement with religion head on.

There are perhaps two things at stake in this shift that bear specific relevance here. First of all, returning to the founding moments of Christianity might be considered as part of a move to radically contest all subsequent religious and political categories of thought, institutional authority and academic disciplines. According to Ward Blanton, the recent appropriations of Christian motifs do not merely call for a rethinking of boundaries, but constitute in themselves the very process of rethinking or reconfiguring existing categories of the religious and secular.[1] Thinking about recent shifts in continental philosophy as a "return" to religion is therefore not particularly helpful, given that, as Blanton, puts it, "secular thought never really left the orbit of religion." (19) Instead, a more useful activity might involve consideration of the reconfigurations of existing relationships and boundaries between both academic disciplines and state and religious institutions.

Secondly, any such "return" or reconfiguration of the relationship between religious and secular does not simply involve bracketing out all that came after the founding moments of Christianity. After an initial attempt to do away with centuries of institutional discourse, such discourse becomes itself subjected to a rereading in light of what Žižek, Badiou, and others have referred to as the "new" and "urgent" status of early Christian motifs. A twofold process occurs where Saint Paul is cast by Badiou as a militant revolutionary and, in turn, his theology of the event becomes the lens through which social and political revolution, whether secular or religious, is read.

While remaining critical to the specific motives driving the recent blurring of religious and secular categories of thought, the dismantling of such categories has at certain points resulted in the articulation of new methodologies for thinking about the secularization thesis. Most notable here is Giorgio Agamben's development and critique of Carl Schmitt's *Political Theology*. Agamben's work constitutes an attempt to rethink modern forms of government in terms of what he terms an "economic theology" in contradistinction to Schmitt's political theology. Therefore, in order to explore one of the ways in which a fruitful dialogue might be set up between the recent turn to religion in continental thought and the contestations of traditional categories of thought pertaining to the early modern period, this essay will focus on Agamben's theory of the signature that he develops in relation to his recent work on economic theology. I will suggest how the signature provides a useful methodological tool for rethinking the secularization process.

The Signature of All Things

As Philip S. Gorski explains, the secularization debate can be articulated in terms of two major, well-documented paradigms. Put very simply, the first identifies a trend of religious decline occurring in Europe from the eighteenth century onwards, whereas the second or "new" paradigm looks to increased participation in religious worship and activity, in order to demonstrate how religion has continued to flourish up until the present day. Taking into account the enormous divergence between thinkers associated with the first paradigm, including among others Comte, Durkheim, and Weber, Gorski suggests that what all these thinkers have in common is their recognition of the process of differentiation that occurs through secularization, and which results in increasingly defined parameters delineating secular and religious practices and institutions.[2] Secularization, in that case, might be defined not as the process whereby God and belief are removed from society at large but, rather, cordoned off into specific areas of daily life. Thus, where the first paradigm is primarily taken up with this process of demarcation, the "new" paradigm assumes as its object of study the participation in activities falling within areas demarcated as "religious." Hence, rather than considering the two paradigms as irreconcilable, according to Gorski, it is actually possible to see how they complement one another (143).

However, what is at stake in our own current moment is the refusal of religion to remain relegated to the "sacred" spaces of society, forcefully reimposing itself on all spheres of life, most notably those deemed categorically "secular": education, healthcare, and politics. The ongoing debates surrounding the 2004 law prohibiting the "foulard" and other forms of religious dress in French schools is just one pertinent example. The reconciliation of the two paradigms no longer seems relevant or even possible in light of recent political and social events worldwide. Simply attempting to maintain some sort of balance between their respective objectives seems counterintuitive and has led to violent repercussions. Here, it is useful to consider Agamben's "theory of signatures" as a potential "third" paradigm, enacting a radical revision of what is at stake for modern and contemporary forms of government in the processes whereby Church and state, the religious and the political, became separate entities. Agamben offers us a historical appreciation of this process of differentiation, while at the same time denying the possibility that such a process can ever be fulfilled or completed.

Agamben's point of departure is *Les Mots et les choses*, where Foucault identifies the signature as located within the Renaissance episteme of resemblance and similitude. During the Renaissance, a number of "sciences" including astrology and physiognomy emerged, whose main objective consisted of decoding a series of outer signs considered as key to acquiring a deeper understanding and knowledge of an object's inner being.[3] For example, according to Paracelsus, a sixteenth-century astrologer and alchemist, every object bears a number of external signs or marks that, when deciphered, reveal a concealed essence or nature.[4] Physiognomy is perhaps the most obvious example of how outer physical properties, the shape of the skull or distance between the eyes, bears witness to an individual's innate character (34). Thus conceived, a signature does not constitute a sign or a mark as such, but denotes a practice; the act of reading signs and marks appearing on the surface of an object. The conclusions drawn by this practice render it at the same time a form of writing, as the essence or inner nature is inscribed onto the object (56).

Combining Foucault's notion of signature with his subsequent analysis of the *énoncé* in *L'Archéologie du savoir*, Agamben develops a more complex yet clearer conception of signature. For Foucault, the *énoncé* can be defined as a phrase, proposition, statement, or, indeed, a set of statements that can be made or uttered within the parameters of a specific socio-historic context.[5] Foucault is not concerned here with the conformity of a phrase or statement to grammatical and syntactical rules, but rather that which he refers to as the "enunciative function": the efficacy of the utterance. How successfully does it perform its prescribed function at a given moment? Hence, it is the social conditions which render a certain statement possible and effective that are of relevance here, as opposed to the linguistic tools employed in making such a statement. Agamben suggests that Foucault's concept of the *énoncé* might be better understood if we were to situate it in the interstice of what Émile Benveniste has called the unbridgeable gap that separates semiology (the system of signs) and hermeneutics (the art of interpretation) (60–1). This is also the space where signatures come into play. It is by supplementing existing theories of linguistic signification with a theory of signatures that this unbridgeable gap might eventually be bridged (61). A signature functions both as a sign, a form of marking and, at the same time, offers up an interpretation of the sign. Considering the *énoncé* in terms of action or practice belonging to a specific moment is essential to Agamben's understanding of signature. This is because the *énoncé* attests to the impossibility of the sign that pre-exists or transcends the discursive moment. There is no such thing as the "pure and unmarked sign." A sign can never signify or designate "univocally and once and for all" (64).

The ability of a sign to signify is dependent upon it carrying the signature. However, the latter will always determine in advance its interpretation, conveying its use and efficacy according to the rules and practices that demand recognition within a specific context (64). There are three main implications of this. First, it is important to reiterate that a signature does not take the form of a concept. Second, it should instead be conceived in terms of a movement, the process of reading that is also an act of writing, and not as a static, fixed identity or term. Third, the signature is the process whereby a given doctrine, discourse, or practice is transferred from one domain to another by way of a series of displacements and substitutions.

Secularization constitutes one of Agamben's major examples of the signature. Secularization, he points out, should not be conceived as a concept but as a signature. It is the process not, as Max Weber claimed, whereby society becomes disillusioned with theology and religion and abandons it outright but, in fact, as Carl Schmitt suggests, the means by which religion remains ever present in modern society.[6] For Schmitt, it is not simply a question of transferring power from the divine to the human sphere. The notion of sovereignty whether considered in terms of God, a monarch, or the State is dependent upon the exception. As Schmitt points out, "Sovereign is he who decides on the exception."[7] Where this once took the form of divine intervention into human affairs in the form of the miracle, with secularization, the exception is transferred to the realm of jurisprudence. For Schmitt, secularization does not simply appropriate existing theological ideas or concepts but in recognizing that the primacy of the exception maintains the same "systematic structure" (36).

Secularization, therefore, does not constitute an emptying out of the religious dimension of social and political practices and structures. The persistence of the religious or transcendental within secular institutions and thought does not take the form of an ever-diminishing residue or trace but, instead, constitutes the means by which the religious embeds itself in the secular via a series of shifts and substitutions. Hence, through secularization, the theological leaves its mark, conceived as a trajectory, on the political while avoiding a direct correlation between political and theological identities. However, in his consideration of an alternative political paradigm to Schmitt's political theology in *Il Regno e la Gloria*, Agamben demonstrates how the secularization process posited by Schmitt is deeply problematic not least in the hierarchical structure it sets up with theology as a point of origin for later secular forms of government.

Agamben defines his project not in terms of establishing a causal hierarchy that posits theology as an originary form of secular mode of government.[8] Like Foucault and Nietzsche before him, Agamben sees any such quest for origins as highly problematic. Thus, in clarifying his use of an archaeological approach, he makes it clear that what is at stake is very much the idea of history as the way of explaining the present but in terms and according to concepts that only belong in the present. Therefore, we must concede that any access we may have to a source or origin can only ever be via tradition, and it is tradition that bars access to the source. Tradition constitutes our way of understanding the past and, as such, never actually belongs to the past and can never allow us access to the past. It refers to an experience that is always a non-experience existing only in the present, never in the past:

> But what does the scholar seek to return to when engaging in a critique of tradition and the canon? Clearly the problem here is not merely philological, because even the necessary philological precautions for such inquiry are complicated when dealing with *Urgeschichte* and *Entsehung*. It is not possible to gain access in a new way, beyond tradition, to the sources without putting in question the very historical subject who is supposed to gain access to them. What is in question, then, is the epistemological paradigm of enquiry itself.[9]

The Empty Throne

Economic theology is proposed by Agamben as an epistemological paradigm in order to provide an in-depth account of how religious assumptions about the relation between power and governmentality are themselves structured upon the notion of management or administration of individuals and resources prevalent in Western society today. Agamben's study of economic theology is not about finding the theological origin of Western modes of government or suggesting the way in which these origins have been concealed from us. Rather, he is interested in the ways in which conceptions of the trinity emerging in the second and third centuries, and which were structured around the notion of *oikonomia* rather than the political, might provide a useful archaeological site for exploring mechanisms of governmentality that continue to operate within Western society.[10]

Agamben distinguishes two major political paradigms as emerging from Christian theology: political theology and economic theology. A very specific notion of paradigm is key to Agamben's archaeological method and it is worth outlining this briefly here before considering in more detail its application to the categories of political and economic theology. Agamben draws on both Foucault's frequent use of paradigm and on Thomas Kuhn's definition of the term. Foucault frequently references the term "paradigm" yet fails to offer any clarification of the term itself. The most notable instance is perhaps his account of the Panopticon as both specific example and theoretical concept. Conversely, Thomas Kuhn provides a twofold definition in *The Structure of Scientific Revolutions*. The first definition involves the identification of common criteria, rules, or values belonging to a certain form of scientific knowledge. The second refers to the example commonly evoked to explain the rules and values pertaining to a group or set and in acting as the example *par excellence* that exceeds its position and function as simply one among many examples or instances.[11] Moreover, where there is an absence of established rules and values, the paradigm becomes the means by which such parameters are formulated. Consequently, the paradigm constitutes both the object of analysis and the conditions under which such analysis might be carried out.

Thus viewed, the paradigms of political and economic theology present us with competing objects or examples of the secularization process, which, in turn, define the conditions of possibility of this process. As such, the two paradigms are mutually exclusive in terms of the specific statements they make, yet co-exist as epistemological modes of enquiry. Where political theology, as most notably articulated by Schmitt, incorporates modern theories of sovereignty and political thought, economic theology, on the other hand, gives rise to biopolitics and the management of all aspects of social life.[12] Moreover, the difference between the two paradigms is not simply conceptual but also structural. Political theology takes as its object the once present sovereign power whose absence has been filled by a series of secular counterparts that assume their power through occupying the site once belonging to the sacred without ever identifying directly with it. Economic theology posits the sacred as having always been absent.

Agamben identifies *oikonomia* as a key problematic in the work of both Schmitt and his adversary Erik Petersen.[13] While working on the debates between Schmitt and Petersen, it becomes apparent that important references to *oikonomia* were deliberately excluded or bracketed from their discussions of political theology. As a result, Agamben became preoccupied with mapping out *oikonomia* as a missing fragment, and in doing so reconstructing it in terms of a political paradigm, an economic theology in contradistinction to political theology. His genealogy of *oikonomia* takes as its starting point Foucault's discussion in *L'Usage des plaisirs* of *oikos*, conceived as the domain of the household and family in contradistinction to the *polis*.[14] However, where Foucault identifies an art of government operating within different domains – the political, the military, and the economic – Agamben emphasizes a sharp opposition between politics and economy. Politics is posited in terms of the legal and judicial, whereas economy constitutes management and administration. Agamben stresses this opposition in order to bring these two spheres together under the notion of government. He achieves this via the paradigm of the trinity that emerged during the second and third centuries.

Agamben explains how the use of the Greek term *oikonomia* was employed in early Christian doctrine. As such, his work complements much recent scholarship, which is focused on identifying a strong Stoic and Cynic influence in the teachings of Paul.[15] According to Agamben, references to *oikonomia* can be traced back to the Pauline epistles where the term used to explain the task that God has given the apostle, the duty that God has conferred upon him to preach the message about Jesus Christ. In 1 Corinthians 9:17 and Colossians 1:25, Paul defines his role as being commissioned or administered to him by God. Moreover, the use of the term *oikonomia* in Ephesians 3 makes it clear that what is being administered is precisely God's mystery: "for surely you have already heard of the commission [*oikonomia*] of God's grace that was given to me for you, and how the mystery was made known to me by revelation" (Ephesians 3.2-3). Yet, in the centuries that followed, a radical reversal of the terms "mystery" and "economy" takes place. This reversal is largely attributed to the third-century theologians Hippolytus and Tertullian. The focus shifts from divine power as a mystery that defies human comprehension to its administration on earth. *Oikonomia*, administration, becomes the mystery itself and no longer simply refers to its management. Of central importance in this shift are the categories of divine being and activity or praxis.

The doctrine of the trinity, which emerges in the fourth century, functions as the means of explaining God's ability to govern on earth while remaining transcendent (94). The distinction made between father, son, and Holy Spirit should not be considered as denoting ontological categories; it is not a question of different beings or even modes of being but, rather, the distinction between being and praxis initially set out by Hippolytus and Tertullian. The paradigm of the trinity facilitates this relationship between the immanent and transcendent (75).

Subsequently, we arrive at a paradox whereby God governs the world, yet the world always remains other. As a result, the relationship between sovereignty and governmentality is always vicarious. Moreover, it is impossible to access ultimate power since it is always deferred from one realm to the other. This is why, Agamben claims, in modern forms of government, there can never be one person held accountable or absolutely responsible. There is no substance to power. It is pure economy, the art of management.

Hence, where political theology is concerned with maintaining a noncoincidence between secular and religious forms of political authority, economic theology attests to the absence of such authority, the gap between divine power and its administration. Hence, the motif of the empty throne often found in Byzantine churches is described by Agamben as "possibly the most pregnant symbol of power."[16] Power operates most effectively when its source is indicated yet absent. The empty throne constitutes the space left empty by and for God, suggesting a presence that has been and will be again. Action and decisions may be made in the name of the absent authority, while at the same time answerability and responsibility for such action can always be deferred to the higher authority who is not there to respond. For Agamben, this is precisely how modern forms of government function in their abdication of culpability for actions they have committed in the name of others.

Using his theory of the signature to map out a genealogy of the economic, theology emerges not as a point of origin but, rather, as being itself caught up in the process whereby the sacred absents itself through the deferral and administration of its power. In this sense, an archaeology of the secularization thesis based on the paradigm of an economic theology involves what Agamben terms a "retroactive effect" on theology itself (19). The moment in which the sacred is perpetually deferred occurs not during secularization but has already taken place within Christian theology. Conceived thus, it is secularization and not its perceived religious "origins" that comes to represent the point of departure for a doubling back, in which the very grounds of its relationship to religious doctrine and practice are radically contested.

Moreover, in his identification of a new paradigm through which we might rethink existing secularization debates, much of what is at stake in such debates also undergoes critical re-evaluation. The diachronic and synchronic categories defining the parameters of research in terms of historical period and geographical location are displaced by the analogical in the paradigm. As singularity, the example operating as paradigm is isolated from its context in order to provide both the definition and problematization of the context as such.[17] Thus, within this volume, the secularization thesis should be considered not simply as one aspect or area of enquiry in relation to the diachronic and synchronic categories of early modern France. Rather, the political events regarded as belonging to these categories and symptomatic of the secularization process should instead be considered as defining the very conditions under which terms such as "modernity" are brought into existence as epistemological categories.

Conclusion – Toward a New Form of Historical Enquiry

Agamben's signature unravels a process of folding whereby theology is always already caught up in the process whereby the sacred is substituted, deferred, and absented, thus challenging what is at stake in secularization itself. His reworking of Foucault's archaeology as the study of *what will have been* highlights the importance of mapping out an economic theology in order to rethink modern forms of government beyond Schmitt's original paradigm. In doing so, Agamben's project not only provides new epistemological categories for thinking about the relationship between politics and theology, but his methodology, which involves a return to long-abandoned structuralist motifs, most notably Foucault's archaeological method, demonstrates both the importance and difficulty of reconciling philosophical and historical analysis in thinking through secularization.

The secularization process cannot be pinned down as something that occurred or even which is still occurring within Western society. For Agamben, an "archeological philosophy" is concerned with the future anterior, *what will have been.* In this sense, his method should not be considered as purely structuralist. Rather than emptying out historical contingency, Agamben's method is imbued with an ethico-moral dimension heavily influenced by Walter Benjamin's weak messianic power. In *On the Concept of History*, Benjamin describes history as a promise, the weak power that represents the hold which the past has over the present.[18] The role of the historian is therefore to redeem this past. In its redemption of history from the "tradition" that blocks our very access to it – the tradition, moreover, which retroactively legitimizes the violence of sovereign exception – archaeology involves intertwining the past and future in the form of *what will have been.*[19]

To go backwards through the course of history, as the archaeologist does, means returning, through the work of creation, in order to give back to the salvation from which it originates. Similarly, Benjamin made redemption a fully historical category, one opposed in every sense to the apologia of bad historians. And not only is archaeology the immanent a priori of historiography, but the gesture of the archaeologist constitutes the paradigm of every true human action (108).

It is worth noting the theologico-salvific dimension by way of conclusion, albeit briefly. While on the one hand it rescues Agamben's method from the criticism of ahistoricism leveled at earlier structuralist accounts of historical process, it nevertheless raises issues in terms of the specific relationship between theology and politics in his own work. Moreover, understanding this relationship is perhaps essential to any subsequent adoption or appropriation of his method. Secularization is not complete and, according to Agamben's economic theology, cannot ever be completed since it does not constitute an emptying out but rather a perpetual deferral of sovereign authority. Identifying what is at stake in the secularization process therefore has as much to do with contemporary political concerns as it does with earlier moments in the history of Western government.

Notes

1. Ward Blanton, *Displacing Christian Origins: Philosophy, Secularity and the New Testament* (Chicago, IL and London: Chicago University Press, 2007), 5.
2. Philip S. Gorski, "Historicizing the Secularization Debate: Church, State, and Society in Late Medieval and Early Modern Europe, ca 1300 to 1700," *American Sociological Review*, 65:1 (February, 2000), 138–67, 140.
3. Michel Foucault, *Les Mots et les choses: une archéologie des sciences humaines* (Paris: Gallimard, 1966).
4. Giorgio Agamben, *Signatura Rerum: Sul Metodo* (Torino: Bollati Boringhieri, 2008); page references are to the English translation *The Signature of All Things: On Method*, translated by Luca D'Isanto (New York, NY: Zone Books, 2009), 33ff.
5. Michel Foucault, *L'Archéologie du savoir* (Paris: Gallimard, 1969).
6. See Max Weber, *The Protestant Ethic and the Spirit of Capitalism* (London: Unwin University Books, 1971); Carl Schmitt, *Political Theology: Four Chapters on the Concept of Sovereignty* (Chicago: University of Chicago Press, 2005).
7. Schmitt, 5.
8. Agamben, *Il regno e la gloria. Per una genealogia teologica dell'economia e del governo* (Milano: Neri Pozza, 2007). Page references are to the French translation *Le Règne et la gloire: pour une généalogie théologique de l'économie et du gouvernement*, translated by Joël Gayraud and Martin Rueff (Paris: Seuil, 2008). 13.
9. Agamben, *Signature of All things*, 89.
10. *Signature of All Things*, 113.
11. *Signature of All Things*, 11.
12. Agamben, *Il regno e la gloria*, 17.
13. The debate between Schmitt and Petersen emerged as a result of a footnote in Petersen's *Der Monotheisms* in which he argued for the theological impossibility of Schmitt's political theology. This is said to have prompted to Schmitt to write *Political Theology II: The Legend of the Elimination of any kind of Political Theology*. Petersen's claim is based on the theological argument that the eschatological kingdom of God can in no way resemble secular, earthly existence. Striving toward a political utopia can only ever be commensurate with the coming of the Anti-Christ. For a full discussion of the Schmitt–Petersen debate, see György Geréby, "Carl Schmitt and Erik Peterson on the Problem of Political Theology: A Footnote to Kantorowicz" in *Monotheistic Kingship: The Medieval Variants*, edited by Aziz Al-Azmeh and János M. Bak (Budapest: CEU Medievalia, 2004), 31–61.

14 Foucault. *L'Usage des plaisirs. Histoire de la sexualité II* (Paris: Gallimard, 1984), 199ff.
15 See, for example, Troels Engberg-Pedersen, *Paul and the Stoics* (Edinburgh: T&T Clark, 2000); Abraham J. Malherbe, *Paul and the Popular Philosophers* (Minneapolis: Fortress Press, 1989); Gerald F. Downing, *Cynics, Paul and the Pauline Churches* (London and New York, NY: Routledge, 1998). Foucault's works on Stoic and Cynic forms of self-transformation and care have also been co-opted into discussions of the Greek influence on Pauline doctrine and early Christianity. See, in particular, Halvor Moxnes, "Asceticism and Christian Identity in Antiquity: A Dialogue with Foucault and Paul," *Journal for the Study of the New Testament*, 26:1 (2003), 3–29.
16 "le symbole sans doute le plus prégnant du pouvoir," 15.
17 *Signature of All Things*, 18.
18 Walter Benjamin, "On the Concept of History" in *Selected Writings: Volume Four* (Cambridge, MA: Belknap Press, 2003), 389–411.
19 *Signature of All Things*, 106.

Bibliography

Primary Sources

Anon. *Relation de l'Autho-da-Fé de Lisbonne* (Paris: 1761).

Archives parlementaires de 1787 à 1860 (Paris: 1875).

Bailly, Jean-Sylvain. *Lettres à M. Bailly sur l'histoire primitive de la Grèce* (Paris: 1787).

Bergier, Nicolas-Sylvestre. *Examen du matérialisme*. 2 vols. (Paris: Humblot, 1771).

Berruyer, Isaac-Joseph. *Histoire du Peuple de Dieu depuis son origine jusqu'à la naissance du Messie, tirée des seuls livres saints, ou le texte sacré des livres de l'ancien Testament, réduit en un corps d'histoire*. Nouvelle édition. 10 vols. (Paris: 1753).

—. *Histoire du peuple de Dieu, depuis la naissance du Messie jusqu'à la fin du Synogogue* (La Haye: 1753).

Bertereau, Martine. *La restitution de Pluton a Monseigneur l'Eminentissime cardinal duc de Richelieu: des mines & minieres de France, cachées & detenuës jusques à present au ventre de la terre: par le moyen desquelles les finances de sa majesté seront beaucoup plus grandes que cells de tous les princes chrestiens . . . : ensemble la raison pourquoy les ditesmines . . . ont estè iusques à present presque inutiles & sans profit* (Paris: Hervé du Mesnil, 1640).

Biblia sacra vulgatam versionem. Edited by Bonifatio Fischer, Johannae Gribomont, H. D. F. Sparks, and W. Thiele. 2 vols. 3rd ed. (Stuttgart: 1983).

Bodin, Jean. *Les Six Livres de la République* (Paris: Fayard, 1986).

Bossuet, Jacques Bénigne. *Politique tirée des propres paroles de l'Écriture sainte 1709*. Edited by Jacques Le Brun (Geneva: Librairie Droz, 1967).

—. *Instruction sur les estats d'oraison, où sont exposées les erreurs des faux mystiques de nos jours: Avec les actes de leur condamnation* (Paris: Chez Jean Anisson, 1697).

—. *De la Connaissance de Dieu et de soi-même*. Edited by Émile Charles (Paris: Librairie classique d'Eugène Belin, 1875).

—. *Relation sur le quiétisme* (Paris: J. Anisson, 1698).

Bourdeille, Pierre de. *Œuvres complètes de Pierre de Bourdeille, Seigneur de Brantôme*. Edited by Ludovic Lalande (Paris: Société de l'histoire de France, 1864–82).

Boursier, Laurent. *De l'action de Dieu sur les créatures* (Paris: Babuty, 1713).

Butel-Dumont, Georges-Marie. *Théorie du luxe; ou Traité dans lesquel on entreprend d'établir que le Luxe est un ressort non-seulement utile, mais même indispensablement nécessaire à la prosperité des Etats*. 2 vols. (1771).

Calvin, Jean. *Traitté des reliques* (Geneva: Pierre de la Rouiere, 1599).

Campanella, Tommaso. *Monarchie d'Espagne et Monarchie de France*. Edited by Germana Ernst (Paris: Presses Universitaires de France, 1997).

Casteglione, *Il Cortegiano* (Paris: Garnier-Flammarion, 1991).

Catéchisme du Concile de Trente (Bouère: Éditions Dominique Martin Morin, 1984).

Caussade, Jean-Pierre de. *Instructions spirituelles, en forme de dialogues sur les divers états d'oraison* (Perpignan: Jean-Baptiste Reynier, 1741).

Concina, Daniele. *Della storia del probabilismo e del rigorismo: dissertazioni teologiche, morali, e critiche* (Venice: 1748).

Condamnation et prohibition faite par nostre tres-Saint Pere le Pape Innocent XII. du livre imprimé à Paris l'an MDCXCVII. qui a pour titre: 'Explication des maximes des saints sur la vie intérieure, &c.' In *Relation des actes et déliberations concernant la Constitution en forme de bref de N. S. le Pape Innocent XII* (Paris: Chez François Muguet, 1700).

Condorcet, Marie Jean Antoine Nicolas de Caritat, marquis de. *Esquisse d'un tableau historique des progrès de l'esprit humain* (Paris: 1795).

Court de Gébelin, Antoine. *Histoire du monde primitive, analysé et comparé avec le monde moderne* (Paris: 1773–83).

Descartes, René. *Discours de la méthode.* Introduction and notes by Etienne Gilson (Paris: J. Vrin, 1989).

Dictionnaire de l'Académie française. 4th ed. 2 vols. (Paris: Brunet, 1762).

Dupuis, Charles-François. *Abrégé de l'origine de tous les cultes* (Paris: 1797).

Encyclopédie, ou Dictionnaire raisonné des sciences, des arts et des métiers, par une société de gens de lettres. 17 vols. (Paris: Chez Briasson; Neufchâtel: Chez Samuel Faulche et Compagnie, 1751–65).

Fénelon, François de Salignac de La Mothe. *Explication des maximes des saints sur la vie intérieure.* In *Oeuvres.* Edited by Jacques Le Brun. 2 vols. (Paris: Gallimard, 1983).

—. *Démonstration de l'existence de Dieu. Oeuvres* [op. cit.].

—. *Oeuvres spirituelles de Messire François de Salignac de la Mothe-Fénelon.* 2 vols. (Anvers: Henri de la Meule, 1718).

—. *Traité de l'existence et des attributs de Dieu.* In *Oeuvres complètes.* Edited by Jean-Edme-Auguste Gosselin. 10 vols. (Paris, 1848–52; Geneva: Slatkine, 1971).

—. *Plans de gouvernement. In Oeuvres complètes* [op. cit.].

Ferrière, Claude-Joseph de. *Dictionnaire de droit et de pratique.* 2 vols. (Paris: V. Brunet, 1769).

François, Laurent. *Preuves de la religion de Jésus-Christ, contre les spinosistes et les deistes.* 3 vols. (Paris: La Veuve Estienne & Fils, 1751).

Godefroy, Denys. *Advis presenté à la Royne, Pour reduire les Monnoies à leur juste prix & valeur, empescher le surhaussement & empirance d'icelle* (Paris: Pierre Chevalier, 1611).

Grotius, Hugo. *Hugo Grotius: Mare Liberum 1609–2009.* Edited and translated by Robert Fennstra (Leiden: Brill, 2009).

Guyon, Jeanne-Marie. "Le Moyen court et très facile de faire oraison." *Le Moyen court et autres écrits spirituels* (1685). Edited by Marie-Louise Gondal (Grenoble: Éditions Jérôme Millon, 1995).

—. *Lettres chrétiennes et spirituelles sur divers sujets qui regardent la vie intérieure.* 5 vols. (London: 1767).

—. *Correspondence.* 3 vols. Edited by Dominique Tronc (Paris: Honoré Champion, 2003–5).

d'Holbach, Paul Henri Thiry, baron. *Système de la nature, ou Des loix du monde physique & du monde moral.* New ed. 2 vols. (London: 1771).

—. *Le Christianisme dévoilé ou examen des principes et des effets de la religion chrétienne* (London: 1767).

Jamyn, Amadis. *Œuvres poétiques d'Amadis Jamyn. Avec sa vie par Guillaume Colletet.* Edited by Charles Brunet (Paris: Léon Willem, 1878).

Jodelle, Estienne de. *Les œuvres et meslanges poétiques d'Estienne Jodelle.* Edited by Marty-Laveaux (Paris: LeMarre, 1868–70).

—. *Œuvres completes.* Edited by Eneas Balmas. 2 vols. (Paris: Gallimard, 1965).

Karlstadt, Andreas. "On the Removal of Images." *A Reformation Debate: Three Treatises in Translation.* Translated by Bryan D. Mangrum and Giuseppe Scavizzi (Ottawa: Dovehouse Editions, 1991).

[Médicis, Catherine de]. *Lettres de Catherine de Médicis.* Edited by Hector de la Ferrière and Gustave Baguenault de Puchesse (Paris: Imprimerie nationale, 1880–1943).

Le Sainte Concile de Trente oecuménique et général, célébré sous Paul III. Jules III. et Pie IV. souverains pontifes. Translated by Martial Chanut. 3rd ed. (Paris: Sébastien Mabre-Cramoisy, 1686).

Loppin, Isaac. *Advis très juste et légitime au Roy Très Chrétien, pour le repos et soulagement des III Ordres de son Estat et le moyen de dresser une milice de cinquante mil hommes. Ensemble une police exemplaire à tous les Estats, Empires et Républiques de l'Univers, pour la descharges de toutes tailles, taillons, aydes, gabelles et généralement tous subsides et imposts . . .* (Paris: 1648).

—. *Les Mines gallicanes, ou le Thrésor du royaume de France, où sont montrez les droicts du Roy et les moyens justes et légitimes par lesquels . . . Sa Majesté peut avoir . . . les richesses et les utilitez suivantes: I. Mettre par chacun mois, dans ses coffres, neuf millions de livres . . . II. Dresser promptement et entretenir, à peu de frais, une milice de cinquante mil hommes de guerre . . . III. Et . . . l'establissement d'une juste, saincte et chrestienne police* (Paris, 1638).

Maistre, Joseph de. *Œuvres.* Edited by Pierre Glaudes (Paris: Robert Laffont, 2007).

—. *St Petersburg Dialogues or Conversations on the Temporal Government of Providence.* Translated and edited by Richard A. Lebrun (Montreal and Kingston: McGill-Queen's University Press, 1993).

—. *Letters on the Spanish Inquisition.* Translated by John Fletcher (London: Keating, Dolman and Jones, 1838).

Malebranche, Nicolas. *Entretiens sur la Métaphysique et sur la Religion* (Rotterdam: Reinier Leers, 1688).

—. *Traité de Morale* (Rotterdam: Reinier Leers, 1684).

—. *Méditations Chrétiennes et Métaphysiques* (Lyon: Leonard Plaignard, 1707).

—. *Réflexions sur la Prémotion Physique* (Paris: Michel David, 1715).

Marguerite de Navarre. *L'Heptaméron des nouvelles.* Edited by Nicole Cazauran (Paris: Gallimard, 2000).

Marsile Ficin. *Sur le banquet de Platon ou de l'Amour.* Edited by Raymond Marcel (Paris: Les Belles Lettres, 1956).

Masselin, Jehan. *Journal des États Généraux de France tenus à Tours en 1484.* Edited by A. Bernier (Paris: Imprimerie Royale, 1835).

Montesquieu, Charles de Secondat, baron de. *The Spirit of Laws.* Translated and edited by Anne M. Cohler, Basia C. Miller, and Harold S. Stone (Cambridge: Cambridge University Press, 1989).

Morellet, André. *Abrégé du Manuel des Inquisiteurs.* Edited by Jean-Pierre Guicciardi (Grenoble: Jérôme Millon, 2000).

—. *Mémoires de l'abbé Morellet de l'Académie française.* Edited by Jean-Pierre Guicciardi (Paris: Mercure de France, 2000).

Noailles, Louis-Antoine de. *Instruction pastorale de M.l'Archevêque de Paris, sur la perfection chrétienne et sur la vie intérieure, contre les illusions des faux mystiques,* in Fénelon, *Oeuvres complètes* [op. cit.].

Nouvelles ecclésiastiques, ou Mémoires pour servir de l'histoire de la constitution Unigenitus. 3rd ed. (Utrecht, 1728–1803).

Rabaut de Saint-Etienne. *Lettres à M. Bailly sur l'histoire primitive de la Grèce* (Paris: 1787).

Recueil général des anciennes lois françaises. Edited by François-André Isambert et al. (Paris: Plon, 1821–33).

[Richelieu]. *Testament Politique de Richelieu.* Edited by Françoise Hildesheimer (Paris: Société de l'histoire de France, 1995).

Robespierre, Maximilien. "On the Principle of Political Morality." *Robespierre: Virtue and Terror* (London: Verso, 2007).

Romme, Gilbert. *Rapport sur l'ère de la République fait à la Convention nationale dans la séance du 20 septembre de l'an II de la République. Archives parlementaires 77.* 499–506.

Ronsard, Pierre de. *Œuvres complètes* (Paris: P. Jannet, 1857–67).

Rousseau, Jean-Jacques. *The Social Contract.* Translated by Maurice Cranston (London: Penguin Books, 1968).

Sieyès, Émmanuel-Joseph. *Sieyès: Political Writings.* Edited by and translated by Michael Sonenscher (Indianapolis: Hackett, 2003).

—. *Écrits Politiques.* Edited by Roberto Zapperi (Paris: Éditions des archives contemporaines, 1985).

Spinoza, Benedict de. *Ethics. A Spinoza Reader.* Edited and translated by Edwin Curley (Princeton, NJ: Princeton University Press, 1994).

—. *Dieu, l'homme et la béatitude.* Translated and introduction by Paul Janet (Paris: G. Balière, 1878).

Stendhal, *Chroniques pour l'Angleterre.* Translated by Renée Dénier, edited by Keith G. McWatters. 7 vols. (Grenoble: ELLUG, 1993).

Le violier des histoires romaines. Edited by M. G. Brunet (Paris: P. Jannet, 1858).

Volney, Constantin-François. *Les ruines, ou méditation sur les révolutions des empires.* tome 1 (Paris: Firmin Didot, 1826 [1791]).

Voltaire, François-Marie Arouet. *Questions sur l'Encyclopédie* in *Oeuvres complètes de Voltaire.* Edited by Louis Moland. 52 vols. (Paris: Garnier, 1877–85).

—. "De Constantine." *Oeuvres de 1753–1757 II, Mélanges de 1756, Les Oeuvres complètes de Voltaire* (Oxford: The Voltaire Foundation, 2010).

—. *Candide and Other Stories.* Translated and edited by Roger Pearson (Oxford: Oxford University Press, 1990).

—. *Philosophical Letters.* Translated by Prudence L. Steiner and edited by John Leigh (Indianapolis: Hackett, 2007).

—. *Œuvres historiques.* Edited by René Pomeau (Paris: Gallimard, 1957).

Secondary Sources

Abrams, M. H. *Natural Supernaturalism: Tradition and Revolution in Romantic Literature* (New York: W.W. Norton and Company, 1971).

Agamben, Giorgio. *Homo Sacer: Sovereign Power and Bare Life*. Translated by Daniel Heller-Roazen (Stanford: Stanford University Press, 1998).

—. *The Signature of All Things: On Method*. Translated by Luca D'Isanto (New York, NY: Zone Books, 2009).

—. *Le Règne et la gloire: pour une généalogie théologique de l'économie et du gouvernement*. Translated by Joël Gayraud and Martin Rueff (Paris: Seuil, 2008).

Arasse, Daniel. *La Guillotine et l'imaginaire de la Terreur* (Paris: Flammarion, 1987).

Arendt, Hannah. "The Concept of History: Ancient and Modern." *Between Past and Present* (London: Penguin, 1977).

Armenteros, Carolina and Richard A. Lebrun, eds. *Joseph de Maistre and the Legacy of Enlightenment* (Oxford: SVEC, 2011).

Asad, Talal. *Formations of the Secular: Christianity, Islam, Modernity* (Stanford: Stanford University Press, 2003).

Badiou, Alain. *Saint Paul: The Foundations of Universalism*. Translated by Ray Brassier (Stanford: Stanford University Press, 2003).

Baker, Keith Michael. "Enlightenment and the Institution of Society: Notes for a Conceptual History." *Main Trends in Cultural History: Ten Essays*. Edited by Willem Melching and Wyger Velema (Amsterdam and Atlanta, GA: Rodopi, 1994).

—. *Inventing the French Revolution* (Cambridge: Cambridge University Press, 1990).

— and Peter H. Reill, eds. *What's Left of the Enlightenment?: A Postmodern Question* (Stanford: Stanford University Press, 2001).

Barthes, Roland. *The Rustle of Language*. Translated by Richard Howard (Berkeley, CA: University of California Press, 1989).

Bataille, Georges. *Théorie de la religion*. Edited by Thadée Klossowski (Paris: Gallimard, 1973).

—. *Literature and Evil*. Translated by Alastair Hamilton (London: Marion Boyars Publishers, 2001).

Beaune, Colette. *The Birth of an Ideology: Myths and Symbols of Nation in Late Medieval France*. Edited by Fredric Cheyette and translated by Susan Ross Huston (Berkeley, CA: University of California Press, 1991).

Becker, Carl, L. *The Heavenly City of the Eighteenth Century Philosophers* (New Haven: Yale University Press, 1932).

Bell, David A. *The Cult of the Nation in France: Inventing Nationalism, 1680–1800* (Cambridge, MA: Harvard University Press, 2001).

Benjamin, Walter. *Illuminations*. Edited by Hannah Arendt and translated by Harry Zohn (New York: Schocken Books, 1977).

—. "On the Concept of History." *Selected Writings: Volume Four* (Cambridge, MA: Belknap Press, 2003).

Bethencourt, Francesco. *The Inquisition: A Global History, 1478–1834*. Translated by Jean Birrell (Cambridge: Cambridge University Press, 2009).

Bitterling, David. *L'invention du Pré Carré: Construction de l'espace français sous l'Ancien Régime* (Paris: Albin Michel, 2009).

Blanton, Ward. *Displacing Christian Origins: Philosophy, Secularity and the New Testament* (Chicago: Chicago University Press, 2007).

Bloch, Marc. *The Royal Touch: Sacred Monarchy and Scrofula in England and France.* Translated by J. E. Anderson (London: Routledge and Kegan Paul, 1973).

Blumenberg, Hans. *The Legitimacy of the Modern Age.* Translated by Robert M. Wallace (Cambridge, MA: MIT Press, 1983).

Boutier, Jean, Alain Dewerpe, and Daniel Nordman. *Un tour de France royal. Le voyage de Charles IX 1564–1566* (Paris: Éditions Aubier 1984).

Bradley, James E. and Dale Van Kley, eds. *Religion and Politics in Enlightenment Europe* (Notre Dame, IN: University of Notre Dame Press, 2001).

Bremond, Henri. *L'Invasion mystique*, vol. II *of Histoire littéraire du sentiment religieux en France.* 12 vols. (Paris: Bloud et Gay, 1915–36).

Burson, Jeffrey D. *The Rise and Fall of Theological Enlightenment: Jean-Martin de Prades and Ideological Polarization in Eighteenth Century France* (Notre Dame, IN: University of Notre Dame Press, 2010).

Buttigieg, Joseph A and Thomas Kselman, eds. *European Christian Democracy: Historical Legacies and Comparative Perspectives* (Notre Dame, IN: University of Notre Dame Press, 2003).

Cassirer, Ernst. *Philosophy of the Enlightenment.* Translated by Koelln and Pettegrove (Princeton, NJ: Princeton University Press, 1951).

Céard, Jean. "Au travers du voile: *L'Hymne de l'Hyver* de Ronsard." *Les fruits de la Saison. Mélanges de littérature des XVIe et XVIIe siècles offerts au professeur André Gendre.* Edited by Philippe Tessier, Loris Petris, and Marie-Jeanne Liengme Bessire (Neuchâtel-Genève: Droz, 2000), 209–22.

—. "Les mythes dans les Hymnes de Ronsard." *Les mythes poétiques au temps de la Renaissance.* Edited by Marie-Thérèse Jones-Davies (Paris: J. Touzot, 1985), 21–34.

Chartier, Roger. *The Cultural Origins of the French Revolution.* Translated by Lydia Cochrane (Durham, NC: Duke University Press, 1991).

Cherel, Albert. *Fénelon au XVIIIe siècle en France 1715–1820: Son Prestige – Son Influence* (Paris, 1917; reprint, Geneva: Slatkine, 1970).

Choudhury, Mita. "'Carnal Quietism': Embodying Anti-Jesuit Polemics in the Catherine Cadière Affair, 1731." *Eighteenth-Century Studies* 39(2), 2006: 173–86.

—. "A Betrayal of Trust: The Jesuits and Quietism in Eighteenth-Century France." *Common Knowledge* 15(2), 2009: 164–80

Christin, Olivier. *Une Révolution symbolique: l'iconoclasme huguenot et la reconstruction catholique* (Paris: Editions de minuit, 1991).

Cobban, Alfred. *In Search of Humanity: The Role of the Enlightenment in Modern History* (London: J. Cape, 1960).

—. "The Enlightenment and the French Revolution." *Aspects of the French Revolution* (New York: J. Cape, 1968).

Coleman, Charly. "Resacralizing the World: The Fate of Secularization in Enlightenment Historiography." *Journal of Modern History* 82, 2010: 368-95.

Cottret, Monique. *Jansénismes et lumières: Pour un autre XVIIIe siècle* (Paris: Michel Albin, 1998).

Crocker, Lester. *An Age of Crisis: Man and World in Eighteenth Century French Thought* (Baltimore: Johns Hopkins University Press, 1959).

Crouzet, Denis. *Dieu en ses royaumes: une histoire des guerres de la religion* (Seyssel: Champ Vallon, 2008).

—. *La genèse de la réforme française vers 1520–1562* (Paris: Belin, 2008).

—. *La nuit de la Saint-Barthélemy; un rêve perdu de la Renaissance* (Paris: Fayard, 1994).

—. *Les guerriers de Dieu: la violence au temps des troubles de religion* (Seyssel: Champ Vallon, 1990).

—. *La sagesse et le malheur. Michel de l'Hospital chancelier de France* (Seyssel: Champ Vallon, 1998).

Darnton, Robert. "The High Enlightenment and the Low Life of Literature in Pre-Revolutionary France." *Past and Present* 51, 1971: 81–115

—. *The Forbidden Best-Sellers of Pre-Revolutionary France* (New York: W.W. Norton, 1995).

Davis, Kathleen. *Periodization and Sovereignty: How Ideas of Feudalism and Secularization Govern the Politics of Time* (Philadelphia: University of Pennsylvania Press, 2008).

Desan, Susan. *Reclaiming the Sacred: Lay Religion and Popular Politics in Revolutionary France* (Ithaca: Cornell University Press, 1990).

Downing, Gerald F. *Cynics, Paul and the Pauline Churches* (London: Routledge, 1998).

Durkheim, Émile. *Les Formes élémentaires de la vie religieuse* (Paris: Presses Universitaires de France, 1960).

Echeverria, Durand. *Mirage in the West: A History of the French Image of America to 1815* (New York: Octagon Books, 1966).

Ehrard, Jean. *L'idée de la nature en France à l'aube des lumières* (Paris: Flammarion, 1970).

Ehrmann, Jean. *Antoine Caron, peintre des fêtes et des massacres* (Paris: Flammarion, 1986).

Engberg-Pedersen, Troels. *Paul and the Stoics* (Edinburgh: T&T Clark, 2000).

Favreau, Robert. "La datation dans les inscriptions médiévales françaises." *Construire le temps: normes et usages chronologiques du moyen âge à l'époque contemporaine* (Paris and Geneva: Champion and Droz, 2000).

Feeney, Denis. *Caesar's Calendar: Ancient Time and the Beginnings of History* (Berkeley, CA: University of California Press, 2007).

Ferguson, Margaret. "Recreating the Rules of the Games: Marguerite de Navarre's *Heptaméron*." *Creative Imitation: New Essays on Renaissance Literature in Honor of Thomas M. Greene.* Edited by David Quint, Margaret Ferguson, G.W. Pigman III, and Wayne A. Rebhorn (Binghamton: Medieval & Renaissance Texts & Studies, 1992).

Figuier, Louis. *Histoire du merveilleux dans les temps modernes* (Paris: Hachette, 1860).

Foucault, Michel. *Surveiller et punir* (Paris: Gallimard, 1975).

—. *Les Mots et les choses: une archéologie des sciences humaines* (Paris: Gallimard, 1966).

—. *L'Usage des plaisirs. Histoire de la sexualité* II (Paris: Gallimard, 1984).

Franchi, Anna. *Caterina de' Medici, regina di Francia* (Milan: Casa Editrice Ceschina, 1933).

Frank, Stephanie. "The General Will Beyond Rousseau: Sieyès' Theological Arguments for the Sovereignty of the National Assembly." *History of European Ideas* 37, 2011: 337–43.

—. "Re-imagining the Public Sphere: Malebranche, Schmitt's Hamlet, and the Lost Theatre of Sovereignty." *Telos* 153, 2010: 70–93.

Gabor, Gary and Herbert de Vriesse, eds. *Rethinking Secularization: Philosophy and the Prophecy of a Secular Age* (Newcastle upon Tyne: Cambridge Scholars Press, 2009), 138–67.

Gauchet, Marcel. *The Disenchantment of the World: A Political History of Religion.* Translated Oscar Burge (Princeton: Princeton University Press, 1997).

Gay, Peter. *The Enlightenment: An Interpretation.* 2 vols. (New York: Knopf, 1967–9).

—. "Carl Becker's Heavenly City." *Carl Becker's Heavenly City Revisited.* Edited by Raymond O. Rockwood (Ithaca: Cornell University Press, 1958).

Geréby, György. "Carl Schmitt and Erik Peterson on the Problem of Political Theology: A Footnote to Kantorowicz." *Monotheistic Kingship: The Medieval Variants.* Edited by Aziz Al-Azmeh and János M. Bak (Budapest: CEU Medievalia, 2004).

Gidel, Gilbert. *La Politique de Fénelon* (Paris, 1906; reprint, Geneva: Slatkine, 1971).

Gorski, Philip S. "Historicizing the Secularization Debate: Church, State, and Society in Late Medieval and Early Modern Europe, ca 1300 to 1700." *American Sociological Review* 65(1), February 2000: 138–67.

Greengrass, Mark. *Governing Passions: Peace and Reform in the French Kingdom, 1576–1585* (Oxford: Oxford University Press, 2007).

Groethuysen, Bernhard. *Die Entstehung der bürgerlichen Welt-und Lebensanschauung in Frankreich.* 2 vols. (Halle/Saalle: M. Niemeyer, 1927–30).

Habermas, Jürgen. *Religion and Rationality: Essays on Reason, God, Modernity.* Edited by Eduardo Mendieta (Cambridge, MA: MIT Press, 2002).

— and Joseph Cardinal Ratzinger. *Dialectics of Secularization: On Reason and Religion.* Translated by Brian McNeil (San Francisco: Ignatius Press, 2006).

Havens, George R. *The Age of Ideas: From Reaction to Revolution in Eighteenth-Century France* (New York: Holt, 1955).

Hazard, Paul. *La Crise de la conscience européenne* (Paris: Boivin, 1935).

—. *La pensée européenne au XVIIIe siècle de Montesquieu à Lessing* (Paris: Boivin, 1946).

Headley, John M. *The Emperor and His Chancellor: A Study of the Imperial Chancellery under Gattinara* (Cambridge: Cambridge University Press, 1984).

Heller, Henry. *Labour, Science and Technology in France, 1500–1620* (Cambridge: Cambridge University Press, 1996).

Hildesheimer, Françoise. *Relectures de Richelieu* (Paris: Publisud, 2007).

Hoffman, George. "Doubles, Crosses: *Heptameron,* Story 71." *Approaches to Teaching Marguerite de Navarre's Heptaméron.* Edited by Colette Winn (New York: Modern Language Association of America, 2007), 102-5.

Holford-Strevens, Leofranc. *The History of Time: A Very Short Introduction* (Oxford: Oxford University Press, 2005).

Hont, Istvan. *Jealousy of Trade: International Competition and the Nation-State in Historical Perspective* (Cambridge, MA: The Belknap Press, 2005).

Horkheimer, Max and Theodor Adorno. *Dialectic of Enlightenment.* Translated by John Cumming (New York: Continuum, 1999).

Huet, Marie-Hélène. *Mourning Glory: The Will of the French Revolution* (Philadelphia: University of Pennsylvania Press, 1997).

Hunt, Lynn. *Measuring Time, Making History* (Budapest: Central European University Press, 2008).

Israel, Jonathan. *The Radical Enlightenment: Philosophy and the Making of Modernity* (Oxford: Oxford University Press, 2001).

—. *Enlightenment Contested: Philosophy, Modernity and the Emancipation of Man 1650–1752* (Oxford: Oxford University Press, 2006).

Jacob, Margaret C. *The Radical Enlightenment: Pantheists, Freemasons, and Republicans.* 2nd ed. (Lafayette, LA: Cornerstone, 2006).

Jaspers, Karl. *Origin and Goal of History.* Translated by Michael Bullock (London: Routledge and Kegan Paul, 1953).

Julliot, Caroline. *Le Grand Inquisiteur, naissance d'une figure mythique au XIXe siècle* (Paris: Champion, 2010).

Kahn, Didier. *Alchimie et Paracelsisme en France 1567–1625* (Geneva: Droz, 2007).

—. "The Rosicrucian Hoax in France 1623–24." *Secrets of Nature: Astrology and Alchemy in Early Modern Europe.* Edited by W. R. Newman and A. Grafton (Cambridge, MA: The MIT Press, 2001).

Kaiser, Thomas E. "This Strange Offspring of Philosophie: Recent Historiographical Problems in Relating the Enlightenment to the French Revolution." *French Historical Studies* 15, 1988: 549–62.

Kantorowicz, Ernest. *The King's Two Bodies: A Study in Medieval Political Theology* (Princeton, NJ: Princeton University Press, 1966).

Kelley, Donald R. *Foundations of Modern Historical Scholarship: Language, Law and History in the French Renaissance* (New York: Columbia University Press, 1970).

Kleuting, Harm, Norbert Hinske, and Karl Hengst. *Katholische Aufklärung: Aufklärung in Katholischen Deutschland* (Hamburg: Meiner, 1993).

Kölbl-Ebert, Martina. "How to Find Water: The State of the Art in the Early Seventeenth Century, Deduced from Writings of Martine de Bertereau 1632 and 1640." *Earth Sciences History* 28(2), 2009: 204–18.

Koselleck, Reinhart. "Remarks on the Revolutionary Calendar and Neue Zeit." *The Practice of Conceptual History: Timing History, Spacing Concepts.* Translated by Todd Samuel Pressner and Others (Stanford: Stanford University Press, 2002).

— "Time and History." *The Practice of Conceptual History: Timing History, Spacing Concepts* (Stanford: Stanford University Press, 2002).

Kselman, Thomas. *Death and the Afterlife in Modern France* (Princeton: Princeton University Press, 1993).

Kuznicki, Jason. "Sorcery and Publicity: The Cadière-Girard Scandal of 1730–1731." *French History* 21(3), 2007: 289–312.

Kwass, Michael. "Ordering the World of Goods: Consumer Revolution and the Classification of Objects in Eighteenth-Century France." *Representations* 82(1), 2003: 87–116.

Lajarte, Philippe de. "Le prologue de l'*Heptaméron* et le processus de production de l'œuvre" *La nouvelle française à la Renaissance.* Edited by Lionello Sozzi (Geneva: Slatkine, 1981), 397–423.

Lamur, Ingrid. *L'Œuvre manuscrite de Louis Dorleans: Histoire de l'origine de la Ligue et Poezies*. Mémoire de maîtrise under the direction of Denis Crouzet, 1999–2000, Université de Paris IV-Sorbonne.

Landes, David S. *A Revolution in Time: Clocks and the Making of the Modern World* (Cambridge, MA: Harvard University Press, 1983).

Lapide, Pinchas. *The Sermon on the Mount: Utopia or Program for Action* (Orbis Books, 1986).

Lazard, Madeleine. *Les aventures de Fémynie. Les femmes à la Renaissance* (Paris: Fayard, 2001).

Leduc-Fayette, Denise. "Fénelon et infini véritable" *L'Infini entre science et religion au XVIIe siècle*. Edited by Jean-Marie Lardic (Paris: J. Vrin, 1999).

Lefort, Claude. "On the Permanence of the Theologico-Political?" *Democracy and Political Theory* (Minnesota, MN: University of Minnesota Press, 1989).

—. "The Revolution as New Religion." *Writing: The Political Test*. Edited and translated by David Ames Curtis (Durham: Duke University Press, 2000).

Lehner, Ulrich and Michael Printy. *A Companion to the Catholic Enlightenment in Europe* (Leiden: Brill, 2010).

Lepinois, S. E. Nicolas Houel. *Apothicaire et bourgeois parisien fondateur du jardin de l'Ecole des apothicaires de Paris. Notes biographiques d'après des documents inédits* (Dijon: Therèse Jacquet, 1911).

Lerner, Bettina. "Michelet, Mythologue." *Yale French Studies* 111, 2007: 61–72.

Lestringant, Frank. *Une sainte horreur, ou le voyage en Eucharistie XVIe-XVIIe siècle* (Paris: Presses Universitaires de France, 1996).

Lilla, Mark. *The Still-Born God: Religions, Politics and the Modern West* (New York: Knopf, 2007).

Lougee, Carolyn C. *Le Paradis des Femmes: Women, Salons, and Social Stratification in Seventeenth-Century France* (Princeton, NJ: Princeton University Press, 1976).

Löwith, Karl. *Meaning in History: The Theological Implications of the Philosophy of History* (Chicago: University of Chicago Press, 1949).

MacIntyre, Alaistar. *After Virtue: A Study in Moral Theory* (Notre Dame, IN: University of Notre Dame Press, 1981).

Malherbe, Abraham J. *Paul and the Popular Philosophers* (Minneapolis: Fortress Press, 1989).

Malia, Martin. *History's Locomotives: Revolutions and the Making of the Modern World* (New Haven: Yale University Press, 2006).

Manuel, Frank E. *The Prophets of Paris* (Cambridge, MA: Harvard University Press, 1962).

Martin, Kinsley. *French Liberal Thought in the Eighteenth Century: A Study of Political Ideas from Bayle to Condorcet* (Boston: Little, Brown and Co, 1929).

Masuzawa, Tomoko. *The Invention of World Religions, or How European Universalism was Preserved in the Language of Pluralism* (Chicago: University of Chicago Press, 2005).

McMahon, Darrin M. *The Enemies of Enlightenment: The French Counter-Revolution and the Making of Modernity* (Oxford: Oxford University Press, 2001).

McManners, John. *French Ecclesiastical Society under the Ancien Régime: A Study of Angers in the Eighteenth Century* (Manchester: Manchester University Press, 1960).

Medlin, Dorothy and Jeffrey Merrick, eds. *André Morellet 1727–1819 in the Republic of Letters and the French Revolution* (New York: Peter Lang, 1995).

Mellon, Stanley. *The Political Uses of History: A Study of Historians in the French Revolution* (Stanford: Stanford University Press, 1958).

Merrick, Jeffrey W. *The Desacralization of the French Monarchy in the Eighteenth Century* (Baton Rouge, LA: Louisiana State University Press, 1990).

Michelet, Jules. *Histoire de la Révolution française* (Paris: Éditions Robert Laffont, 1979).

Miernowksi, Jan. "Fiction and Ritual in the *Heptameron*." *Approaches to Teaching Marguerite de Navarre's* Heptaméron. Edited by Colette Winn (New York: Modern Language Association of America, 2007), 106–12.

Miller, Samuel J. "Enlightened Catholicism on a European Scale." *Portugal and Rome, c. 1748–1830: An Aspect of Catholic Enlightenment* (Rome: Gregorian University Press, 1978), 1–27.

Monnier, Geneviève and William MacAllister-Johnson. "Caron antiquaire: à propos de quelques dessins du Louvre." *Revue de l'Art*, 14, 1971: 23–30.

Monod, Albert. *De Pascal à Chateaubriand: Les défenseurs français du Christianisme de 1670 à 1802* (Paris: F. Alcan, 1916).

Mornet, Daniel. *Les origines intellectuelles de la Révolution française* (Paris: A.Colin, 1933).

Moxnes, Halvor. "Asceticism and Christian Identity in Antiquity: A Dialogue with Foucault and Paul." *Journal for the Study of the New Testament* 26(1), 2003: 3–29.

Nancy, Jean-Luc. *A Finite Thinking*. Edited by Simon Sparks (Stanford: Stanford University Press, 2003).

Niderst, Alain. "Le Quiétisme de *Télémaque?*" *Fénelon mystique et politique 1699–1999*. Edited by F.-X. Cuche and J. Le Brun (Paris: Honoré Champion, 2004).

Northeast, Catherine M. *The Parisian Jesuits and the Enlightenment* (Oxford: Oxford University Press, 1991).

O'Connor, Thomas. "Théologie et lumières chez Luke Joseph Hooke." Thèse de doctorat, Sciences des religions, Paris IV and l'Institut catholique, 1993.

Ozouf, Mona. *La Fête révolutionnaire* (Paris: Gallimard, 1976).

—. "Republican calendar." *A Critical Dictionary of the French Revolution*. Edited by François Furet and Mona Ozouf and translated by Arthur Goldhammer (Harvard, MA: Belknap Press, 1989).

Palmer, Robert, R. *Catholics and Unbelievers in Eighteenth Century France* (Princeton, NJ: Princeton University Press, 1939).

—. *The Age of the Democratic Revolution: A Political History of Europe and America, 1760–1800*. 2 vols. (Princeton, NJ: Princeton University Press, 1959–64).

—. "Turgot: Paragon of the Continental Enlightenment." *Journal of Law and Economics* 19, 1967: 607–19.

Pappas, John Nicholas. *Berthier's Journal de Trevoux and the Philosophes* in *Studies on Voltaire and the Eighteenth Century* 3 (Geneva: Institut et musée Voltaire, 1957).

Péruse, Jean de La. "Médée." *Théâtre français de la Renaissance: La tragédie à l'époque d'Henri II et de Charles IX, Vol. I.* (Florence: Leo S. Olschki; Paris: Presses universitaires de France, 1989), 120–73.

Plongeron, Bernard. *Théologie et politique au siècle des lumières 1770–1820* (Geneva: Droz, 1973).

—. "Recherches sur l' 'Aufkläring' catholique en Europe occidental, 1770–1830." *Revue d'histoire moderne et contemporaine* 16, 1969: 555–605.

Poole, Robert. "Calendar Reform in Eighteenth-Century England." *Past and Present*, 149(November), 1995: 95–139.

Potter, David. *A History of France, 1460–1560: The Emergence of a Nation State* (New York: St. Martin's Press, 1995).

Printy, Michael. *Enlightenment and the Creation of German Catholicism* (Cambridge: Cambridge University Press, 2009).

Randall, Catherine. *Earthly Treasures: Material Culture and Metaphysics in the "Heptaméron" and Evangelical Narrative* (West Lafayette, IN: Purdue University Press, 2007).

Ravitch, Norman. *Sword and Mitre; Government and Episcopate in France and England in the Age of Aristocracy* (The Hague: Mouton, 1966).

Reichart, Rolf. "Light Against Darkness: The Visual Representations of a Central Enlightenment Concept." *Representations* 61(Winter), 1998: 95–148.

Reid, Jonathan A. *King's Sister, Queen of Dissent: Marguerite de Navarre 1492–1549 and her Evangelical Network* (Leiden: Brill, 2009).

Rétat, Pierre. *L'Attentat de Damiens: discours sur l'événement au XVIIIᵉ siècle* (Lyon: Presses Universitaires de Lyon, 1998).

Richet, Denis and François Furet. *La Révolution française* (Paris: Hachette, 1965).

Rigolot, François. "Magdalen's Skull: Allegory and Iconography in *Heptameron 32*." *Renaissance Quarterly* 47(1), 1994: 57–73.

Riley, Patrick. *The General Will Before Rousseau: The Transformation of the Divine into the Civic* (Princeton, NJ: Princeton University Press, 1988).

—. "Fénelon's 'Republican' Monarchism in *Telemachus*." *Monarchisms in the Age of Enlightenment: Liberty, Patriotism, and the Common Good*. Edited by Hans Blom, John Christian Laursen, and Luisa Simonutti (Toronto: University of Toronto Press, 2007).

—. "Malebranche and Cartesianized Augustianism." *A Treatise of Legal Philosophy and General Jurisprudence*. Edited by Enrico Pattaro, Damiano Canale, Paolo Grossi, Hasso Hofmann, and Patrick Riley (Amsterdam: Springer, 2009), 463–90.

Rosa, Mario. "Jésuitisme et anti-jésuitisme dans l'Italie du XVIIIe siècle." *Les anti-jésuites: Discours, figures et lieux de l'antijésuitisme à l'époque moderne*. Edited by Pierre-Antoine Fabre and Catherine Maire (Rennes: Presse universitaire, 2010).

Rosenblatt, Helena. "The Christian Enlightenment." *Christianity, Enlightenment, Reawakening and Revolution 1660–1815, The Cambridge History of Christianity*. Edited by Stewart J. Brown and Timothy Tackett (Cambridge: Cambridge University Press, 2006), 283–301.

Rothkrug, Lionel. *Opposition to Louis XIV: The Political and Social Origins of the French Enlightenment* (Princeton: Princeton University Press, 1965).

Schmitt, Carl. *Political Theology: Four Chapters on the Concept of Sovereignty*. Translated by George Schwab and edited by Tracey B. Strong (Chicago: University of Chicago Press, 2005 [1922]).

—. *Political Theology II: the Myth of the Closure of any Political Theology* (Cambridge: Polity Press, 2008 [1969]).

Sepinwall, Alyssa. *The Abbé Grégoire and the French Revolution: The Making of Modern Universalism* (Berkeley, CA: University of California Press, 2005).

Sewell, William. *A Rhetoric of Bourgeois Revolution: The Abbé Sieyès and What Is the Third Estate?* (Durham, NC: Duke University Press, 1994).

Sheehan, Jonathan. *The Enlightenment Bible: Translation, Scholarship, Culture* (Princeton, NJ: Princeton University Press, 2005).

Smith, Pamella H. *The Business of Alchemy: Science and Culture in the Holy Roman Empire* (Princeton, NJ: Princeton University Press, 1994).

Sommers, Paula. *Celestial Ladders: Readings in Marguerite de Navarre's Poetry of Spiritual Ascent* (Geneva: Droz, 1989).

—. "Marguerite de Navarre's *Heptaméron*: The Case for the Cornice." *French Review* 57(6), 1984: 786–93.

Sonenscher, Michael. "Introduction." *Sieyès: Political Writings* (Indianapolis: Hackett, 2003).

Sorkin, David. *The Religious Enlightenment: Protestants, Jews, and Catholics from London to Vienna* (Princeton, NJ: Princeton University Press, 2008).

Spink, John. "L'affaire de J.-M. de Prades." *Dix-huitième siècle* 3, 1971: 150–80.

Tallon, Alain. *Conscience nationale et sentiment religieux en France au XVIe siècle. Essai sur la vision gallicane du monde* (Paris: Presses Universitaires de France, 2002).

Taylor, Charles. *A Secular Age* (Cambridge, MA: Harvard Belknap Press, 2007).

—. *Sources of the Self: The Making of the Modern Identity* (Cambridge, MA: Harvard University Press, 1989).

Tetel, Maurice. *Marguerite de Navarre's Heptameron: Themes, Language and Structure* (Durham, NC: Duke University Press, 1973).

Thomson, Erik. "France's Grotian Moment? Hugo Grotius and Cardinal Richelieu's Commercial Statecraft." *French History* 21(4), 2007: 377–94.

—. "The Dutch Miracle, Modified: Hugo Grotius's *Mare Liberum*, Commercial Governance and Imperial War in the Early Seventeenth Century." *Grotiana* 30, 2009: 88–106.

Thysell, Carol. *The Pleasures of Discernment: Marguerite de Navarre as Theologian* (New York: Oxford University Press, 2000).

Trevor-Roper, Hugh. "Paracelsianism made Political, 1600–1650." *Paracelsus: The Man and His Reputation, His ideas and Their transformation.* Edited by Ole P. Grell (Leiden: Brill, 1998).

Vallet, Michel. *L'aventure Magique de Martine de Bertereau* (Nice: Collection Belisane, 1976).

van Ittersum, Martine. "The Long Goodbye: Hugo Grotius' Justification of Dutch expansion overseas, 1615–1645." *History of European Ideas* 36(4), 2010: 386–411.

Van Kley, Dale. *The Religious Origins of the French Revolution: from Calvin to the Civil Constitution* (New Haven: Yale University Press, 1996).

—. *The Jansenists and the Expulsion of the Jesuits from France* (New Haven: Yale University Press, 1975).

—. *The Damiens Affair and the Unraveling of the* Ancien Régime *1750–1770* (Princeton, NJ: Princeton University Press, 1984).

—. "Piety and Politics in the Century of Lights." *New Cambridge History of Eighteenth-Century Political Thought.* Edited by Mark Goldie and Robert Wokler (Cambridge: Cambridge University Press, 2006).

—. "The Rejuvenation and Rejection of Jansenism in History and Historiography: Recent Literature on Eighteenth-Century Jansenism in French." *French Historical Studies* 29, 2006: 649–84.

Vernière, Paul. *Spinoza et la pensée française avant la Révolution* (Paris, 1954; reprint, Geneva: Slatkine, 1979).

Vovelle, Michel. *Piété baroque et déchristianisation en Provence au XVIIIe siècle: Les attitudes devant la mort d'après les clauses de testaments* (Paris: Seuil, 1978).

Vries, Hent de. *Philosophy and the Turn to Religion* (Baltimore: Johns Hopkins University Press, 1999).

—. *Religion and Violence: Philosophical Perspectives from Kant to Derrida* (Baltimore: Johns Hopkins University Press, 2001).

Wade, Ira O. *The Intellectual Origins of the French Enlightenment* (Princeton, NJ: Princeton University Press, 1971).

Weber, Max. "Science as a Vocation." *From Max Weber: Essays in Sociology*. Edited and translated by H. H. Gerth and C. Wright Mills (New York: Routledge, 2003 [1948]).

—. *The Protestant Ethic and the Spirit of Capitalism* (London: Unwin University Books, 1971).

Webster, Charles. *Paracelsus: Medicine, Magic and Mission at the End of Time* (New Haven: Yale University Press, 2009).

White, Lynn Jr. "The Historical Roots of our Ecologic Crisis." *Science* 155, 1967: 1203–7.

Wolloch, Isser. "Robert R. Palmer, 11 January 1909–11 June 2002." *Biographical Memoirs Proceedings of the American Philosophical Society* 2002(148), 2004: 393–8.

Wright, Johnson Kent. "The Pre-Postmodernism of Carl Becker." *Post Modernism and the Enlightenment: New Perspectives in Eighteenth-Century French Intellectual History*. Edited by Daniel Gordon (London: Routledge, 2001), 161–76.

Zorach, Rebecca. *Blood, Milk, Ink, Gold: Abundance and Excess in the French Renaissance* (Chicago: University of Chicago Press, 2005).

Index